OLD HISTORY NEW GEOGRAPHY

BIFURCATING ANDHRA PRADESH

JAIRAM RAMESH

RUPA

Published by
Rupa Publications India Pvt. Ltd 2016
7/16, Ansari Road, Daryaganj
New Delhi 110 002

Sales Centres:
Allahabad Bengaluru Chennai
Hyderabad Jaipur Kathmandu
Kolkata Mumbai

Copyright © Jairam Ramesh 2016

The views and opinions expressed in this book are the author's own and the facts are as reported by him which have been verified to the extent possible, and the publishers are not in any way liable for the same.

The international boundaries on the maps of India are neither purported to be correct nor authentic by Survey of India directives.

All rights reserved.
No part of this publication may be reproduced, transmitted, or stored in a retrieval system, in any form or by any means, electronic, mechanical, photocopying, recording or otherwise, without the prior permission of the publisher.

ISBN: 978-81-291-3963-4

First impression 2016

10 9 8 7 6 5 4 3 2 1

The moral right of the author has been asserted.

Printed by Replika Press Pvt. Ltd.

This book is sold subject to the condition that it shall not, by way of trade or otherwise, be lent, resold, hired out, or otherwise circulated, without the publisher's prior consent, in any form of binding or cover other than that in which it is published.

*Dedicated to KVR who unfortunately passed away a day before
I started on this book and from whom I learnt so much...*

*When I am not thanked at all, I am thanked enough
I've done my duty and I've done no more*

HENRY FIELDING

Contents

Chronology of Key Dates Relating to the Bifurcation of Andhra Pradesh (2001–14)   xi

I. OLD HISTORY
1. The Long Background   3
2. Ten Days That Shook Andhra Pradesh and After   43
3. My Earlier Brush with Telangana   58

II. NEW GEOGRAPHY
4. The GoM Summons   65
5. Getting the GoM Going   71
6. Freezing Telangana   75
7. The Tussle for Hyderabad   78
8. A New Capital for a New Andhra Pradesh   82
9. Two States, One Governor   85
10. Internal Security Concerns   90
11. Managing Water Resources   93
12. The Polavaram Saga   100
13. Education and Article 371-D   109
14. Economic and Financial Matters   113
15. The GoM Completes Its Main Task   117

III. HIGH DRAMA AND AFTER
16. The Lok Sabha Drama, Act I   125

17. The Lok Sabha Drama, Act II	128
18. The Rajya Sabha Drama	134
19. The Final Touches	144

IV. RECOLLECTIONS

20. Amusing GoM Musings	155
21. A Last Word	168
Annexures	175
References	231
Acknowledgements	235
Index	237

Chronology of Key Dates Relating to the Bifurcation of Andhra Pradesh (2001–14)

27 April 2001	K. Chandrasekhar Rao (KCR) forms the Telangana Rashtra Samithi (TRS).
30 October 2001	The Congress Working Committee (CWC) passes the resolution on Telangana and second States Reorganisation Commission (SRC).
4 March 2004	The Congress and TRS reaffirm alliance for the 2004 Lok Sabha and state assembly elections based on the CWC resolution of 30 October 2001.
27 May 2004	The UPA (United Progressive Alliance) government releases the National Common Minimum Programme (NCMP) that formulates its approach on the Telangana issue.
7 June 2004	President A.P.J. Abdul Kalam addresses the joint Houses of Parliament. He repeats the NCMP formulation on the Telangana issue.
12 September 2006	KCR resigns from Union Cabinet.
12 February 2009	Y.S. Rajasekhara Reddy (YSR), Chief Minister of Andhra Pradesh, makes a statement on Telangana in the Andhra Pradesh assembly.

2 September 2009	YSR dies in a helicopter crash.
3 September 2009	K. Rosaiah takes over as Chief Minister of Andhra Pradesh.
29 November 2009	KCR goes on a hunger strike demanding the creation of Telangana.
7 December 2009	K. Rosaiah calls an all-party meeting in Hyderabad to discuss the situation arising out of the hunger strike and to deliberate on the next steps on Telangana.
9 December 2009	Home Minister P. Chidambaram issues a statement at 11:30 p.m. that gives the impression that Telangana will be created. KCR calls off the hunger strike.
10 December 2009	P. Chidambaram and Finance Minister Pranab Mukherjee respond to queries on the 9 December statement in the Rajya Sabha and the Lok Sabha respectively.
23 December 2009	P. Chidambaram issues a statement giving further clarifications on the 9 December statement and sets out the way forward.
5 January 2010	P. Chidambaram calls a meeting in New Delhi of eight recognized political parties of Andhra Pradesh.
3 February 2010	The Government of India constitutes the Srikrishna Committee to examine the issue of the bifurcation of Andhra Pradesh.
24 November 2010	K. Rosaiah resigns as Chief Minister and is replaced by Kiran Kumar Reddy the following day.
30 December 2010	The Srikrishna Committee submits its report.
6 January 2011	P. Chidambaram calls an all-party meeting in New Delhi and makes the Srikrishna Committee report public.
5 August 2011	A Calling Attention Motion is heard on

	Telangana in the Lok Sabha. P. Chidambaram speaks at length.
2 May 2012	A debate on demands-for-grants of the Home Ministry ensues in the Lok Sabha. P. Chidambaram speaks on Telangana.
1 August 2012	P. Chidambaram returns as Finance Minister and Sushilkumar Shinde takes over as Home Minister.
28 December 2012	Home Minister Sushilkumar Shinde convenes an all-party meeting on Telangana in New Delhi, and announces that the final decision will be taken within a month.
30 July 2013	The CWC passes a resolution calling for the bifurcation of Andhra Pradesh and the creation of Telangana.
3 October 2013	The Cabinet meets to consider the note of the Home Ministry recommending (i) the bifurcation of Andhra Pradesh and (ii) the constitution of a Group of Ministers (GoM); it approves both.
8 October 2013	A GoM is constituted to prepare legislation to give effect to the Cabinet decision of 3 October 2013.
11 October 2013	The first formal meeting of the GoM takes place.
19 October 2013	The second formal meeting of the GoM takes place.
7 November 2013	The third formal meeting of the GoM takes place.
12, 13 November 2013	The GoM meets leaders of political parties of Andhra Pradesh.
18 November 2013	The GoM meets Union ministers from Seemandhra and also the Chief Minister of Andhra Pradesh.
21 November 2013	The fourth formal meeting of the GoM takes place.

27 November 2013	The fifth and the final formal meeting of the GoM takes place.
3 December 2013	The GoM finalizes its report and the Reorganisation Bill.
5 December 2013	The Cabinet meets to consider the GoM report and the Andhra Pradesh Reorganisation Bill, 2013. It approves the Bill.
12 December 2013	President Pranab Mukherjee refers the Andhra Pradesh Reorganisation Bill, 2013 to the Andhra Pradesh legislature.
16 December 2013	The Andhra Pradesh Reorganisation Bill, 2013 is introduced in the Andhra Pradesh legislative assembly and council.
30 January 2014	The Andhra Pradesh legislative assembly and council approve the resolution tabled on 26 January 2014 by the Chief Minister, rejecting the Andhra Pradesh Reorganisation Bill, 2013 by voice vote. Communication from the state is received by the GoM on 3 February 2014.
4, 5, 6 February 2014	The GoM meets informally to finalize the Bill to be introduced in the Lok Sabha.
7 February 2014	The Cabinet approves the Andhra Pradesh Reorganisation Bill, 2014.
12 February 2014	The Cabinet considers further changes to the Andhra Pradesh Reorganisation Bill, 2014 relating to the Polavaram project and approves changes. Prime Minister Manmohan Singh meets Bharatiya Janata Party (BJP) leaders over lunch.
13 February 2014	The Andhra Pradesh Reorganisation Bill, 2014 is introduced in the Lok Sabha. Chaos prevents debate.
17 February 2014	The Home Minister and the author meet BJP leaders.

18 February 2014	The Lok Sabha passes the Andhra Pradesh Reorganisation Bill, 2014.
19 February 2014	The Home Minister and the author meet BJP leaders, after which the Prime Minister meets them. Kiran Kumar Reddy resigns as Chief Minister.
20 February 2014	The Rajya Sabha passes the Andhra Pradesh Reorganisation Bill, 2014.
1 March 2014	The Andhra Pradesh Reorganisation Act, 2014 is notified in the Gazette of India.
1 March 2014	President's Rule is imposed in Andhra Pradesh and the assembly is placed in suspended animation.
1 March 2014	The Cabinet formally approves the Prime Minister's commitment of 20 February 2014 in the Rajya Sabha, including the grant of special category status to the successor state of Andhra Pradesh for five years.
4 March 2014	2 June 2014 is notified as appointed day for the formation of Telangana.
10 April 2014	A detailed review of the implementation of the Andhra Pradesh Reorganisation Act, 2014 is carried out by author with Andhra Pradesh Governor and senior state government officials in Hyderabad.
29 May 2014	The Polavaram Ordinance is notified in the Gazette of India.
2 June 2014	The Telangana government takes over.
8 June 2014	The new government takes over in the successor state of Andhra Pradesh.
8 July 2014	The Andhra Pradesh Reorganisation (Amendment) Bill, 2014, replacing the 29 May 2014 Ordinance with retrospective effect, is introduced in the Lok Sabha.
11 July 2014	The Lok Sabha passes the Andhra Pradesh Reorganisation (Amendment) Bill, 2014.

14 July 2014	The Rajya Sabha passes the Andhra Pradesh Reorganisation (Amendment) Bill, 2014.
17 July 2014	The Andhra Pradesh Reorganisation (Amendment) Bill, 2014 is notified with retrospective effect.

I
OLD HISTORY

I

The Long Background

In October 1953, India's first linguistic state, Andhra, came into being. In November 1956, Parliament formed the unified Telugu-speaking state of Andhra Pradesh, by merging Andhra and the Telugu-speaking areas of the Nizam of Hyderabad's erstwhile empire. These areas were known as Telangana.

In February 2014, Parliament bifurcated Andhra Pradesh, and created a separate state of Telangana.

The wheel had turned a full circle in fifty-eight years.

Why did it happen?

How did it happen?

And when it happened, what exactly did happen?

This book throws light on these questions—questions that continue to inflame passions on both sides. I was closely involved with the process of bifurcation for seven months, beginning October 2013. This is my narrative of that tumultuous period, one born out of personal experience.

But the text of this narrative has a chequered historical context.[1] It has even a long political subtext.

Note: All letters from C. Rajagopalachari (Rajaji) to Jawaharlal Nehru are from the Rajaji collection in the Nehru Memorial Museum & Library, New Delhi. All letters from Nehru to Rajaji are from different volumes of the *Selected Works of Jawaharlal Nehru*.
[1] A good historical account for the period up to 1956 is Rao, 1973.

Therefore, before I begin my story of how India's twenty-ninth state emerged, I go back in time, to set the stage as it were, for what was to take place in February 2014.

◆

During British rule, both Tamil- and Telugu-speaking areas were part of Madras province. This province also had a few Kannada- and Malayalam-speaking districts. The demand to recognize Andhra as a separate linguistic province went back to 1913. In 1920, at its Nagpur session, the Indian National Congress formally made a commitment to the linguistic reorganization of provinces. It made a beginning the very next year by establishing its twenty-one provincial bodies along linguistic lines. Then, at its Madras session in May 1927, the Congress demanded the creation of separate Andhra, Karnataka and Sind provinces. In 1928, the Nehru (Motilal) Report emphasized the desirability of creating linguistic provinces. In March 1938, the Madras legislative assembly passed a resolution calling for the formation of 'separate provinces for the Tamil, Telugu, Kannada and Kerala regions'. But the British did not respond positively.[2]

Meeting between 24 and 27 June 1939 in Bombay, the Indian National Congress passed a resolution that concluded, 'The All-India Congress Committee is strongly of the opinion that immediate steps should be taken for the formation of [a] separate Andhra province'. This resolution was drafted by none other than Mahatma Gandhi himself.[3] He had written earlier (on 23 December 1938) to S. Radhakrishnan, then Vice Chancellor of Banaras Hindu University (BHU), supporting the creation of a separate Andhra province. He was to repeat his stance in a stinging article in *Harijan* on 29 March 1942, caustically chiding Maharaj Kumar of Vizianagaram (later to be a cricket commentator known as 'Vizzy') for calling into question his [Gandhi's] support for

---

[2]Why the British did not accede to the demands of those who wanted to create an Andhra province but created the Orissa and Sind provinces in April 1936 is discussed in Schwartzberg, 2009.
[3]*The Collected Works of Mahatma Gandhi* (henceforth CWMG), Volume 69, 1977, p. 368.

an Andhra province.[4]

The Indian Union came into being on 15 August 1947 with Madras province as an integral part. On 27 November 1947, Jawaharlal Nehru, while replying to a question by the prominent Andhra leader N.G. Ranga in the Constituent Assembly, underplayed the urgency for linguistic reorganization. But India's first prime minister also had this to say, 'The demand for the province of Andhra which if I may say so is a perfectly legitimate demand, raises relatively few difficulties and it can be included among the provinces in the Constitution as was done in the case of Orissa and Sind under the Government of India Act of 1935. This decision can be implemented soon after the Constitution is adopted.'[5] This was the only concession Nehru was prepared to make, as he clearly stated 'first things must come first' and linguistic reorganization would have to wait.

Subsequently, on 16 June 1948, the President of the Constituent Assembly, Dr Rajendra Prasad, appointed a commission under the chairmanship of a retired judge of the Allahabad High Court, S.K. Dar, to examine and report on the formation of the new provinces of Andhra, Karnataka, Kerala and Maharashtra. The Dar Commission submitted its report on 18 December, on the eve of the Jaipur session of the Indian National Congress. Considering the political and economic circumstances prevailing at that time and keeping in view the larger national challenges it considered to be of higher priority, the Dar Commission came out strongly against the formation of provinces exclusively or even mainly along linguistic considerations. While recognizing that different linguistic groups had conflicts amongst themselves in composite provinces, it believed that administrative solutions should be found to deal with such problems. In the specific context of Andhra it also highlighted the fact that a huge majority of the members of the Madras legislative assembly hailing from the Rayalaseema region, which was to be part of the new Andhra province, were themselves opposed to its formation. In other words, the

---

[4]CWMG, Volume 75, 1979, pp. 414–15, carries Gandhiji's article 'The Andhras' which appeared in *Harijan,* 29 March 1942.
[5]Gopal, Volume 4, 1986, pp. 530–31.

commission found the Telugu-speaking MLAs (members of legislative assembly) divided on the issue of a new Andhra province.

In its arguments in favour of postponing the creation of new linguistic provinces, the Dar Commission echoed the strongly-held views of almost every single key personality of the Constituent Assembly, including Nehru, Sardar Vallabhbhai Patel, Dr Rajendra Prasad, Maulana Azad and C. Rajagopalachari (Rajaji). Dr B.R. Ambedkar had presented a memorandum to the Dar Commission laying out both the advantages and the risks associated with linguistic provinces and categorically stated, 'My solution of the problem therefore is that, while accepting the demand for the re-constitution of Provinces on linguistic basis, the Constitution should provide that the official language of every Province shall be the same as the official language of the Central Government. It is only on that footing that I am prepared to accept the demand for linguistic provinces'.[6]

At the Jaipur session of the Congress itself, a three-member committee was set up, comprising Nehru, Sardar Patel and Pattabhi Sitaramayya[7] the incoming Congress president. The committee—known to posterity as the JVP Committee, after the first letter of the first name of the three members—was set up to examine the Dar Commission report and make recommendations to the Government of India.

On 10 January 1949, a little over three weeks after the Congress' Jaipur conclave was over, Nehru wrote to the legendary Andhra leader, T. Prakasam, saying that he agreed with the latter's suggestion to create a separate Andhra province and its inclusion in the draft Constitution. But after promising to give every consideration to Prakasam's demand, he went on to write, 'But you will appreciate that no one who is in a responsible position can, at this present juncture, do anything which might upset a very delicate balance. I should like to have a little peace

---

[6]The background to the establishment of the Dar Commission is described well in Austin's classic, *The Indian Constitution*, 1966.

[7]A veteran Congressman from the Krishna district in coastal Andhra; a freedom fighter, incarcerated in the Ahmednagar Fort jail with Nehru, Patel, Maulana Azad and others between 10 August 1942 and 28 March 1945; the founder of Andhra Bank.

or the semblance of peace for some time. After that we can go ahead in many directions'.

Thereafter, Nehru personally wrote up the JVP Committee report in the last days of March 1949. It was a comprehensive assessment and, once again, while not advocating large-scale linguistic reorganization, made special mention of Andhra: 'In some ways, the demand for an Andhra province has a larger measure of consent behind it than similar demands... On the whole, therefore, we feel that if an Andhra province is to be formed its protagonists will have to abandon their claims to the city of Madras... We feel that the case of Andhra province should be taken up first and the question of its implementation examined before we can think of considering the question of any other province.'[8]

On 2 October 1949, Nehru wrote to Sardar Patel after meeting three deputations on the Andhra province issue. He noted, 'I am convinced that the report of the three-man committee appointed by the Jaipur Congress is correct. That report suggests the postponement of the partitioning of provinces for a more favourable time. It further suggests that if there is agreement between the parties concerned, further steps can be taken without much difficulty.' Nehru asked Patel to read out his note 'either in the Congress Working Committee or at the Party meeting whenever this question of linguistic provinces arises'. He made this request since he was going to be away in the USA for a month from 7 October—on his first ever visit to that country.

On Nehru's return, the Congress Working Committee (CWC) met on 16 November 1949 and passed a resolution:

> The Working Committee considered the resolutions of the Madras Government, the Andhra Provincial Congress Committee and the Tamil Nad Congress Committee in regard to the formation of the Andhra Province. In view of their general agreement that the Andhra Province may be constituted in accordance with the report of the Linguistic Provinces Committee appointed by the Jaipur

---

[8]Gopal, Volume 10, 1990, pp.128–37. Gopal writes that, on the basis of Pattabhi Sitaramayya's suggestion, Nehru made the following change in his original draft: 'We are of *opinion*, therefore, that if an Andhra province is to be formed, its protagonists will have to abandon their claims to the city of Madras (p. 136).'

Congress [the Working Committee] resolves that the Government of India be requested to take steps to form forthwith the Andhra Province consisting generally of the undisputed Andhra districts but without the city of Madras. The exact demarcation should be made by a Boundary Commission to be appointed therefor. The Committee trusts that these steps shall enable the inclusion of the Andhra Province in Schedule I of the new Constitution.

But there seems to have been no agreement on the time schedule. Immediately following the CWC meeting, Pattabhi Sitaramayya was quoted as having said that 'a number of preliminaries would have to be settled' and as having expressed the hope that 'before the next general elections, the Andhra Province would be functioning in full swing.'[9] Two days later, Nehru wrote to Sardar Patel saying that 'we should take immediate steps to this end now'. He also wrote to Governor General C. Rajagopalachari saying that he had asked the Home Ministry to consult the Governor General's office which would have to issue the order regarding the Andhra province. Taking a cue from this decision, the Madras legislative assembly formed an eight-member Partition Committee under the chairmanship of Madras' Premier P.S. Kumaraswamy Raja to work out the modalities for creating the Andhra province.

The Partition Committee submitted its report by the end of December 1949 with a solitary but strong note of dissent from Prakasam. Prakasam was not reconciled to the loss of Madras city. This was also a time when the fissures amongst the Andhra leaders—between those from Rayalaseema like N. Sanjiva Reddy and those from the coastal districts like Prakasam—came to the fore. But Prakasam's stature was such that his views could simply not be brushed aside.[10] In the

---

[9] *The Hindu*, 17 November 1949.

[10] That Prakasam was not easy to work with is borne out by a letter that none other than Sardar Patel wrote to him on 13 April 1950: 'I am distressed to find that at the evening of your great career, you are undoing this good and great work of your life-time. After all, you were and have been one of the pioneers and builders of that great organisation to which we have the honour to belong. How can you be guilty of destroying your own creation? Please do not succumb to anger and lose your reason and self-control. Listen to the advice of friends and well-wishers. Why

background was the towering figure of Rajaji, for whom Prakasam's demands were anathema. Like Nehru and Patel, Rajaji was also distinctly unenthusiastic about linguistic reorganization with a view that 'it would impede national intercourse and economic advance'.[11]

It is clear that Nehru wished that the new Andhra province be incorporated into the Constitution of India that would come into effect on 26 January 1950. But this was not to be. He realized that while the CWC had taken a decision, its implementation was proving to be a huge headache. On 5 January 1950, while talking to reporters at Madras airport on his way to Colombo, Nehru publicly admitted that the chances of a separate Andhra being formed before 26 January 1950 were zero and that there were 'far too many practical issues which still needed to be sorted out'. He followed this up with a letter on 21 January to Kumaraswamy Raja saying that it would be impossible to create Andhra before the Constitution came into effect because of the 'irreconcilable differences of a fundamental nature between Tamil and Telugu leaders in the Madras assembly'. These differences, Nehru noted, were on a host of issues including, 'the status of Madras city, the boundaries of the new state and the future of the Tungabhadra project'. He went on to say that once these issues were sorted out to the satisfaction of both sides, the Government of India would move ahead with the creation of Andhra. He, however, firmly ruled out any arbitration from New Delhi which Prakasam had been advocating all along.[12]

On 26 January 1950, all provinces, including Madras, were re-designated as states (Map 1) and all premiers as chief ministers. On that historic day, the state of Hyderabad also came into being. This Hyderabad state, corresponding to what had been the Nizam of Hyderabad's erstwhile empire, had predominantly Telugu-speaking areas (called Telangana) but also had a few largely Marathi-speaking and Kannada-speaking districts in Aurangabad and Gulbarga divisions, respectively.

Rajaji was Home Minister of India between December 1950 and

---

not come to meet us if you have any grievance instead of breaking all canons of discipline.' Das, 1974, p. 298

[11] Gandhi, 1997.

[12] Gopal, Volume 14, Part I, 1992, pp. 317–18.

MAP 1: INDIA AS ON 26 JANUARY 1950

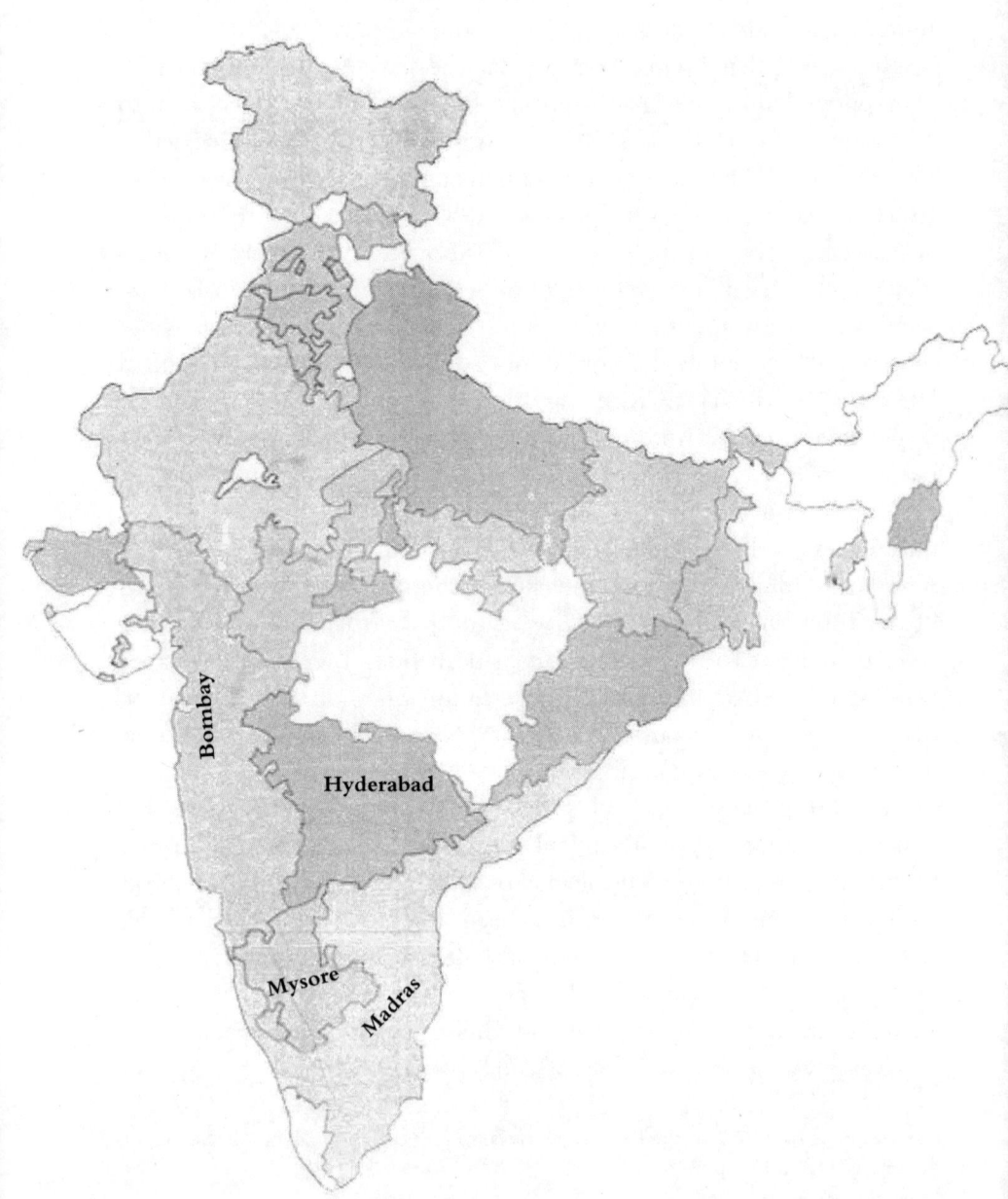

Note: Map not to scale

November 1951. During his tenure, on 15 August 1951, Swami Sitaram, a prominent Congressman from Andhra, announced a fast-unto-death to bring about the creation of a new Andhra state. A week after, Nehru made a statement in the Lok Sabha once again supporting the creation of an Andhra state along the lines suggested by the JVP Committee. On 20 September, Swami Sitaram ended his fast at the intervention of Acharya Vinoba Bhave who conveyed to him Nehru's reassurance that 'everything possible would be done to expedite the creation of a separate Andhra State'. Nine days later, Nehru wrote to Sitaram reiterating the assurance while also highlighting the obstacles to the formation of a new state which he felt could be overcome with 'goodwill and a friendly approach'.[13] Nehru repeated his position at a public meeting in Vijayawada on 27 December 1951 saying, 'The Government of India does not want to delay or to stand in the way of the creation of an Andhra State. You have got the Andhra province, take it but take it in the right way and not in the wrong way, go about it in a friendly way and you will proceed much faster than by any other way'.[14]

The early part of 1952 was taken up with the country's first general election, an exercise which had started on 25 October 1951. The Congress swept the polls but fared poorly in Madras state where it won just 152 seats in an assembly of 375, failing to win a majority by a considerable margin. Its performance in the Andhra seats of Madras state was even worse—all its stalwarts lost, and the party won just 39 of the 117 seats. In a desperate move to keep the communists at bay, Sri Prakasa, the Governor of Madras, nominated Rajaji to the legislative council so that he could become Chief Minister and form the government that would have reasonable stability. Rajaji took over as Chief Minister on 10 April 1952.[15] Immediately thereafter, the Nehru-Rajaji exchange on the Andhra issue started.

---

[13]The events of 1951 and Nehru's correspondence during the period of Swami Sitaram's fast can be found in Gopal, Volume 16, Part II, 1994.
[14]Gopal, Volume 17, 1995. This volume also contains Nehru's correspondence with the President of India, Dr Rajendra Prasad, on Swami Sitaram.
[15]The controversial manner in which Rajaji took over as Chief Minister is best described in Gandhi, 1997. Nehru seemed to have been unaware of Sri Prakasa's move but did not object once it happened.

Nehru's authoritative biographer, S. Gopal, succinctly summarized Nehru's views on Andhra, thus: 'On the Andhra demand in particular Nehru was inclined to be sympathetic, for he realised that it had its root not so much in a narrow love of language as in a widespread feeling among the Andhras that they were not getting a fair deal in the composite province'.[16] On 26 May 1952, Nehru wrote to Rajaji saying that he had come to the conclusion that the consideration of linguistic provinces, especially the formation of Andhra, could not be postponed any longer. Responding a day later, Rajaji advised Nehru to postpone such a decision by a year as he feared that communist influence would be strong in the Andhra state where 'a Communist-led non-Congress alliance government was distinctly possible'. On 28 May, Nehru replied, 'If the Andhra issue is raised before me I can put forward my general principle. That will involve an agreement about the city of Madras. If that is not forthcoming then we need not go ahead. If it is forthcoming, then I have no excuse for delay.'

On 7 July 1952, Nehru made a detailed intervention in the Lok Sabha during a debate on the demand for linguistic states. He used the opportunity to spell out his approach to the demand in general and on the Andhra issue in particular.[17] On 18 July 1952, he wrote an unusually brief letter to Rajaji saying: 'You must have followed our debates on the linguistic provinces and specially Andhra. I have promised to help in arriving at a settlement. I have little doubt that this Andhra matter will continue worrying us till something is done. How am I to proceed about it?'

On 21 July 1952, Nehru spoke in the Rajya Sabha, and reiterated his support for a separate Andhra state but along the lines suggested by the JVP Committee. He rejected the idea of the central government imposing its will on either party and wanted both sides to arrive at an amicable separation. The next day, Rajaji wrote to him saying, 'The Tamil people are fed up with the unfair suspicion and agitation that has been going on among Andhra friends; but the question has

---

[16]Gopal, 1979, p. 258.
[17]Gopal, Volume 18, 1996. This volume also contains the letters of 26 and 28 May 1952 from Nehru to Rajaji.

to be considered from more important angles than mere emotional distrust and fatigue.'

Through all of August, September and October 1952, there appears to have been no correspondence between Nehru and Rajaji on the Andhra issue. This is most uncharacteristic for two prolific letter writers. I can only surmise that they would have been in touch with each other but no records are available. However, Nehru's press conference on 28 September in Hyderabad was devoted almost entirely to Andhra. In response to a question, Nehru said, 'I have never been an advocate of the formation of linguistic States and the disintegration of Hyderabad. But, if however, there is a strong demand for the same, and the rival claims of adjacent areas are settled by mutual adjustment, I would agree to it.'[18]

Six days later, at another press conference, this time in Madras, Nehru was asked to spell out the Government of India's stand on the formation of an Andhra state. He said, 'The Government of India will act on any generally accepted plan for the formation of a separate state for Andhras, subject to financial and other considerations that are important. I have conferred, corresponded and talked to people about it and I have also stated the most feasible way of achieving it. I cannot be expected to issue a decree like a Grand Moghul sitting in Delhi, because I am not a Grand Moghul.'

It is then that events took a dramatic turn which neither Rajaji nor Nehru could have envisioned. On 19 October 1952, Potti Sriramulu, an energetic follower of Mahatma Gandhi, announced a fast-unto-death in Madras city for meeting two demands: carving out an Andhra state from the state of Madras comprising its Telugu-speaking areas and making Madras city the joint capital of the two states. Sriramulu had undertaken fasts before. Gandhi had written a couple of letters to him between 1939 and 1946 supporting the causes Sriramulu took up but also chiding him for his propensity to go on fasts. During 1946-48, Sriramulu undertook three fasts in support of opening temples to people of all castes in Nellore and other places. On 4 January 1947, Gandhi wrote to Prakasam from Noakhali expressing his happiness that the most recent fast of Sriramulu had ended successfully and added,

---

[18]Gopal, Volume 19, 1996.

'I know he is a solid worker though a little eccentric'.[19]

The immediate background to Sriramulu's October 1952 fast appears to have been Rajaji's proposal to divert the waters of the Krishna to Madras. This proposal was turned down by an expert committee appointed by Nehru but it had further fuelled the apprehensions of Andhra leaders and convinced them that Rajaji did not particularly care for the interests of their region. Sriramulu really did not require anybody's prodding to go on fast but there is some evidence to suggest that he did so 'in consultation with and the blessings of Swami Sitaram'.[20]

The location of the fast was the residence of the Speaker of the Madras legislative assembly, Bulusu Sambamurthy, a strong champion of an Andhra state. Initially, the fast itself did not seem to evoke public interest—*The Hindu*, the leading daily published from Madras, buried the news on the ninth page. But statements by Rajaji and counter-statements by Prakasam and his colleagues certainly evoked curiosity.

On 24 November 1952, Rajaji resumed his exchanges with Nehru on Andhra, protesting strongly against the proposal of Prakasam, Swami Sitaram, Sambamurthy and N. Sanjiva Reddy to make Madras city a chief commissioner's state[21] and allow it to function as a common capital for the rest of Madras state and Andhra. He told Nehru that 'if indeed Madras is to be split into three States and the city of Madras and its environments should be made into a 'C' state, it would be the saddest curse that freedom would have brought on Madras.' Strangely, there is no mention of Sriramulu's fast in this letter.

On 3 December, the forty-ninth day of the fast, twenty-eight MLAs supporting the Andhra cause appealed to Sriramulu to withdraw his fast. The same day, the Rajya Sabha also took note of it and Nehru wrote to Rajaji: 'Some kind of a fast is going on for the Andhra Province and I get frantic telegrams. I am totally unmoved by this and I propose to ignore it completely. But it is not easy to ignore the basic question. I wrote to you about it some months ago. You

---

[19] I owe this reference to the noted historian, Ramachandra Guha.
[20] Rao, 1973, p. 248.
[21] What today would be called a union territory. Chief commissioner's (or 'C' category) states were introduced in the Constitution but abolished by the States Reorganisation Act, 1956.

then suggested that it had to be taken up but not now. There can be little doubt that this will remain a running sore and some time or the other we shall have to take steps... I do not want to be driven to any action... Merely to go on repeating what we have said seems to me rather inadequate. I should like your advice in the matter.'

Rajaji's reply of 6 December was emphatic. 'It is true to repeat the same thing over and over is not adequate. But truth and the conclusions of administrative examination cannot be altered for the sake of novelty. I feel, therefore, we should not be ashamed of re-stating what was arrived after long consideration by you three. There seems to be no end to the troubles we have to face. You are cheerful and brave but I am too feeble for all this.' Rajaji's reference to 'you three' was to the conclusions of the JVP Committee report. This letter, too, has no mention of Sriramulu and his fast.

On 7 December, referring to the telegrams he had been receiving on Sriramulu and his condition, Nehru wrote to Rajaji saying that 'he cannot proclaim any decision because somebody is fasting to death' and that 'no government can function in this way'. But he also expressed the view that the issue of an Andhra state could not be postponed any longer. On 8 December, Nehru made a brief statement in the Lok Sabha saying that 'major decisions on major matters could not be taken under pressure', and appealed to Sriramulu to give up his fast.

On 9 December, he followed this up in the Rajya Sabha. He drew attention to the JVP Committee report and re-emphasized that the government was prepared to concede to the demand for an Andhra state comprising the undisputed Telugu-speaking areas of Madras state but ruled out making Madras city part of that new state. After his interventions, the Chairman of the Rajya Sabha, Vice President S. Radhakrishnan, announced that he had himself spoken to the Chairman of the Vijayawada Municipal Council, and his understanding was that 'Potti Sriramulu had either given up his fast, or would soon do so'. On 11 December, Prakasam and others met with Sriramulu to plead with him to withdraw his fast in view of Nehru's statements in Parliament. But Sriramulu remained unmoved.

That very day Rajaji wrote to Nehru saying that there was 'considerable satisfaction expressed in generally unbiased quarters over your statement'. Rajaji bemoaned the fact that Prakasam and other Congress leaders like N. Sanjiva Reddy were 'putting forward untenable conditions because they knew that in the undisputed Telugu-speaking areas that would form the new state of Andhra, the communists would have been in a clear majority.' To Nehru's suggestion of appointing an outsider to get on with the work of carving out the new state, Rajaji suggested the name of 'our retiring Commander-in-Chief Cariappa!' The next day, Nehru wrote to Rajaji asking for the latter's reaction to the suggestion that the Andhra state function with Madras as its capital for two–three years till its own capital took shape. However, this proposal was completely unacceptable to the Madras Chief Minister.

On 13 December, twenty MLAs appealed to Sriramulu again to break his fast. That too had no effect. With his health rapidly deteriorating, the denouement took place at 11:20 p.m. on 15 December when Sriramulu became a martyr to the Andhra cause. He was, incidentally, only the second man ever in Indian political history to have died in this manner—the first being Jatin Das, a colleague of Bhagat Singh, who had sacrificed his life in a Lahore jail on 13 September 1929 after being on a hunger strike for sixty-three days. Making a statement in the Lok Sabha the very next day after the Sriramulu tragedy, 'deeply regretting this ultimate consummation, in death, of the fast undertaken by Sriramulu', Nehru yet again expressed his readiness to move ahead with the formation of Andhra state along the lines recommended in the JVP Committee report. This he said, 'had already been decided independent of Sriramulu's martyrdom'. The same day he wrote to Rajaji again on the need to move forward with creating an Andhra state. But Rajaji continued to be difficult. Prakasam's statements had added fuel to the fire. On 16 December, he had made a statement that Nehru was 'under an evil influence and was being guided by interested persons'. The target was unmistakably Rajaji.

Nehru had been of the opinion that the new Andhra state may have to use Madras city for a couple of years till its own capital became fully ready. Rajaji wrote to Nehru on 17 December, that Sriramulu's tragedy was 'precipitated and pushed up to the fatal end by people whose motives I do not admire or appreciate and it would not be desirable to have the headquarters of the Andhra State temporarily to be in Madras. This opinion of mine may at first sight appear to be born of prejudice or cantankerousness. I respectfully submit that it would be the most inexpedient and maintain all the bitterness with which the current context is affected.' Two days later, Nehru made a formal statement in the Lok Sabha announcing the establishment of 'an Andhra state consisting of the Telugu-speaking areas of the present Madras State, but not including the city of Madras'. Clearly, Nehru had kept Rajaji's strong feelings in mind and changed his view on the status of Madras city. He also announced that the Chief Justice of the Rajasthan High Court, Justice K.N. Wanchoo, would 'consider and report on the financial and other implications of this decision and the questions to be considered in implementing it'.[22]

On 20 December, the Governor of Madras, Sri Prakasa, wrote to Nehru conveying Rajaji's extreme anger at Andhra leaders like Swami Sitaram, Prakasam and Sambamurthy who 'never missed a single meal' but 'egged on a good and innocent man to die in that cruel manner'.[23] He went on to add that Rajaji would not permit of any 'joint property' quoting him as having said, 'It is not the Tamil people who had asked for the separation and if the Andhras wanted it, they may as well have it and have done with it. They must get out lock, stock and barrel.'

Nehru replied to this two days later saying, 'A period of transition is inevitable...The one thing we must be clear about is that the city of Madras is not going to Andhra... Rajaji's attitude can be understood because he is feeling hurt at the turn events took. Nevertheless it is not a reasonable attitude; nor is it one which will lead to a cooperative settlement of the problem... (B)oth from the reasonable and practical point of view, a complete and sudden divorce is neither desirable nor possible. I still do not know why there should not be a common Governor and common High Court, at least to begin with'. Nehru also wrote to Rajaji the very same day expressing his concern with the latter's continuing rigidity and beseeching him to permit the new

---

[22]Gopal, Volume 20, 1997, pp. 235–59.
[23]Sri Prakasa to Jawaharlal Nehru, 20 December 1952, Sri Prakasa Papers, Nehru Memorial Museum & Library.

MAP 2: INDIA AS ON 1 OCTOBER 1953

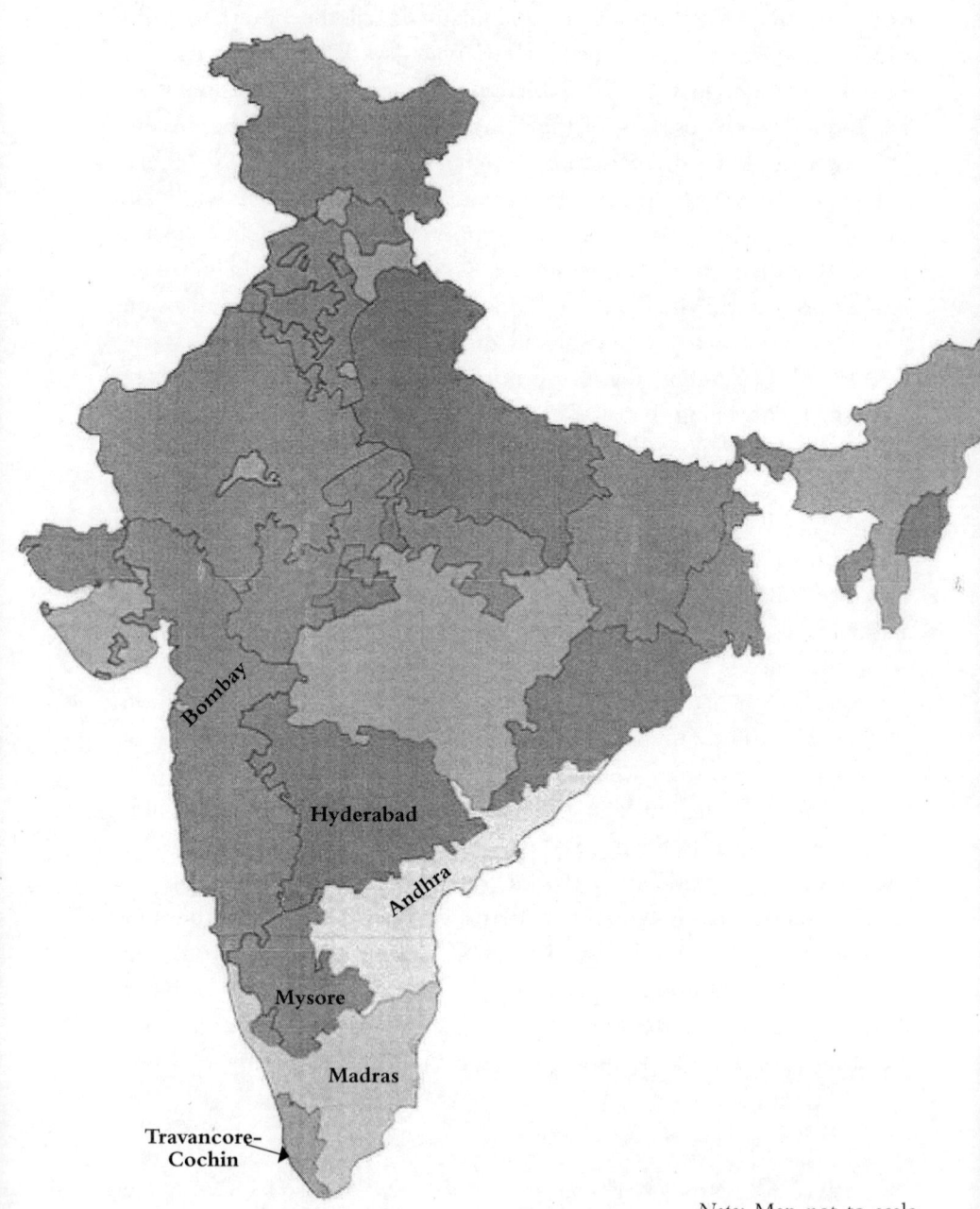

Note: Map not to scale

Andhra state to function from Madras temporarily.

The CWC formally approved the creation of an Andhra state on 15 January 1953 (Map 2). But Rajaji was still in a foul mood. When President Dr Rajendra Prasad met Prakasam on his visit to Madras on 23 February 1953, Rajaji was incensed. He later wrote to Nehru, 'I have truly fallen on unfortunate days… This special invitation without any request on the other side from anyone boosts what was already bad enough. The slender thread of my faith and courage are weakening rapidly. Forgive me if I make any decision at any time without consulting anyone any more.'

Nehru wrote to him on 19 March 1953, 'I would earnestly suggest to you…you should make a friendly gesture to the Andhras and assure them that you will give them full facilities for their offices, etc. in Madras city till they find it convenient to take them away. Otherwise also you might give them your goodwill and your assurance about facilities for them in Madras city in regard to education, hospitals and the like'. Nehru ended this typed letter with a handwritten plea, 'If I may further suggest, even before a declaration about the capital, etc., you might make friendly references to the Andhras and your wish to cooperate with them and help them.'

Rajaji replied three days later saying, 'the atmosphere was continually being poisoned' and 'all the groups in Andhra find it will pay to be making false allegations against me'. Thereafter, on 25 March, Nehru wrote to Rajaji, 'Last night I sent you the draft of the statement I propose to make today in Parliament in regard to the Andhra State. In that statement I had said that many offices of the Andhra State might continue to be located in the city of Madras till arrangements are made for their transfer to Andhra territory. I am changing the word "many" to "some". I think this meets your point.' But given the frame of mind he was in at that time, Rajaji was unrelenting. He was at his acerbic best while replying to Nehru the next day: '"many" and "some" are the same; however in the present context dealing with people who may not be up to the mark in the nuances of the English language, "some" may be better than "many". I had objected only to the word "most" which was in Sukthankar's letter… Madras city is calm and observes its traditional equanimity. It is lucky it is not a city on the banks of the Krishna.' Rajaji was reacting to Cabinet Secretary Y.N. Sukthankar's letter to him of 20 March 1953 conveying eleven decisions of the Cabinet on the formation of an Andhra state (based on Justice Wanchoo's recommendations), including the fact that 'most of the offices of the Andhra State should continue to be located in the City of Madras till arrangements are made for their transfer to the Andhra territory'.

Subsequently, India's first state to be created on a linguistic basis, namely Andhra, came into being on 1 October 1953. It was undoubtedly an agonizing process, and it could well have come three or four years earlier had Rajaji been more cooperative, had Prakasam been more accommodating and had Nehru been less of a democrat and not been adamant about consensus. The new state came into being with Kurnool in Rayalaseema as its capital and with the High Court at Guntur in the coastal region. This split location was the outcome of the 1937 Sri Bagh Pact signed between the leaders of Rayalaseema and the coastal districts according to which if the capital was located in one region, the High Court would be situated in the other.[24]

Nehru addressed a public meeting in Kurnool on 1 October 1953, and spoke extensively on other demands for creating new linguistic states following the formation of Andhra. At a press conference immediately after his public meeting he expressed his annoyance at a question posed to him on 'Visala Andhra' (that is, a larger unified state comprising Andhra and Telangana) but cooled down quickly to say that it was for the 'proposed States Reorganisation Commission to examine the demand'. The very next day he was in Madras assuaging Rajaji, praising Madras and speaking at length on the essential unity of India. In that speech, he also announced that a commission would soon be set up to consider the reorganization of states. But he was at pains to explain that this was not going to be about the linguistic division of India, something that was unacceptable to him as well as to Rajaji, who considered linguistic provinces to be a 'tribal idea'.

Prakasam became the first Chief Minister of the new Andhra state, and soon made his intent clear. Speaking in the assembly on

---

[24]Sri Bagh, incidentally, was the name of the house in Madras city of the Andhra leader, Kasinathuni Nageswara Rao, who is perhaps now better known as the founder of the company that makes Amrutanjan.

28 November 1953, he said, 'Kurnool town would not be a permanent capital. That it was a temporary arrangement had already been noted separately in the resolution passed by all the members of the Andhra Legislative Assembly at Madras. Not only this. The Prime Minister has given an assurance that all the provinces in India are going to be reorganised on a linguistic basis... I am fully confident that a larger Andhra is going to be formed before long. Then Hyderabad will become our permanent capital. It may take another two or three years.'[25] In this, the venerable Prakasam was to prove remarkably prescient.

Incidentally, the idea of having a commission to consider the linguistic reorganization of states seems to have been born on 17 December 1952 when the then President Dr Rajendra Prasad wrote to the Prime Minister saying, 'Sriramulu's death is only a burst up of something that has been brewing for a long time. So instead of having to deal with it every year, it is much better to deal with the whole question all at once. If the idea is to appoint a commission, it might be asked to consider the question of separate Kanarese-speaking, Malayali-speaking, Maharashtra-speaking [sic] and Gujarati-speaking provinces'.[26] The very same day Nehru replied, 'I agree with you that we shall have to face other demands for linguistic provinces in the near future'. On 19 February 1953, Nehru wrote to Morarji Desai, then Chief Minister of Bombay state, 'After waiting for the Andhra State to be established and got [sic] going, we should think of a really high level commission which can go fully into this subject all over India keeping in mind all the various factors'. That Home Minister Govind Ballabh Pant and he had decided to go ahead with appointing such a body is clear from a letter Nehru wrote on 20 July to R.K. Patil, a minister in the Madhya Pradesh government that 'we have decided to appoint a high-powered Commission to go into all these matters'.

Thereafter, following up on what he had said in Kurnool and Madras on 1 and 2 October 1953 respectively, Nehru made a statement in the Lok Sabha[27] on 23 December announcing the appointment of a

---

[25]Quoted in Viswanatham, 1992.
[26]Choudhary, 1991.
[27]Jawaharlal Nehru's evolving position on the issue of language and the linguistic reorganization of states is well captured in King, 1998. With the benefit of hindsight,

States Reorganization Commission (SRC) to examine 'objectively and dispassionately the question of the reorganization of the States of the Indian Union so that the welfare of the people of each constituent unit as well as the nation as a whole is promoted'. Each of the members of the commission—Justice S. Fazl Ali, H.N. Kunzru and K.M. Panikkar—was selected by Nehru personally and received fairly detailed letters of invitation from him to serve on it. There was a minor flutter when Fazl Ali in his letter of acceptance referred to the proposed body as 'the Boundary Commission'. Nehru promptly corrected him and reminded him that he was accepting the 'Chairmanship of the Commission on the reorganization of states'.[28] It also speaks volumes of that extraordinary generation that when S.G. Vaze, a member of the Servants of India Society, objected to Kunzru becoming a member of the SRC saying that the work of the society would suffer, Nehru had to write to Vaze with a personal plea while also invoking the authority of the President of India himself to overcome his objections and bring Kunzru on board.[29]

The SRC submitted its report on 30 September 1955. Among other things, it recommended that the Telugu-speaking areas of Hyderabad state, which historically had constituted the Telangana region, be made into a separate state, called Hyderabad. The commission appreciated the strong sentiments that existed in favour of such a separate state but it also recognized the substantial benefits that would materialize if it were combined with the Andhra state to create a 'Visalandhra',[30] an

---

it may appear that he prevaricated on the issue and indeed he has been criticized for this. But such criticism ignores the larger political context—of an India emerging from the trauma of Partition; making the transition to a republic; dealing with communist violence in some parts, particularly in Hyderabad state; and wanting to establish the foundations of economic development with undivided attention.

I might add here that that the views of Dr B.R. Ambedkar evolved as well. His book, *Thoughts on Linguistic Provinces* (reprinted in Moon, 1989), has a somewhat different philosophy from that contained in his memorandum to the Dar Commission in 1948. Acutely aware of this, in the Preface to his book he wrote 'More important than consistency is responsibility...A responsible person must have the courage to rethink and change his thoughts'.

[28]Gopal, Volume 24, 1999, pp. 242–44.
[29]Ibid., p. 252.
[30]*Selected Works of Jawaharlal Nehru* uses the term 'Visala Andhra' while the SRC used

idea that had been first mooted by the Andhra Mahasabha in October 1942. Perhaps unable to clearly make up its mind, the commission said that the new state of Hyderabad should come into being immediately and after five years, if two-thirds of its legislature so wished, it should be merged with Andhra.

The CWC met in New Delhi on 9 November 1955 to consider the SRC's recommendations. It passed a detailed resolution, drafted as always by Nehru himself, in which it said, 'The division of the present Hyderabad State is generally accepted. The Committee are of the opinion that it would be desirable, subject to the wishes of the people concerned, for the Telangana area to be attached to the Andhra State, at the beginning of this reorganisation and advise accordingly.' To be sure, Nehru was aware of the sentiments for a separate Telangana but felt that the balance of advantage lay in a larger, unified Andhra state, or Andhra Pradesh, as it would soon be called.

A major influence on Nehru accepting the need for immediate integration must have been Home Minister Govind Ballabh Pant who was of the firm view that unification was better done right away rather than five years later as recommended by the SRC. Speaking in a debate on the SRC Report in the Lok Sabha on 14 December 1955, Pant signalled the government's intention to combine the Telugu-speaking part of Hyderabad state with Andhra. Nine days later, again in the Lok Sabha, Pant reiterated his stance: 'The Commission had suggested that Telangana should be unified with Andhra after 5 years if two-thirds of the people [sic] are in its favour. Prima facie it does not seem to be in the interests of any smaller unit to be kept apart because the prospect of its being merged in another State comes in the way of the progress of both, and arrangements that are finalised in a way facilitate the progress of either and of both. So, theoretically, it would be much better if the two States could be unified now.' When an MP (member of Parliament) whose identity is unfortunately not known shouted 'no no', Pant replied, 'I am only trying to analyse but this does not conclude the matter completely. It still remains open to

---

the term 'Vishalandhra'. Both have identical meanings.

you to convert others.'[31]

Nehru was still worried about Telangana. He was well aware that the region suffered in comparison to the coastal districts of the imminent Andhra Pradesh. These districts had seen the expansion of education, irrigation and economic development during the time they were part of Madras province. Therefore, on 20 February 1956, Nehru and Pant got eight leaders from both the Andhra and Hyderabad states to meet in Delhi and arrive at a written understanding regarding how the new unified state would function and what special safeguards would be put in place for the people of Telangana. The understanding that these eight leaders finalized is known as the Gentlemen's Agreement (Annexure 1).

Thereafter, on 5 March, Nehru spoke extensively on the SRC's recommendations at a public meeting in Nizamabad in the Telangana region, around 150 kilometres from Hyderabad. His remarks are worth quoting in full since they have contemporary relevance as well:

> ...we have given a great deal of thought to the issue of Hyderabad and Telangana. The Congress Working Committee gave its recommendations. We met the people who were in favour of a greater Andhra and the others who wanted a separate Telangana. As I said, both sides had some logical arguments to advance. It is not that either side is wrong. On the one hand, it seemed wrong to postpone something, to be done after five years, to keep it pending for that long. On the other hand, there was fear in the hearts of the people of Telangana, of being displaced by the people of Andhra. Both these things had to be resolved.
>
> Some took all these things into account including the new thinking which favours large states, rather than small ones so that the barriers are fewer and progress is faster. In these circumstances, it seemed improper to have two separate states of Andhra and Telangana. The new outlook pointed to a greater Andhra. Then we had to think how to reassure the people of Andhra and assuage their fears. So you may have heard of the new proposal

[31]Nanda, 2002.

that a greater Andhra should be created with its two regions having their own separate identity and say in their development. It also envisages safeguards for the people of Telangana regarding their land, admissions to schools and colleges, language, jobs, etc.

This is broadly what has been decided and the proposal will soon be presented to you. This decision has been arrived at after prolonged discussions with both sides and great care has been taken to see that feelings on either side are not exacerbated...I hope all of you will accept this new proposal wholeheartedly and put it into practice. I want that you should become part of greater Andhra and benefit by it.[32]

On 18 April 1956, the States Reorganisation Bill, 1956 was introduced in the Lok Sabha. It is generally not known that this Bill had proposed that the new unified Telugu-speaking state actually be called Andhra-Telangana. Obviously, this had the approval of the Cabinet. (Interestingly, Pattabhi Sitaramayya, then Governor of Madhya Pradesh, had written to the Home Minister on 4 March 1956 saying that the new unified state be called Andhra Pradesh 'just as there is Uttar Pradesh and Madhya Pradesh'. But the Cabinet had not agreed to this suggestion.) The Bill then went for examination to a joint select committee of Parliament which had fifty-one members and was chaired by Pant himself. Two Andhra stalwarts—Lanka Sundaram and A. Satyanarayana Raju—were among the members.

In its report of 16 July 1956, the select committee suggested that in accordance with the resolution adopted by the legislative assemblies of Andhra and Hyderabad, the reorganized state of Andhra should be known as Andhra Pradesh, and not as Andhra-Telangana. Nehru and Pant had then changed their minds on the name of the new state and had agreed to the name Andhra Pradesh instead of Andhra-Telangana. The States Reorganisation Act, 1956 was notified on 31 August 1956, after the Bill got approved in the Lok Sabha on 10 August 1956 and in the Rajya Sabha fifteen days later. Thereafter, Nehru formally inaugurated it on 1 November 1956 with Hyderabad as its capital (Map 3). He spoke

[32]Gopal, Volume 32, 2003, p. 5.

at Fateh Maidan in the city and exhorted the people to go beyond arguments and suspicions and work unitedly—although much of the speech was devoted to the Anglo-French-Israeli invasion of Egypt that had rocked the world a few days before.

The question does arise: why did Nehru, who was fascinated by the cosmopolitan, multi-lingual, multi-religious character of Hyderabad city and indeed of Hyderabad state itself, agree to its immediate merger with the Andhra state? I can think of three reasons.

First, Nehru gave the highest priority to large irrigation projects, which he referred to as the 'temples of modern India'. On 10 December 1955, he had laid the foundation stone for the construction of the giant Nagarjuna Sagar Dam on the right bank of the Krishna River in Andhra state. A little later on the very same day, he crossed over by ferry to Hyderabad state where he unveiled a pylon to mark the commencement of the construction of the Nagarjuna Sagar Dam on the left bank of the Krishna River. The dam was a joint venture project of the two states and Nehru attached the greatest importance to its successful and speedy completion. Incidentally, that the site had Buddhist heritage value added to its sanctity in his eyes. He may well have felt that it would be easier if this prestigious project were to be executed by one state instead of two—especially two who could not always be expected to agree with each other.

Second, Nehru must have been influenced by the views expressed in the two state assemblies. In December 1955, 147 of the 174 MLAs in the Hyderabad assembly (barring the Speaker) who spoke on a merger resolution, 103 favoured immediate integration. However, there had been no vote. Naturally, the vote for merger in the Andhra assembly was unanimous. Nehru spent three days visiting both states between 8 and 10 December. Speaking in Kurnool on 9 December, he acknowledged that he was not in favour of breaking up the composite Hyderabad state but was going along with the recommendations of the SRC. Some of his senior colleagues, particularly Pant and Lal Bahadur Shastri, were in favour of a single unified Telugu-speaking state and it is perfectly possible that he deferred to their views. Only Maulana Azad was against merging the states of Hyderabad and Andhra.

Third, Nehru was very concerned about communist agitations in

MAP 3: INDIA AS ON 1 NOVEMBER 1956

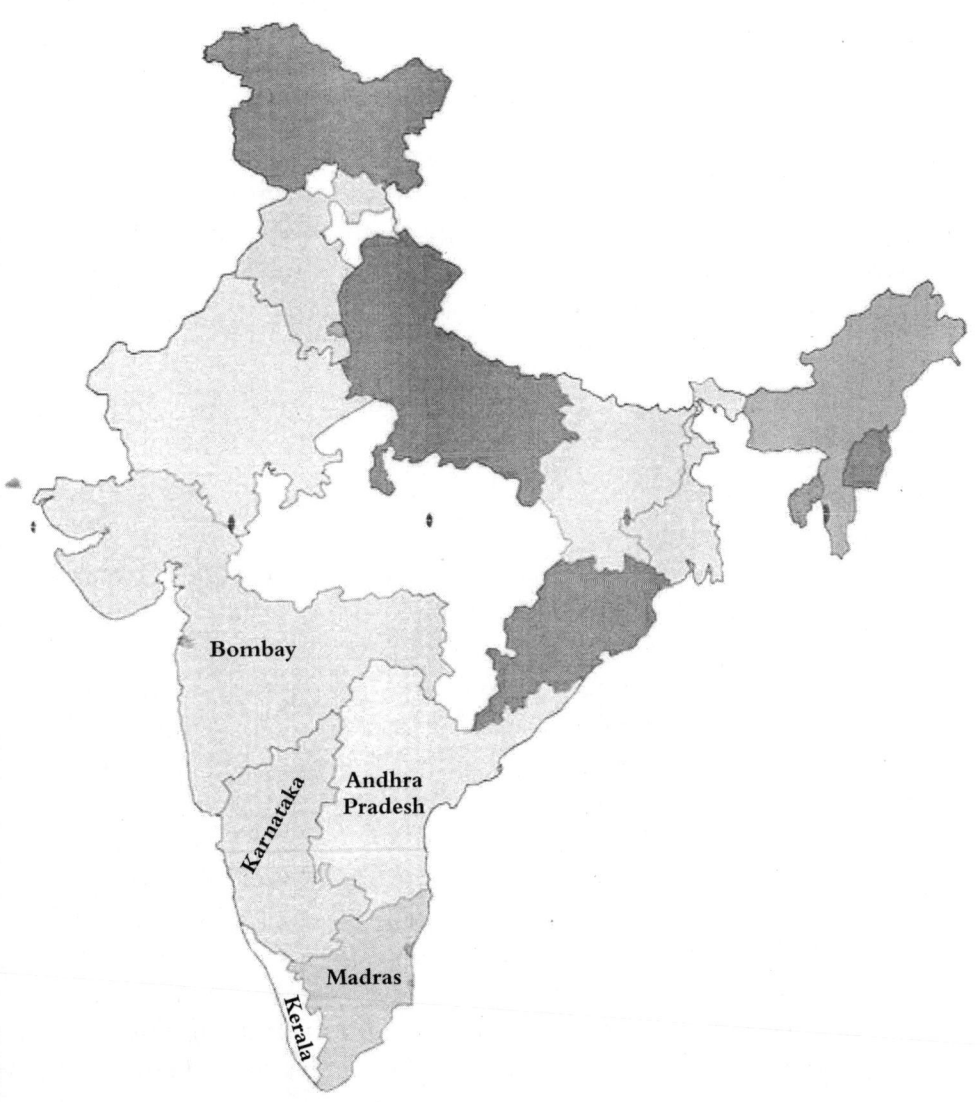

Note: Map not to scale

the Hyderabad state that went back to the late 1940s. Although the communists had formally ended their armed struggle in 1951, they still held considerable sway, given the continued prevalence of feudal landownership. It is not a coincidence that Vinoba Bhave launched the Bhoodan movement in April 1951 from Pochampally village in Nalgonda district of the Telangana region. There is incontrovertible evidence to suggest that Nehru went to the extent of raising this matter with the visiting Soviet leaders, Nikita Khrushchev and N.A. Bulganin, on 12 December 1955.[33] Nehru may have believed that the communist threat could be more effectively managed in a larger state. Incidentally, the communists themselves were in favour of Vishalandhra, perhaps also because of the caste background of their leadership in the state.

◆

Till about mid-1968, Andhra Pradesh moved ahead relatively peacefully under the leadership of N. Sanjiva Reddy, D. Sanjeevaiah and K. Brahmananda Reddy—all excellent administrators. But the Telangana issue, muted for well over a decade, surfaced again in the latter half of 1968. There were, to my mind, a variety of reasons for this.

First, every agitation needs a political spark and for the Telangana issue it was the return of M. Chenna Reddy to Hyderabad from New Delhi. He was a prominent leader from Telangana who had been shifted from the state to the centre as Minister of Steel and Mines in April 1967. But in early 1968, the Supreme Court invalidated his election to the state legislature the previous year and debarred him from holding any government position for six years. Chenna Reddy resigned on 27 April 1968 convinced that he had been a victim of intra-party machinations masterminded by Chief Minister K. Brahmananda Reddy. He then used the Telangana issue to keep himself in the limelight.

Second, right through his seventeen-year tenure as the Prime

---

[33]Gopal, Volume 31, 2002, pp. 334–45 and p. 547. A good analysis of the communist influence in the 1950s in Andhra and Hyderabad states, and its link with caste, is Harrison, 1960.

Minister, Nehru had been steadfastly refusing the demand of Sikh leaders, led by Master Tara Singh, for a Punjabi-speaking state as he was convinced that this was actually a cover for the creation of a separate state based on religion. However, Indira Gandhi, who became Prime Minister in January 1966, quickly reversed her father's stance in September that year and agreed to the reorganization of Punjab to create a new state of Haryana and a larger Himachal Pradesh. Earlier, she had played a key role in persuading India's first Prime Minister to create Maharashtra and Gujarat in May 1960 with the city of Bombay firmly in the former state.[34] It is entirely possible that political leaders from Telangana now sensed an opportunity for reviving their demand for a separate state.

Third, every agitation needs ammunition to sustain itself and for Telangana this was provided by the perceived non-implementation of the Gentlemen's Agreement of 1956. This perception was not entirely wrong.[35] To make matters worse, from a Telangana point of view at least, the Andhra Pradesh High Court delivered a judgement on 3 January 1969 which exempted employment in autonomous bodies of the state government from the domicile rules in place. These rules had a long history; the Nizam had put them in place way back in 1919 to protect the residents of the Telangana area and give them preference in government employment in their own region. These 'Mulki Rules' had, however, become inoperative from 21 March 1959 when a law passed by Parliament—the Public Employment (Requirements as to Residence) Act, 1957—came into effect. Nevertheless, Parliament had taken care to say in the law that government employment in the Telangana area would be open only to those who had been residing there for not less than fifteen years and could provide written evidence to this effect.

In July 1968, employment in the state electricity board had been brought under the purview of this law. It was *only* this that

---

[34]In his recent memoirs, Pawar (2015), quotes Y.B. Chavan, Maharashtra's first Chief Minister as having told him and other colleagues about Indira Gandhi's crucial role in creating Gujarat and Maharashtra in May 1960.
[35]This is described in detail in K.V. Ranga Reddy's autobiography (2009). He was a leading figure of the Telangana movement in the 1950s and 1960s.

the 3 January 1969 High Court judgement, invalidated, leading to an immediate furore because employment opportunities in electricity boards were substantial. But the 1957 Act in its entirety was not held unconstitutional. Nevertheless, the Telangana region, and more particularly Hyderabad city, witnessed mass protests—no doubt egged on by disgruntled Congressmen like M. Chenna Reddy and others. Indira Gandhi forced Chief Minister Brahmananda Reddy to convene an all-party meeting on 19 January in Hyderabad when an agreement was reached among the forty-four leaders present. This agreement, while rejecting the creation of a separate Telangana state, presented a detailed plan of action for addressing the grievances of the youth from Telangana as well as the concerns of domiciled employees (Annexure 2).

However, this agreement provided only short-lived respite. On 3 February, a single-judge bench of the Andhra Pradesh High Court held that the key provisions of the Public Employment (Requirements as to Residence) Act, 1957 were themselves unconstitutional. This went beyond the earlier judgement of 3 January. As expected, this added fuel to the fire even though, on 20 February 1969, a two-judge bench of the High Court set aside the judgement of the single-judge bench. This new order could have cooled passions for a while but a final blow was delivered by the Supreme Court on 28 March 1969 when, in response to a separate writ petition filed before it, it too held the entire domicile rules to be unconstitutional.

This decision spurred further agitations by youth, lawyers and dissident Congressmen, and a new outfit called the Telangana Praja Samithi (TPS) was formed. Indira Gandhi was forced to step in and, on 11 April 1969, she announced an eight-point programme in the Lok Sabha to restore normalcy in the state and address the numerous grievances of the Telangana agitators meaningfully (Annexure 3). But she firmly rejected the demand for a separate state. Her intervention, however, did not have the desired impact and protests continued unabated, forcing her to fly to Hyderabad late at night on 4 June.

Writing about her nocturnal air-dash, T.V. Rajeswar, who was then the Intelligence Bureau officer in charge of the Prime Minister's security, has this to say:[36] 'On the night before the Prime Minister's departure for Kabul, Hyderabad was in total turmoil. The agitation for the creation of a separate state of Telangana was getting out of hand. Mrs. Gandhi had to fly to Hyderabad late in the night to assess the situation, meet the leaders of the agitation and sort out the mess to the extent possible. She returned to Delhi in the early hours the next day and took off for Kabul soon thereafter.' Home Minister Y.B. Chavan then went to Hyderabad to follow-up on the Prime Minister's visit. The position of Brahmananda Reddy as Chief Minister was getting increasingly tenuous. Ministers from the Telangana region, led by Konda Lakshman Bapuji, resigned from his Cabinet.

Though largely unappreciated by historians, Chavan played an important role. All through the later half of 1969, he sought to bring about a rapprochement between the warring parties in the state. He went to Hyderabad twice in the space of three months. There was talk of creating a new state of Telangana based on the Meghalaya model. (In January 1967, Chavan had suggested the formation of a separate hill state of Meghalaya out of Assam as part of a regional federation in which the two states would be constituent units with equal status.) The proposal as it related to Telangana did not move forward.[37] Brahmananda Reddy survived because he sided with Indira Gandhi when the Congress split in November 1969—a momentous year in many ways. This was the year that saw not just the presidential election in which V.V. Giri defeated N. Sanjiva Reddy, the official Congress candidate, but also the nationalization of banks. It was in 1969 also that the Naxalite movement gathered significant momentum in Srikakulam, Warangal and other districts of Andhra Pradesh.

The disquiet in Andhra Pradesh continued, although at a lower pitch, all through 1970. In December that year, Indira Gandhi called for Lok Sabha elections, to be held in mid-February 1971, about fourteen months before they were due. She scored a stunning victory and stormed back to power with a two-thirds majority. However, in Telangana, it was the TPS that did very well, winning 10 of the 14

---

[36] Rajeswar, 2015.
[37] Chavan's role is discussed in Kunhi Krishnan, 1971.

Lok Sabha seats in the region, with Indira Gandhi's Congress winning just 3 of the 12 seats it contested there. While Indira Gandhi was now the undisputed leader of the country, having received a huge overall mandate, she knew that her weakness in Telangana could play havoc with the Congress' fortunes in Andhra Pradesh. She invited the TPS leaders, led by M. Chenna Reddy, for talks and succeeded in getting them to merge their party with the Congress in August 1971.

Indira Gandhi then moved to assuage Telangana sentiments by appointing P.V. Narasimha Rao as Chief Minister of Andhra Pradesh on 30 September 1971. Rao was a Brahmin in a state whose politics was dominated by the Reddys and the Kammas. But, more importantly, he hailed from Karimnagar in the Telangana region, although he was known as an integrationist—that is, a believer in a unified Andhra Pradesh. He had a none-too-distinguished record as an MLA and a minister; undoubtedly he had been selected in the knowledge that he would be a complete Indira-loyalist.

Rao's appointment as Chief Minister had necessarily to be accepted by everybody in the state because of the all-powerful position of Indira Gandhi at that time. But it was clear that sooner or later his authority would be challenged. Ironically, this began to happen immediately after he led the Congress to a spectacular victory in the February 1972 assembly elections in which the Congress won an unprecedented 219 of the 287 seats it contested and got 53 per cent of the popular vote. Of course, there was a definite Indira factor at work here but Rao was the sitting Chief Minister. He would later claim that his land reform policies, implemented as part of Indira Gandhi's own socio-economic agenda, alienated powerful sections of Andhra Pradesh's political class who then conspired to get rid of him. This is not without foundation but there was another major event that sealed his fate. This had to do with the Mulki Rules issue once again.

On 4 February 1972, a full five-judge bench of the Andhra Pradesh High Court ruled on a writ petition that domicile rules for employment in the Telangana area, put in place by Parliament in March 1959, through the Public Employment (Requirements as to Residence) Act, 1957, were unconstitutional. This reiterated what the

Supreme Court had said on 28 March 1969 but on a different case. Both the state and central governments appealed to the Supreme Court which, in its judgement handed down on 3 October 1972, reversed the Andhra Pradesh High Court decision and now upheld the domicile rules to be in accordance with the Constitution. This was a complete turnaround by the Supreme Court itself within a short span of three years. Narasimha Rao welcomed the Supreme Court judgement as providing finality to the vexed issue and said he would implement the domicile rules in public employment. This at once triggered unrest in the coastal districts of the state where the feeling grew that employment opportunities in Hyderabad would now not be available to those living outside the Telangana region. While Telangana was joyous with what the Supreme Court had to say, the rest of Andhra Pradesh was very angry. If a Jai Telangana movement had rocked Andhra Pradesh in 1969–70, the state witnessed a Jai Andhra movement in 1972–73. The movement now was for the more advanced and prosperous coastal districts to separate from Telangana.[38]

The agitation got out of hand and the army had to be called in. Indira Gandhi announced a five-point peace formula in the Lok Sabha on 27 November 1972 but that did not seem to work as intended. In her statement (Annexure 4), she bemoaned the fact that state leaders had not been able to arrive at an amicable solution to the situation arising out of the Supreme Court judgement and had, instead, passed the buck on to the central government. She reiterated her opposition to bifurcation but announced measures to soften the impact of the Supreme Court judgement. Very soon thereafter, in January 1973, she got Narasimha Rao to resign and imposed President's Rule in the state. She then appointed H. C. Sarin as one of the two advisors to the Governor. Sarin, an ICS (Indian Civil Service) officer, had spent years in the Ministry of Defence and had a reputation for being a tough, no-nonsense administrator.

With Sarin in Hyderabad, Indira Gandhi deputed her Minister of State in the Home Ministry, K.C. Pant, to negotiate a settlement that

---

[38]The Jai Andhra, Jai Telangana and Naxalite movements are described very well in Sen, 2003.

would end the political agitation. Pant had worked closely with the Prime Minister earlier. He was also known to her personally, since he was the son of Govind Ballabh Pant who, as Home Minister, had played a pivotal role in the formation of Andhra Pradesh in November 1956. Pant (the son, that is), a most patient listener as I can testify from my experience, held numerous rounds of negotiations both in New Delhi and Hyderabad. Finally, a six-point formula (Annexure 5) for restoring peace in Andhra Pradesh was made public on 21 September 1973,[39] with more clarifications issued a month later.

The formula itself was an agenda for reviving the elected government, addressing concerns of regional disparities within the state, and ensuring that there was no injustice in access to employment and education to anyone in the state, while at the same time recognizing some historical legacies that the state had to carry. The six-point formula led to the Constitution (32nd Amendment) Act, 1973 that inserted Article 371-D in Part XXI of the Constitution of India dealing with 'Temporary, Transitional and Special Provisions'. It is Part XXI that contains, for instance, Article 370 concerning Jammu and Kashmir and Article 371-A concerning Nagaland. Article 371-D, which became effective from 1 July 1974, was included to ensure equitable opportunities to all people from different parts of Andhra Pradesh mainly in matters of public employment and education.

Indira Gandhi did not stop with this. Normally, central universities are created by laws passed by Parliament. But mindful of the seriousness of the issue and determined to send out the right political signals during a troubled period in the state, she also got Article 371-E inserted in the Constitution at the same time as Article 371-D. This provided for the establishment of a central university in Andhra Pradesh

---

[39]Interestingly, though the declaration's title was 'Statement Issued by Leaders of Andhra Pradesh', it had no signatories. It is only through the efforts of Syed Jafri, a senior journalist and now a member of the Telangana legislative council, that I was able to access issues of the *Deccan Chronicle* newspaper of those days which reported 76 'signatories' comprising MPs, MLAs, MLCs and others from both regions of the state. Prominent supporters of the statement were Brahmananda Reddy, P.V. Narasimha Rao, T. Anjaiah, J. Chokka Rao and Jaipal Reddy, with M. Chenna Reddy unreconciled to it, at least publicly.

which later came to be located in Hyderabad.[40] Subsequently, an extraordinarily detailed presidential order called the Andhra Pradesh Public Employment (Organisation of Local Cadres and Regulation of Direct Recruitment) Order, 1975 was issued on 18 October 1975. The seriousness with which the issue was taken by Indira Gandhi can be judged by the fact that a presidential order was issued under powers conferred on the President of India by the Constitution itself. By its very nature, such an order would have vastly greater sanctity than a mere executive order issued by a ministry of the Government of India. The Supreme Court was to later hold that orders issued under Article 371-D cannot be challenged as unconstitutional. That was exactly what Indira Gandhi and her key advisors like Pant had intended.

Indira Gandhi is justifiably given credit for the North-Eastern Areas (Reorganisation) Act, 1971 that established the states of Manipur and Tripura and that led to the formation of the state of Meghalaya and the union territories of Arunachal Pradesh and Mizoram. She is also rightly given credit for the Punjab Reorganisation Act, 1966. But her grand achievement in having Article 371-D (and Article 371-E) included in the Constitution has been inadequately analyzed and commended.[41] It is this that brought peace back to Andhra Pradesh and gave it a huge development boost.

When President's Rule was revoked after a long eleven-month spell in December 1973, Indira Gandhi appointed J. Vengal Rao another leader from Telangana as the Chief Minister. Vengal Rao, a Velama by caste and a fine administrator, consolidated on Brahmananda Reddy's

---

[40]Munshi (1967) writes that both Nehru and he had wanted Osmania University to become a central university after the successful 'police action' in Hyderabad in September 1948 but Sardar Patel and Maulana Azad had disagreed. On 22 June 1952, Nehru sent a detailed note to Maulana Azad and other Cabinet ministers advocating that Osmania University be made a central university. But this proposal went nowhere because of opposition in the Hyderabad assembly. The note is in Gopal, Volume 18, 1996, pp. 134–37.

[41]It is strange that none of the noted biographies of Indira Gandhi—by, for example, Dom Moraes, Uma Vasudev, Inder Malhotra, Pranay Gupte, Pupul Jayakar and Katherine Frank—have any worthwhile discussion of her role in managing the Andhra Pradesh crisis of 1969–73.

achievements and brought Andhra Pradesh to the front rank of India's states in both agriculture and industry.[42] However, when the Congress split for a second time in January 1978, Vengal Rao left Indira Gandhi and sided with Brahmananda Reddy, who became president of the rival Congress. But M. Chenna Reddy and P.V. Narasimha Rao stayed with her. In the February 1978 assembly elections,[43] Indira Gandhi's Congress won handsomely and M. Chenna Reddy, who Indira Gandhi had earlier appointed as Governor of Uttar Pradesh when Vengal Rao was appointed Chief Minister of Andhra Pradesh, finally achieved his ambition and became Chief Minister. He continued in that position for two years before he was replaced by T. Anjaiah (also from Telangana) who also had a two-year stint.

◆

For the next two decades, the Telangana movement lay dormant even if the sentiment had not altogether vanished.[44] Throughout the late 1960s and 1970s, it was clear that real socio-economic issues apart, factional politics within the Congress party in the state at the highest levels had kept the Telangana agitation going. It was also clear that both Nehru and Indira Gandhi had repeatedly given solemn assurances regarding safeguards for Telangana. In retrospect, had these assurances been implemented in letter and spirit by the state leadership within the Congress party, the Telangana sentiment would not have been kept alive in the manner it came to be.

[42]Vengal Rao's memoirs, made available to me in its English translation in a manuscript form by his son Jalagam Venkat Rao, are not particularly revealing on the Telangana issue but are very disparaging of Narasimha Rao.
[43]It may appear puzzling as to why elections were held in February 1978 when the previous polls were in February 1972. That was because Article 172 of the Constitution had been amended during the Emergency (42nd Amendment). This took effect from 3 January 1977 to extend the term of state legislatures from five years to six years. Subsequently, the 44th Amendment restored it to five years with effect from 6 September 1979.
[44]A scholarly study of the early Telangana movement is Reddy and Sarma, 1979. Reddy, 1989, is also noteworthy. Another valuable book is Weiner, Katzenstein and Rao, 1981.

Why was there no visible Telangana movement for almost two decades between 1980 and 2000, even after Indira Gandhi's assassination in October 1984? I would suggest two main reasons for this.

First was the dramatic political emergence of the film star N.T. Rama Rao, popularly known as NTR, on the plank of Telugu pride in January 1983—after the Congress had given the state four chief ministers in five years. NTR was a complete newcomer to politics, a colourful man in every way. He had broken the decades-long Congress hegemony in the state in a spectacular manner by stitching together a broad social coalition which, for the first time, gave prominence to backward classes and scheduled castes.[45] Given his charismatic personality, he was initially acceptable to all regions of Andhra Pradesh, a point he hammered home in the mid-term March 1985 assembly elections that he had called to secure a fresh mandate. NTR contested from Gudiwada (coastal Andhra), Nalgonda (Telangana) and Hindupur (Rayalaseema) and won all three seats. His entry into politics and his tenure as Chief Minister saw the rise of a new generation of political leaders who had not cut their teeth in the Telangana movement. NTR also shrewdly gave the impression that he was addressing emotive issues like discrimination in public employment and the sharing of river waters. People were willing to give him the benefit of doubt and a very long rope as well. This they did till 1989 when they voted massively against him, bringing the Congress back to power.

The second reason is that sometime in the mid-1980s, the People's War Group (PWG) reignited the Naxalite movement. In 1987, a group of Indian Administrative Service (IAS) officers, ironically well-known for their social and pro-tribal sensitivities, were abducted and held hostage for a couple of days in East Godavari district. Thereafter, the decade of the 1990s saw a large number of brazen, high-profile killings by the Naxalites. Between January 1993 and December 2001, three senior IPS

---

[45]This even though the Congress had appointed D. Sanjeevaiah, a scheduled caste leader, as Chief Minister in January 1960 and T. Anjaiah, a backward class leader, as Chief Minister in October 1980. In an obituary of NTR published in *Business Standard* on 25 January 1996, I had myself described NTR as both the product and the creator of social forces.

(Indian Police Service) officers, one MP and six MLAs were shot dead. Not only that, but on 1 October 2003, an attempt was made on the life of Chief Minister Chandrababu Naidu in Tirupati. It was the killing of establishment figures that forced the state government to be ruthless in its pursuit of Naxalite cadres who may well have been providing tacit support to the cause of a separate Telangana. It could certainly be, to use the language of econometrics, a spurious correlation but the fact remains that the Telangana movement was at its lowest point just as Naxalite killings and tough police action were at their peak.

M. Chenna Reddy, the prime mover of the Telangana agitation during 1969–71, came back as Chief Minister on 3 December 1989. His first tenure as Chief Minister lasted two years. His second term lasted just one year. Hyderabad witnessed its worst communal riots in November–December 1990, and he was replaced on 17 December 1990 by N. Janardhana Reddy. With the Ram Janmabhoomi movement of the Bharatiya Janata Party (BJP) gathering momentum all over the country, the politics of communal mobilization now appeared to have the upper hand over the politics of separatism in Andhra Pradesh too.

On 21 June 1991, all of Andhra Pradesh, particularly Telangana, rejoiced as Narasimha Rao became the Prime Minister of India. Resisting calls from various places, he decided to contest the Lok Sabha elections from Nandyal in Telangana. NTR announced that his Telugu Desam Party (TDP) would not oppose him. However, even with Rao at the helm, the old factional politics that had plagued the Congress in the past resurfaced and, on 9 December 1992, Janardhana Reddy was replaced as Chief Minister by K. Vijaya Bhaskara Reddy, a senior leader from Rayalaseema who was then a Union Cabinet Minister.

The Congress was decimated in the 1994 assembly elections and NTR stormed back as Chief Minister on 12 December 1994—although it was now evident that the TDP was in the midst of its own internal power struggle involving NTR on the one side and Chandrababu Naidu on the other. Chandrababu Naidu finally became Chief Minister on 1 September 1995. His single-minded focus on IT, especially in and around Hyderabad, created a whole new discourse. But the real estate boom generated by this strategy came to be seen as delivering huge windfall gains to people from outside the Telangana region. This began to create local resentment. Naidu succeeded in creating Cyberabad but, as Sanjaya Baru, an acute observer of Andhra Pradesh's political economy, was to tell me much later, the benefits of urban development were allowed to be cornered by non-locals. Baru's contention is that the McKinsey Vision 2020 report commissioned by Naidu ignored Telangana's development and Naidu focussed far too much on Hyderabad itself and on the Hyderabad–Vijayawada corridor. This was to provide the required ammunition to a person who almost became an early twenty-first century Sriramulu—K. Chandrasekhar Rao (KCR).

◆

It was in April 2001 that the Telangana issue come back into the nation's political agenda with a vengeance. The Telangana Rashtra Samithi (TRS) was formed on 27 April 2001 by KCR. KCR, a mesmerizing public speaker who was to use this talent to devastating effect later, had, like Chandrababu Naidu, started his political career in the Congress. He later joined the TDP in 1983. He had a lacklustre political career as a minister and a Deputy Speaker. Clearly miffed at not being made full Cabinet Minister by Chandrababu Naidu, he quit the TDP in 2001 and donned the mantle of a crusader for the cause of the people of Telangana—people who he said were being oppressed and denied their legitimate share by powerful and entrepreneurial individuals hailing from outside the Telangana region.

There is nothing in KCR's track record that sets him apart as a crusader for Telangana.[46] It is possible that this zeal lay dormant in him and it took the callousness of Chandrababu Naidu to make it bloom. It is also possible that KCR sensed an opportunity for the creation of Telangana when, in August 2000, the Atal Bihari Vajpayee government bifurcated Bihar, Madhya Pradesh and Uttar Pradesh to meet the long-standing demands for Jharkhand, Chhattisgarh and Uttarakhand respectively.[47] The BJP did not include Telangana in this round of the

[46] A long essay by Praveen Donthi in *Caravan* (April 2014) sheds much light on this subject.
[47] The Bihar Reorganisation Act, 2000; the Madhya Pradesh Reorganisation Act, 2000; and the Uttar Pradesh Reorganisation Act, 2000 were notified in the official gazette

reorganization of states—in spite of its own support for it—because of the opposition of its ally, the TDP.

Though he was strident, KCR was also unsure. He, therefore, entered into an alliance with the Congress for the 2004 assembly and Lok Sabha elections. It suited both parties. The Congress had been out of power for a decade in the state and must have seen in him a valuable ally to defeat the TDP. This alliance was based on a resolution passed by the CWC on 30 October 2001 which reads thus:

> The Committee considered the recommendations of the Pranab Mukherjee Committee which was set up to study the demands for formation of smaller states. The Committee felt that though there were many valid reasons for [the] formation of Vidarbha and Telangana, the reorganisation of existing States raised a large number of issues. The Committee was of the view that the whole matter could be best addressed by another States Reorganisation Commission to look into all the issues involved. The CWC accepted the recommendations of the Pranab Mukherjee Committee and decided to request the Central Government to set up another States Reorganisation Commission for this purpose.

KCR expressed his satisfaction with this resolution on 4 March 2004 in a joint press meet with D. Srinivas, then the president of the Andhra Pradesh Congress Committee (APCC).

Thereafter, the 2004 elections saw a spectacular performance by the Congress and the emergence of the strongman Y.S. Rajasekhara Reddy (YSR) as Chief Minister. The TRS won 26 assembly seats and 5 Lok Sabha seats. However, the Congress, with its very strong showing, was not dependent on the TRS either in the state or at the centre. Nonetheless, KCR was kept in good humour. With YSR at the helm, he was also kept in check. In May 2004, KCR became Minister of Labour and Employment in UPA-1 (United Progressive Alliance).

However, by September 2006, KCR's frustration at not being able to convince Sonia Gandhi and Manmohan Singh to create Telangana

---

of the Government of India on 25 August 2000 after Parliament gave its approval. The new states came into being three months later.

or even establish a second States Reorganisation Commission became evident. He felt that while Pranab Mukherjee was engaged in consultations, these were designed merely to keep a conversation going without conceding anything. KCR resigned as Cabinet Minister and moved back to Hyderabad to resume his agitational programme on a full-time basis. But with YSR there, he made little headway. In fact, all through 2007 and 2008, KCR and his party faced one problem after another and his credibility and relevance kept being called into question.

In the 2009 assembly and Lok Sabha elections, the TRS did a somersault and entered into an electoral alliance with the TDP ostensibly because that party had also done a somersault and committed itself to the formation of Telangana in October 2008. But this made no difference whatsoever. YSR roared back to office and delivered 33 of the 42 Lok Sabha seats in the state to the Congress. As for the TRS, its Lok Sabha strength dwindled to just 2 MPs and its assembly strength plummeted to a mere 10 MLAs. In May 2009, YSR was clearly on top, the undisputed king of the state so to speak, and even more critical to the UPA in New Delhi. As far as Telangana was concerned, just before the elections, on 12 February 2009, YSR had himself made this statement in the assembly:

> The Government of Andhra Pradesh has no objection for the formation of Telangana State in principle and feels that the time has come to move forward decisively on this issue. However, before taking any decision many of the issues need to be resolved as serious concerns have been raised by the stake-holders. The Government has, therefore, decided to constitute a committee of Members of both the Houses to deliberate the issues and concerns on the formation of Telangana and further steps could be taken after the report from the Joint Committee of Members from both the Houses is submitted to the Government.

This was, however, a conditional nod, as YSR's closest aide, K.V.P. Ramachandra Rao, was to admit to me much later. Incidentally, the committee mentioned in the resolution was chaired by K. Rosaiah, the then Finance Minister of Andhra Pradesh. It never met since elections, both for the assembly and Parliament, were announced shortly thereafter.

It was the sudden demise of YSR in a helicopter crash on 2 September 2009 that changed the politics of Andhra Pradesh completely. In YSR's death, KCR found a new life and started putting renewed pressure on the Congress leadership in New Delhi to agree to the creation of Telangana.

This book takes the story forward from YSR's death, which clearly was *the* event that finally made Telangana possible. A statement issued by the then Home Minister P. Chidambaram on 9 December 2009 was to trigger a whole chain of events that culminated in the bifurcation of Andhra Pradesh in February 2014 (Map 4). There were twists and turns no doubt in the intervening period but the die seemed to have been cast that fateful night.

MAP 4: INDIA AS ON 2 JUNE 2014

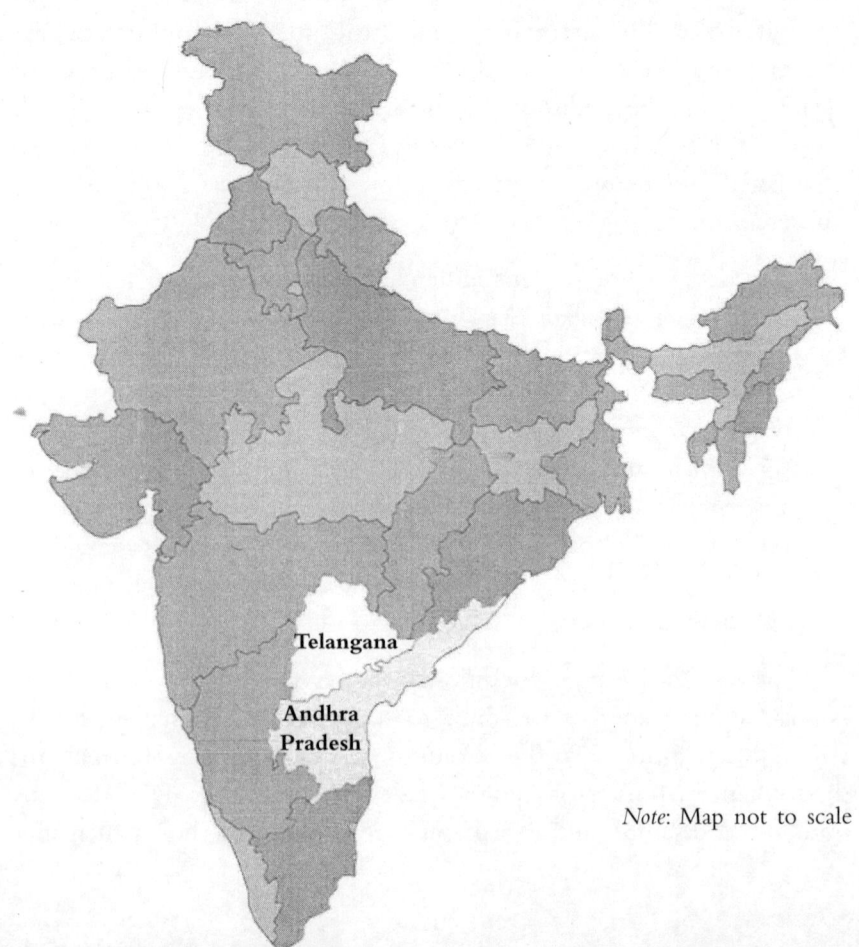

Note: Map not to scale

2

Ten Days That Shook Andhra Pradesh and After

John Reed's classic eyewitness account of the October 1917 Revolution in Russia is called *Ten Days That Shook the World*. The 29 November 2009–9 December 2009 period could well be termed as the 'Ten Days That Shook Andhra Pradesh'.[48]

With the sudden demise of YSR, the elderly K. Rosaiah succeeded him as Chief Minister the very next day. KCR may have felt that the pendulum had swung in his favour. Desperately trying to keep himself politically relevant, he went on a hunger strike on 29 November 2009. The atmosphere in Hyderabad became surcharged. Osmania University, in the heart of the city and at the centre of the agitation those days, was in a state of ferment.

The hunger strike was launched in Khammam jail where KCR had been detained, and continued thereafter from the morning of 3 December in a private ward in Hyderabad's Nizam Institute of Medical Sciences. With KCR's health appearing to deteriorate sharply, the Congress leadership asked Rosaiah to call an all-party meeting to figure out what was to be done regarding Telangana. Rosaiah did so on 7 December. Eight major political parties of the state attended and all of them, barring the Communist Party of India (Marxist) [CPI(M)], supported the proposal to adopt a resolution in the state

---

[48] A highly informative account of this period is Nag, 2011.

assembly for the creation of Telangana. The minutes of this meeting were sent to the Home Minister the very next day.

On 9 December at about 11:30 p.m. Home Minister P. Chidambaram issued a statement that was destined to change the state's history. It appears that the Home Minister did so based on his assessment derived from intelligence and other reports. KCR's health was one major factor influencing the decision-making process. The other related to the role that Maoists and their sympathizers *may* have been playing to aggravate the situation. Clearly, the highest echelons of the government had information that led them to believe that the ground situation in Hyderabad was grave and something really substantive had to be done to retrieve the situation. The Home Minister must have had reason to believe that a Potti Sriramulu moment had arrived once more in Andhra Pradesh. The statement itself was evidently finalized at Prime Minister Manmohan Singh's residence with the Home Minister, Pranab Mukherjee and Rosaiah present, and had apparently followed consultations with other leaders of the Congress.

The Home Minister's statement read thus:

> The process of forming the state of Telangana will be initiated. An appropriate resolution will be moved in the state assembly.
>
> We have requested the Chief Minister of Andhra Pradesh to withdraw the cases filed on or after November 2009, against all the leaders, students and others associated with [the] present agitation. The Chief Minister informed us he will take the necessary steps in this regard.
>
> We are concerned about the health of Shri K Chandrasekhar Rao; we request him to withdraw his fast immediately. We also appeal to all concerned, especially the students, to withdraw their agitation and help restore normalcy.

There was bedlam in Parliament the very next day on the grounds that the Home Minister had made a major policy statement outside Parliament when it was in session. In the Rajya Sabha, M. Venkaiah Naidu of the BJP led the charge. After a semblance of order had been restored, the Home Minister offered this clarification:

Sir, I am deeply grateful to the hon. Member. I know that he hails from Andhra Pradesh and, therefore, his concern can only be greater than the concerns of some other members. When he raised the matter yesterday, [the] Government was not in a position to respond, because, at that time, consultations were under way. When the consultations had been completed and the Government was able to come to a decision, it was very late in the night and, obviously, the matter did not brook any delay and we could not have possibly waited till the next morning to make the statement. Besides, what I said yesterday night at about 11:30 is a re-statement of an earlier decision of the Government, which is very well known to the House. It was a re-statement. And, of course, I said other things like cases will be withdrawn. We have requested the Chief Minister. I appealed to Shri Chandrasekhar Rao to withdraw his fast. Those were necessary to be said yesterday in order to bring the agitation to an end quickly and restore normalcy. I am happy to inform the House that, by and large, normalcy has been restored in Hyderabad and in Andhra Pradesh. Shri Chandrasekhar Rao spoke to me this morning. He has welcomed the statement. He has thanked all sections of the House who have extended support to him. And I have invited him to Delhi to come and discuss the next steps. With this, I humbly request the hon. Member to let the matter rest.

The matter got raised in the Lok Sabha as well when the BJP patriarch L.K. Advani made a longish intervention supporting the decision. Interestingly, on 1 April 2002, L.K. Advani as Home Minister had written to A. Narendra, a TRS MP, turning down the demand for Telangana (Annexure 6). Yet, on 10 December 2009, Advani did a U-turn and said:

Madam Speaker, I am grateful for giving me an opportunity to congratulate the House as you have set a precedent by intervening on the issue of Andhra Pradesh. It is due to the intervention of the Parliament that the Government has taken a very important decision. I would like to congratulate the Government and specially the Parliament. Both the issues on which the House had expressed its concern yesterday have been sorted out. We are in favour of creation of Telangana state as per the wishes of the people of Telangana. We are also wishing that the life of our colleague may not be in danger because he was on a fast for ten days on this issue and his condition had become critical. I am happy that both the issues have been sorted out and I congratulate you for this.

Madam Speaker, I was expecting that the Hon'ble Home Minister would come out with a decision of the Government in this regard. He had announced it outside. He should announce here also and explain the action to be taken on the proposal of the Assembly. Constitutionally, it is not necessary but it will be good if it is done. I would like the Government to take the House into confidence about the procedure and steps to be taken regarding the creation of the twenty-ninth state. I know that much is needed before introducing a Bill to this effect. I would like the Government to complete the groundwork before introducing this Bill. However, I would be happy if the Government takes the House into confidence regarding the further action to be taken in this regard, about their strategy, expectations and the time by which it is likely to be done.

With the Home Minister busy sparring with Venkaiah Naidu in the Rajya Sabha it was left to the then Finance Minister and the top Congress trouble-shooter, Pranab Mukherjee, to respond to the veteran BJP leader in the Lok Sabha, which he did thus:

Madam, I would, first of all, like to thank the Leader of the Opposition and submit that as the decision was taken very late last night we are yet to get information from the State Government about the response to the announcement made by the Home Minister. Some rallies are being organised there. Therefore, we are yet to get the full information from the State Government. So far the collected information is that Shri Chandrasekhar Rao has withdrawn his fast. We are appreciative of it. He has responded to it. The hon. Leader of the Opposition is fully aware that other information also are [sic] required. In regard to the formation of the new State all procedures will be followed. But if we have information from the State which we would like to share with the House, definitely during the day or tomorrow we will keep the House informed.

The 9 December 2009 statement gave ammunition to both sides. Telangana supporters were convinced that the creation of the new state of Telangana was now only a matter of time. On the other hand, proponents of a united Andhra Pradesh ('Samaikya Andhra') felt betrayed and launched a counter-agitation to register their protests. The protests found their echo in Parliament as well with MPs of the Congress and the TDP from the Telangana region supporting the 9 December statement and members from the Seemandhra[49] region expressing their grave concerns.

Passions ran high across Andhra Pradesh. Ministers and MLAs from Seemandhra resigned. The statement had immediate national reverberations as well. Demands for the formation of Vidarbha, Gorkhaland, Bodoland and Maru Pradesh were raised by political leaders of Maharashtra, West Bengal, Assam and Rajasthan respectively. A leading political leader of Tamil Nadu, S. Ramadoss, called for the bifurcation of that state as well. The Chief Minister of Uttar Pradesh wrote to the Prime Minister twice in quick succession asking for the giant state to be split into four smaller states.

There appeared to be all-round confusion. On 10 December, Congress spokesman Abhishek Singhvi went on record to say, 'The first logical step towards the creation of a separate state has to be an expression of consensus through a resolution of the Assembly.' This drew immediate attack from the TRS leaders who were perhaps aware that such a consensus was simply impossible. On 12 December, K. Rosaiah was quoted in the media as having said that 'he was astonished, surprised and anguished by Mr Chidambaram's statement'. He must have been pulled up because the very next day his office issued a clarification saying that his purported astonishment and anguish was not with the 9 December statement of P. Chidambaram but with 'the turn of events in the aftermath of the statement'.

---

[49]Seemandhra refers to undivided Andhra Pradesh minus Telangana (in other words, to the coastal districts plus Rayalaseema).

As this clarification was being issued, Singhvi declared that there was no need for a second SRC, which was surprising, as this was contrary to the Congress' official stance since October 2001. More importantly, that very day, Pranab Mukherjee said in Kolkata, 'The agitation for Telangana has been going on for sixty years. This does not mean everywhere a new state has to be created...The State government concerned has to express its view because the President would like to know the view of the State before recommending a Bill to be considered in Parliament. For the formation of every state these are the preliminary things [that need to be done].'

On 14 December, another Congress spokesman, Shakeel Ahmad, no doubt taking a cue from Mukherjee's statement, went on record to say, 'The Centre would initiate the process of creating a separate state of Telangana only after the Andhra Pradesh Assembly passed a resolution to this effect.' However, he also added that this did not mean that the government was going back on the 9 December statement.

Sensing that the 9 December pronouncement had created a huge crisis, which the central government had perhaps not anticipated, P. Chidambaram issued a second statement exactly a fortnight later. This read as follows:

> At a meeting of all political parties convened by the Chief Minister of Andhra Pradesh on December 7, 2009, a consensus emerged on the question of [the] formation of a separate state of Telangana. A statement was made on behalf of the Central Government on December 9, 2009 on receipt of the minutes of the meeting.
>
> However, after the statement, the situation in Andhra Pradesh has altered. A number of political parties are divided on the issue. There is need to hold wide-ranging consultations with all political parties and groups in the State. [The] Government of India will take steps to involve all concerned in the process.
>
> Meanwhile, it is necessary that peace and harmony are restored in Andhra Pradesh and the State Government is allowed to focus on governance and development.
>
> The Central Government appeals to the people of the different regions of Andhra Pradesh and all political parties and students

to withdraw their agitations and maintain peace, harmony and brotherhood.

In the light of what was claimed subsequently, it is worthwhile to recall that in the meeting convened by the Chief Minister of Andhra Pradesh on 7 December 2009, the TDP categorically stated, 'if Government brings [a] Resolution for separate Telangana, the TDP will support the Resolution'. Indeed, N. Chandrababu Naidu, the president of the TDP, had written to Pranab Mukherjee on 18 October 2008 that the TDP was in favour of the formation of a separate Telangana state (Annexure 7).

The next turn in this saga took place four weeks later when the Home Minister met with eight recognized political parties of Andhra Pradesh in New Delhi on 5 January 2010. He welcomed them with a detailed statement, the crucial parts of which read thus:

> I welcome you to this consultation on the issues arising out of the recent agitations in Andhra Pradesh in favour of and against a separate State of Telangana.
>
> There are a number of misconceptions surrounding the issues that have brought us here today. There is a misconception that the Central Government acted in haste; that the political parties were not consulted; and that I, as Home Minister, acted as an individual. As you are well aware, none of these misconceptions is supported by facts, but I shall not waste your time refuting these misconceptions.
>
> You are all aware of the long history behind the demand for a separate State of Telangana...
>
> The Central Government was concerned when an agitation was started in November 2009 demanding a separate State of Telangana. Quite rightly, the political parties in Andhra Pradesh were the first responders to the agitation. You are aware of the proceedings of the Business Advisory Committee of the Andhra Pradesh State Assembly on December 7, 2009 followed by the proceedings of the all-party meeting convened by the Chief Minister of Andhra Pradesh later in the evening of the same day.
>
> I wish to reiterate that the first statement on behalf of the

Central Government was made on the basis of the minutes of the all-party meeting held on December 7, 2009.

It is true that the situation on the ground has altered significantly since the all-party meeting of December 7, 2009 and the first statement on behalf of the Central Government on December 9, 2009. Taking note of the altered situation, on December 23, 2009, the Central Government promised to hold wide-ranging consultations with all political parties and groups in Andhra Pradesh. It is therefore that we have convened this meeting of the recognised political parties.

I urge each of the political parties represented here to show accommodation and goodwill. Ultimately, you must find the answers and you must help the Central Government find a solution... What is the mechanism that you visualise for the consultations with all political parties and groups in Andhra Pradesh? What is the road map for such consultations?

A few weeks later, on 3 February 2010, the Government of India, undoubtedly at the instance of the Home Minister himself, announced the formation of a five-member committee headed by the eminent jurist, B.N. Srikrishna, who had retired from the Supreme Court in the early 1990s and had earlier headed the inquiry into the communal riots that had rocked Bombay (now Mumbai) following the demolition of the Babri Masjid in Ayodhya on 6 December 1992.

The Srikrishna Committee was given a wide-ranging mandate, but it was generally understood that it had been called upon to examine the case for the bifurcation of Andhra Pradesh to create Telangana. The committee took its work very seriously. It travelled across the state, received thousands of representations and met with hundreds of people from a wide cross-section. It submitted its report on 30 December 2010 in which it laid out six options:

1. Maintaining status quo: Keeping the Andhra Pradesh state as it is with no change in the Telangana, Rayalaseema and coastal Andhra regions.
2. Bifurcating the state of Andhra Pradesh into Seemandhra and Telangana regions with both of them developing their own

capitals in due course of time. Hyderabad to be converted to a union territory like the Chandigarh model.
3. Dividing Andhra Pradesh into two states: one of Rayala-Telangana with Hyderabad as its capital and second one of the coastal Andhra Pradesh.
4. Dividing Andhra Pradesh into Seemandhra and Telangana with the enlarged Hyderabad Metropolis as a separate union territory that will be linked geographically to district Guntur in coastal Andhra via Nalgonda district in the southeast and via Mahabubnagar district in the south to Kurnool district in Rayalaseema.
5. Bifurcation of the state into Telangana and Seemandhra as per existing boundaries, with Hyderabad as the capital of Telangana and Seemandhra to have a new capital.
6. Keeping the state united and providing for creation of a statutorily empowered Telangana Regional Council for socio-economic development and political development of the Telangana region.

Its clear recommendation was option 6—that is, no bifurcation. As far as bifurcation itself was concerned, the committee had this to say: 'Therefore, after taking into account all the pros and cons, the Committee did not think it to be the most preferred, but the second best option. Separation is recommended only in case it is unavoidable and if this decision can be reached amicably amongst all the three regions.'

There was great deal of talk that Justice Srikrishna had submitted, along with his voluminous report that was later made public, a secret report as well. The learned judge had known my parents for over fifty years. Taking advantage of this, I took the liberty of asking him about the truth regarding this perception. This is what he had to say to me in an email communication on 24 November 2015.

Dear Jairam:

Amongst various issues to be considered for the separation of Telangana, one important issue was the issue of security, if the state were to be bifurcated. We had called for intelligence inputs from the security forces including the DG of police and IB as regards the activities of Naxalites in the concerned areas and the possible effect of the formation of Telangana on such activities. This was particularly important as, if you remember, there had been considerable expansion of Naxalite activities in A.P. till the government ruthlessly put it down. There was quite a bit of apprehension that the Naxalites may resume their activities and expand them in a newly formed state. It was to address this issue that a police report was called for. The intelligence authorities desired that their report should not be bandied about. Obviously, a police report on security citing their sources, etc. cannot be a public document. Hence, we decided to shortly state our conclusion but submitted the intelligence report as a separate secret document meant only for the Home Dept. That document is in possession of the Govt. of India. There is no other mystery about the report.

With the submission of the Srikrishna Committee report and with its recommendation[50] it did appear as if the Telangana issue had been settled—that there would be no bifurcation. But right through 2011 and 2012, Telangana MPs belonging to the Congress kept up their pressure in the Lok Sabha forcing frequent adjournments. Agitations in the state also continued and even got violent. I was a little worried because as Minister of Environment and Forests I had managed to get Hyderabad as the venue for the Eleventh Conference of the Parties to the UN Convention on Biological Diversity to be held in October 2012. Ministers from over 150 countries were expected to attend and I wondered whether I had made the right choice after all. There were many who had asked me to have the prestigious conference in Delhi itself, but I had overruled them. Fortunately, the ten-day conclave went off very smoothly.

The Srikrishna Committee report was made public on 6 January 2011 at an all-party meeting convened by the Home Minister. Perhaps having got wind of its recommendations, the BJP, TRS and TDP

---

[50]Rao (2011) is a sober critique by an eminent economist. His *Regional Disparities, Smaller States and Statehood for Telangana*, 2010, is also valuable.

boycotted the meeting. Five other parties—Congress, the Praja Rajyam Party (later to be merged with the Congress in February 2012), the Communist Party of India (CPI), the CPI(M) and the All India Majlis-e-Ittehad-ul Muslimeen (AIMIM)—participated. A statement was issued (to which the AIMIM was not a signatory) appealing to the people of Andhra Pradesh to maintain peace, harmony, and law and order. The Home Minister asked all parties to give 'most careful, thoughtful and impartial consideration to the report and its recommendations'.

The disturbed situation in the state found echo in a Calling Attention Motion moved in the Lok Sabha on 5 August 2011. This turned into a full-fledged debate on Telangana and the Srikrishna Committee report. A number of members, mostly from the Congress and the BJP, took part and the government was under sustained attack for postponing a final decision on the creation of Telangana. It was perhaps for the first and last time that such a prolonged discussion took place on this issue, despite there being interruptions galore and much acrimony. Finally, the Home Minister made another detailed intervention. He bemoaned that the Calling Attention Motion had become a divisive debate and reiterated his belief that the 'solution to the problem which had arisen—demand for Telangana on the one side and the demand for maintaining a united Andhra Pradesh on the other—must come from the Telugu-speaking people'. He underscored that the 'government can only facilitate the solution' and called upon all political parties to go through with their process of consultation. Ironically, he admitted that 'the Congress Party has told me that they have not made up their mind finally'.

The Home Minister was to make yet another pronouncement on Telangana on 2 May 2012 when replying to the debate on the demands for grants of the Ministry of Home Affairs. It was again a combative defense of his 9 December 2009 statement—which was still being seen by most as his solo venture. He said:

> There was a question on Telangana. If any one believes that the Union Home Minister can unilaterally call a few Press persons and make an announcement on Telangana, I think you do not know how the Government functions. No Home Minister can make such

a statement. Now, the circumstances under which that statement was made are well known. Please recall the proceedings of the Business Advisory Committee of the Andhra Pradesh Assembly of 7th December 2009. They unanimously said…(*interruptions*). You are aware of the proceedings of the Business Advisory Committee on 7th December…Followed by the proceedings of the all-party meeting convened by the Chief Minister of Andhra Pradesh later in the evening the same day, two meetings took place on that day. After looking at the Business Advisory Committee meeting's proceedings and the all-party meeting's proceedings—and we have the minutes of the all-party meeting of 7th December—a decision was taken and we made the announcement on December 9th, 2009. But the situation altered dramatically within 24 hours. Virtually every major political party split, including the Party to which I belong, the Congress Party. On this issue, they were divided. Because of the dramatic change in the situation we were obliged to make the revised statement on 23rd December 2009 saying that we have no option now but to call all the political parties to deliberate on the mechanism and lay down a road map for further consultations. That is how all the parties were called again and then the Srikrishna Committee was appointed…The Srikrishna Committee has submitted its report. We are on record that we want all eight political parties to express their opinion.

There was a change of guard in the Home Ministry on 1 August 2012 when, after Pranab Mukherjee's elevation to Rashtrapati Bhavan, P. Chidambaram moved from one end of North Block to another to become Finance Minister for a third time, and Sushilkumar Shinde replaced him as Home Minister. Shinde convened another all-party meeting on 28 December 2012 in order to find a way forward on the Telangana issue. Saying that this would be the last such meeting, the new Home Minister also announced that a final decision on the matter would be taken within a month and that whatever decision would be taken would be 'good' for all sides. As it turned out, that 'one month' was to become something like six months. In fact, on 27 January 2013, a day before Shinde's deadline was to expire his senior colleague, Ghulam Nabi Azad publicly stated that more talks and consultations were needed with state leaders and that a final decision would be taken 'as soon as possible'. With the all-important Budget session of Parliament just a little over three weeks away, Azad was really saying that the decision would be taken only after mid-May 2013 when the Budget session would get over.

The long history (as described in chapter 1) apart, this then was the immediate forty-four-month background to the fateful meeting of the CWC on 30 July 2013. It was at this meeting of the party's top policy-making body that the decision was taken to finally bifurcate Andhra Pradesh and create Telangana.[51] This meeting had been preceded by consultations among all the UPA allies like the Nationalist Congress Party (NCP), Rashtriya Lok Dal (RLD), National Conference (NC) and Dravida Munnetra Kazhagam (DMK). In retrospect, the decision to bifurcate must have been taken between 28 December 2012 and sometime in early June 2013. Not being privy to any of the discussions that took place during that period, I am unable to shed authentic light on why the decision got taken. Besides, there are no written records or a paper trail.

All that I have been able to piece together is that on 1 July 2013, Digvijaya Singh (who was appointed general secretary of the Congress dealing with Andhra Pradesh on 16 June) made a public statement in Hyderabad that the process of taking a decision on Telangana was in the final stages. Then, on 12 July, three leaders from Andhra Pradesh—Chief Minister Kiran Kumar Reddy, Deputy Chief Minister Damodar Raja Narasimha and APCC president Botcha Satyanarayana—were asked to make presentations to a group consisting of Prime Minister Manmohan Singh; Sonia Gandhi, her political secretary, Ahmed Patel; Defence Minister A.K. Antony, Health Minister Ghulam Nabi Azad,

---

[51]The senior Congress leader, M.L. Fotedar, writes that R.K. Dhawan and he were deliberately not invited to the 30 July 2013 CWC meeting because they would have vehemently opposed the division of Andhra Pradesh in keeping with Indira Gandhi's policy. The fact is that Fotedar and Dhawan were not regular members but only permanent invitees to the CWC who sometimes got invited and sometimes did not. Shinde and Chidambaram were also permanent invitees to the CWC but appear to have attended in their respective capacities of home minister and immediate ex-home minister (Fotedar, 2015).

Home Minister Sushilkumar Shinde; and Digvijaya Singh. As expected, the Chief Minister and the APCC president made a strong case against bifurcation, while the Deputy Chief Minister canvassed for a separate Telangana.

A fortnight later, Ghulam Nabi Azad and Digvijaya Singh met the trio separately in the capital. That evening, the Prime Minister hosted Sonia Gandhi, A.K. Antony, Sushilkumar Shinde, Ghulam Nabi Azad, P. Chidambaram, Ahmed Patel and Digvijaya Singh at his residence. This meeting clearly decided that Telangana would finally be created, which was later formalized by the CWC on 30 July.

What happened after the submission of the Srikrishna Committee report for the Congress to have decided to go ahead and bifurcate Andhra Pradesh?

It could well be that the large number of tragic suicides that took place during 2011 and 2012 to push for the creation of Telangana influenced the final decision. Hyderabad particularly had become the arena for continuous agitations mounted by various organizations, most notably the Telangana Joint Action Committee (TJAC) that had mobilized both state government employees and students. In a shocking act, statues of a number of Telugu icons like Krishnadevaraya, Annamacharya and Sir Arthur Cotton—that NTR had got installed along the picturesque Hussain Sagar lake in the city—were vandalized on 10 March 2011. In July 2011, ministers from the Telangana region in the state Cabinet resigned and stopped attending their offices. (They would, however, attend official lunches hosted in my honour by the Chief Minister whenever I visited the state as Union Minister of Rural Development and request for more financial assistance for ongoing programmes and schemes!)

It could also be that with the BJP, TDP and YSR Congress Party (that was formed in March 2011) giving letters and statements in favour of the creation of Telangana, the Congress felt that its hands were strengthened to go ahead with the bifurcation. Chandrababu Naidu wrote to the Home Minister on 27 December 2012, one day before the all-party meeting in Delhi, urging for a quick decision in favour of creating a separate Telangana (Annexure 8). A day later, the Home Minister received a letter from M.V. Mysura Reddy and

K.K. Mahender Reddy on behalf of the YSR Congress Party (Annexure 9) reminding him that the central government had powers under Article 3 of the Constitution to create Telangana and that the continued delay by it to exercise these powers was wreaking havoc in the state.

Of course, it could also well be that the Congress expected the TRS to merge with it before the 2014 Lok Sabha polls. Telangana had 17 seats and Seemandhra 25. It could also well be that the Congress realized its prospects in Seemandhra were bleak in any case because of a ten-year anti-incumbency wave and because of the growing strength of the YSR Congress Party—it was, therefore, trying to minimize its losses by protecting itself in Telangana at least.

But these are all, I must emphasize, only intelligent guesses. The only thing that is incontrovertible is that P. Chidambaram's statement of 9 December 2009 had been a decisive turning point.[52] Also indisputable is that thereafter Ghulam Nabi Azad was able to convince the Congress leadership that bifurcation would yield electoral dividends for the Congress.

It is time now to move on to my own involvement in the bifurcation drama.

---

[52] At this watershed moment, I was far away in Copenhagen, leading the Indian delegation to the UN climate change conference. Considering the role I was to play subsequently in the bifurcation process, few believed that I was completely unaware of the statement and its fallout.

3
My Earlier Brush with Telangana

The Lok Sabha passed the Andhra Pradesh Reorganisation Bill, 2014 on 18 February 2014 and the Rajya Sabha did so two days later. I happened to be a member of the Group of Ministers (GoM) that was set up on 8 October 2013 to prepare this Bill, five days after the Cabinet had given its go-ahead to the bifurcation. For over a hundred days thereafter the GoM became almost my full-time preoccupation. I had not expected to be part of it, so it had come as a complete surprise.

Actually, I have to admit that, while my membership of the GoM was a bolt out of the blue, I did have some connection with the Telangana issue prior to the formation of the GoM. These links certainly had no bearing on my being on the GoM but are of some historical interest in themselves. There were three such occasions over the period spanning 2004 to 2012.

First, a year before the CWC meeting, I got dragged into the Telangana debate in 2012 on account of some remarks I made in Uttar Pradesh. On 17 July 2012, I was touring the district of Sonbhadra in eastern Uttar Pradesh that was affected by left-wing extremism. In the course of a long conversation with two journalists, I mentioned the urgent need to split the state into four for administrative convenience and better governance. I had put forward a strong case for reorganizing India's most populous state, something that I had (and have) been doing for quite some time. I had not even remotely alluded to Telangana in any way. However, over the next two days, my comment was reported widely in the press and the Telangana media speculated that, given my statements on Uttar Pradesh, the creation of Telangana was back on the government's agenda. For instance, on 19 July 2012, *Mission Telangana*, an online news portal reported thus:

Jairam Ramesh's Comments Positive for Telangana

Is the Congress-led UPA government giving a serious thought to creating a Telangana state? The answer seems yes going by the remarks made by Union minister Jairam Ramesh that smaller states can be administered better. Telangana leaders say they have received enough hints that the central government is indeed seized of the issue and is inclined to grant statehood to the region.

Jairam Ramesh, who toured Sonbhadra district of Uttar Pradesh on Tuesday, said it was the right time to end [an] 'administration nightmare' and create smaller states by splitting big states like Uttar Pradesh. The Uttar Pradesh Assembly, during the rule of Mayawati's BSP, adopted a resolution urging the Centre to split the Indian's [sic] biggest state into four. The resolution is pending with the Union government.

Picking up the thread and continuing the debate on smaller states, Ramesh said, 'Uttar Pradesh should be divided. The magnitude of the state's problems is very high with 200 million people, 75 districts and each district with 2.5 million people.'

Ramesh, who assessed developmental works being undertaken under the Centre's Integrated Action Plan, said administration was not reaching the backward regions of the state, particularly eastern UP, because of its size and large population...

Leaders of the TRS and other parties from Telangana said Jairam Ramesh's remarks were significant as he was elected to the Rajya Sabha from Andhra Pradesh and knew well about the Telangana demand and sentiment. He echoed the Telangana leaders' argument that smaller states ensured better administration.[53]

The second connection with the Telangana issue came on 6 April

---

[53] Available on www.missiontelangana.com, accessed on 11 April 2016.

2006 when I was asked a question regarding it in an interaction with the media in Vijayawada. *The Hindu* carried this news report the next day.

Separate Telangana Not Easy, Says Jairam Ramesh

Formation of [a] separate Telangana is not easy as in the cases of Uttaranchal, Chhattisgarh and Jharkhand, for they are not on the same footing, according to Union Minister of State for Commerce, Jairam Ramesh. Mr. Ramesh utilised Thursday's press conference here as an opportunity to push the Telangana ball into TRS President K. Chandrasekhar Rao's court. Mr. Ramesh said that the Congress was committed to the formulation adopted in the National Common Minimum Programme (NCMP) on the issue of [a] separate Telangana.

The NCMP clearly mentioned that a separate state would be 'considered at an appropriate time through a process of consultation and consensus'. The words 'consider', 'appropriate time', 'consultation and consensus' in the formulation had to be understood in their true spirit.

The formulation was not unilateral but several political parties had agreed to it, he said and emphasised that Mr. Rao was also a signatory to the NCMP.

After all, [the] formation of Telangana was not a burning issue. There were much bigger issues like Naxalism and land disputes which needed immediate attention. He said that the state government was trying to reduce imbalances between Telangana and other regions.[54]

My earliest link to the Telangana issue had come about in May 2004. Leaders of the newly-formed UPA had met on the evening of 16 May 2004 at Sonia Gandhi's residence. Thereafter, I had been asked by the Congress leadership to work with all UPA allies and come up with a National Common Minimum Programme (NCMP), which would be an agenda for governance for the coalition government.

By 25 May, I had, in consultation with Prakash Karat and Sitaram

---

[54] *The Hindu*, 7 April 2006.

Yechury of the CPI(M), D. Raja of the CPI, Lalu Prasad Yadav of the Rashtriya Janata Dal (RJD) and Dayanidhi Maran of the DMK, got a draft NCMP ready for the consideration of the UPA leaders. But the section on Telangana was proving sticky. KCR insisted that the NCMP make an unequivocal statement that the state of Telangana would be formed soon. But this was unacceptable not just to Congress leaders but also to some of its allies like the CPI(M). I was also somewhat uncomfortable with including such a direct commitment.

Various formulations were tried out but none of them were found acceptable. I spent considerable time with Pranab Mukherjee, the Congress' ace draftsman for over three decades, trying to find a way out but KCR remained unbending. KCR then invited me to his residence to meet Professor K. Jayashankar, a leading ideologue of the Telangana movement; but even then we could not effect a breakthrough. Then, Mukherjee and I negotiated with KCR and finally agreed on a statement that got incorporated into the NCMP:

> The UPA government will consider the formation of a separate state of Telangana at an appropriate time after due consultations and consensus.

I thought this formulation—which had been suggested by KCR—protected all sides. It was sufficiently clear and ambiguous at the same time—which is what drafting by committee is all about. The NCMP was officially released on 27 May 2004. Its formulation on Telangana was repeated in President A.P.J. Kalam's address to both Houses of Parliament on 7 June 2004.

Incidentally, it could have been his frustration with these 'consultations' promised in the NCMP, being managed by Pranab Mukherjee (then the Defence Minister and later the External Affairs Minister), that may have led KCR to resign from the Cabinet in September 2006.

II
NEW GEOGRAPHY

4

The GoM Summons

It was around lunch time on 8 October 2013 that I received a sealed envelope from the Cabinet Secretariat. I thought it was perhaps an intimation of a Cabinet meeting. Little did I realize that my life was about to be turned upside down and I was soon to earn the undying wrath of Telugus all over the world who were opposed to the bifurcation of Andhra Pradesh.

The communication read thus:

1. The Cabinet Secretariat had, in its meeting held on 3.10.13, considered the note dated 3.10.13 from the Ministry of Home Affairs regarding 'Bifurcating the State of Andhra Pradesh and Formation of a New State of Telangana' and approved the proposal for the creation of a new state of Telangana by bifurcating the existing state of Andhra Pradesh. The Cabinet also decided inter alia that a Group of Ministers (GoM) be constituted to address all the issues that needed resolution at the Central and State Government levels in the matter.

2. The composition of the GoM, as approved by the Prime Minister, will be as under:

Shri Sushilkumar Shinde
Minister of Home Affairs

Shri A.K. Antony
Minister of Defence

Shri P. Chidambaram
Minister of Finance

Shri Ghulam Nabi Azad
Minister of Health and Family Welfare

Shri M. Veerappa Moily
Minister of Petroleum and Natural Gas

Shri Jairam Ramesh
Minister of Rural Development

Special Invitee:

Shri V. Narayanasamy
Minister of State in the Ministry of Personnel, Public Grievances and Pensions, and Minister of State in the Prime Minister's Office

3. The GoM may, if considered necessary, also invite any member of the Union Council of Ministers as a special invitee.

4. The terms of reference of the GoM will be as below:
    (i) determine the boundaries of the new state of Telangana and the residuary state of Andhra Pradesh with reference to the electoral constituencies, judicial and statutory bodies, and other administrative units;
    (ii) look into the legal and administrative measures required to ensure that both the State Governments can function efficiently from Hyderabad as the common capital for 10 years;
    (iii) take into account the legal, financial and administrative measures that may be required for transition to a new capital of the residuary state of Andhra Pradesh;
    (iv) look into the special needs of the backward regions and districts of both the States and recommend measures;
    (v) look into the issues relating to law and order, safety

and security of all residents and to ensure peace and harmony in all regions and districts consequent to the formation of the state of Telangana and the residuary state of Andhra Pradesh, and the long-term internal security implications arising out of the creation of the two states and make suitable recommendations;

(vi) look into the sharing of river water, irrigation resources and other natural resources (especially coal, water, oil and gas) between the two States and also inter-se with other States, including the declaration of Polavaram Irrigation Project as a National Project;

(vii) look into the issues related to power generation, transmission and distribution between the two States;

(viii) look into the issues arising out of the distribution of assets, public finance, public corporations and liabilities thereof between the two States;

(ix) look into the distribution of the employees in the subordinate as well as All India Services between the two States;

(x) look into the issues arising out of the Presidential Order issued under Article 371-D of the Constitution consequent to the bifurcation;

(xi) examine any other matter that may arise on account of the bifurcation of the State of Andhra Pradesh and make suitable recommendations.

The Cabinet Secretariat notification laid out very detailed and specific terms of reference. That is as it should have been. But it was the composition that I found interesting and caused me to raise my eyebrows momentarily. When the Cabinet had met on 3 October,[55] to consider a note on the formation of Telangana and the constitution of a GoM to prepare the necessary legislation by the Ministry of Home

---

[55]In this long Cabinet meeting, the Prime Minister patiently asked every member for his or her view. All, barring M.M. Pallam Raju and K.S. Rao, supported the bifurcation because the CWC had already passed a resolution to this effect on 30 July 2013.

Affairs, it had approved both proposals. A ten-member GoM, with members selecting themselves by virtue of the portfolios they held, was to be set up. In addition to the Home Minister and Finance Minister, the proposal had the ministers of human resource development, power, water resources, urban development, road transport, law and personnel as members, apart from the Deputy Chairman of the Planning Commission. This ten-member group had, in fact, been announced on 4 October, a day after the Cabinet meeting. But four days later, a somewhat different seven-member GoM was notified.

It was clear that while the revised seven-member GoM had members who self-selected themselves by virtue of the portfolios they held (like the Home Minister, the Finance Minister and the Minister of State for Personnel), some had also been selected keeping in mind their political backgrounds.

Sushilkumar Shinde had himself been Governor of Andhra Pradesh between November 2004 and January 2006.

P. Chidambaram was the one who made the official statement on 9 December 2009 that brought the Telangana issue back into sharp focus after five years of discussions. He had been the main anchor for all talks on Telangana as long as he was Home Minister till mid-2012. He had spoken thrice in two-and-a-half years on the subject in Parliament.

A.K. Antony was one of the senior-most leaders of the Congress and a member of the Congress' 'core group' that usually met on Friday evenings at the prime minister's residence during 2004–14. Besides, he had headed the committee set up to confer with Congress MPs and MLAs following the CWC resolution of 30 July 2013. Earlier in the mid-1980s, he had been general secretary of the Congress party dealing with Andhra Pradesh.

Ghulam Nabi Azad, apart from being the most ardent advocate of bifurcation, was also a senior minister. During 2004–07 he had been the general secretary of the Congress party dealing with Andhra Pradesh.

Veerappa Moily, too, had been a general secretary in charge of Andhra Pradesh in the past (specifically at the time of the 9 December 2009 statement made by P. Chidambaram), while Narayanasamy had worked under Azad in the run-up to the 2004 assembly and Lok Sabha elections.

Frankly, I was unable to figure out my inclusion, although I had been an MP representing Andhra Pradesh since July 2004 and had travelled extensively across the state. I queried the Home Minister about it when I called on him almost immediately after receiving the GoM notification. I had enjoyed a warm personal relationship with Shinde for almost two decades. And, during 2008–09, I had worked with him in the Ministry of Power. The ever-smiling Shinde—whom Bal Thackeray had once called 'Hasmukh' to distinguish him from his colleague Deshmukh (Vilasrao)—patted me on the back and said in Hindi, '*Arre yaar, sawal kyoon poochte ho; upar se aaya hoga; ab kaam par lag jao; mazdoori tum hee ko karna hai* (why do you ask questions, buddy; orders may have come from the top; now get going; you will have to do the work)'.

As we know, the CWC resolution on Telangana had been passed on 30 July 2013 and the Cabinet decision came sixty-four days later. I had always been intrigued by this somewhat long gap till I came across a statement by P. Chidambaram—who had by this time become Finance Minister—in the Rajya Sabha on 5 August 2013. I had somehow missed this as I had been caught up in the Lok Sabha that day.

> In the matter relating to the formation of a separate State of Telangana, the Constitution of India lays down a procedure for formation of a new State. Besides, a number of substantive matters have to be addressed in the formation of a new State. These matters are under the consideration of the Government. The Ministry of Home Affairs will bring a comprehensive note to the Cabinet containing both substantive and procedural issues for the decision of the Cabinet. These will include but not be limited to sharing of river waters, generation and distribution of electricity, safety and security of all residents of all three regions, guarantee of fundamental rights of all residents, etc. Once the Cabinet takes decisions on these matters, there will an opportunity for this House to have a structured discussion on the subject. The Government will welcome such a discussion at an appropriate time.

But actually there may well have been another reason for the long gap. After the CWC resolution came out in such direct and unambiguous language, all hell broke loose within the Congress party. The Telangana protagonists, were, of course, exultant, but those opposed to the bifurcation mobilized their forces. The Chief Minister of Andhra Pradesh, Kiran Kumar Reddy, took a strident public stance against it. MPs from coastal Andhra Pradesh, including members of the Union council of ministers from Seemandhra like V. Kishore Chandra Deo, M.M. Pallam Raju, K.S. Rao, K. Chiranjeevi, D. Purandeswari. Killi Kruparani, Panabaka Lakshmi, Kotla Surya Prakash Reddy and J.D. Seelam, gave public expression to their firm opposition to the resolution.

Sensing that the divisions within the party were running deep and seeing the escalation of public agitations in Seemandhra, the Congress leadership constituted a committee headed by A.K. Antony to talk to all Congress MPs and MLAs from the state to explain to them why the CWC had passed the decisive resolution on 30 July 2013 (Annexure 10). The committee had other members like Digvijaya Singh, Veerappa Moily, Ahmed Patel, Ghulam Nabi Azad and Vayalar Ravi. This committee, however, did not visit the state; since tempers were running high, it was felt that such a visit would not have had much value. Instead, the committee resorted to fire-fighting from New Delhi which, in retrospect, was to prove wholly inadequate.

5
Getting the GoM Going

I met the Home Minister a second time on the morning of 9 October 2013 to informally discuss with him how the GoM should function. My immediate request to him was that we should set up a website and invite representations from the public at large. He readily agreed. I then suggested that the GoM consider a couple of sittings in Hyderabad and other places. Given the tense political climate in the state, Shinde didn't think this was a good idea at all. However, he asked me to raise it when the GoM met formally. He told me that we had to complete the work and have a draft law ready by end-November 2013. This meant that we had a little over fifty days to fulfil our mandate. I informed Shinde that I would focus immediately on water and education issues as I believed they were the most important (as well as the most acrimonious). He gave me the go-ahead to speak to the state government.

The first formal meeting of the GoM took place on 11 October. I had prepared a detailed background note putting down the positions of the Telangana and Seemandhra sides as I saw them against each item of our terms of reference. This was briefly discussed and members felt that it was a useful starting point. As expected, the GoM turned down the suggestion to hold any of its sessions in the state. However, it agreed to launch a website. In addition, it decided to invite formal memoranda from all political parties in the state, gave the go-ahead to calling their representatives to meet the GoM and directed the Union Home Secretary to get written reports from the concerned central ministries as well as from the state government on issues we were tasked to cover. Before the GoM meeting ended, I requested that we stop using the phrase 'residuary state of Andhra Pradesh' as was being done and, instead, use the phrase 'successor state of Andhra Pradesh' to refer to that part of the undivided state not included in Telangana. The word 'residuary'—which was in vogue both in the Home Ministry and Law Ministry—sounded, in my view, somewhat disrespectful.

Another issue engaged the GoM's attention at its first meeting. Three Acts had been passed by Parliament in August 2000 for the reorganization of Bihar, Madhya Pradesh and Uttar Pradesh to create the new states of Jharkhand, Chhattisgarh and Uttarakhand, respectively. These Acts were virtually identical in structure and detail. Recognizing the peculiarities of the situation in Andhra Pradesh, the GoM straightaway decided that going by past laws would just not do and that completely new legislation would have to be prepared for its bifurcation.

Chief Minister Kiran Kumar Reddy met me a couple of days after the GoM held its first meeting. I had enjoyed a comfortable relationship with him since July 2004. We had, in fact, worked closely to get the National Dairy Development Board (NDDB) to expand its operations in the state. But he was a changed man now—messianic in his zeal to oppose the CWC resolution tooth and nail. I asked him how, as Chief Minister, he could oppose what the leadership of his own party had decided. But he did not seem to find any incongruity in his behaviour.

The Chief Minister's point was simple. He argued that bifurcation could not take place without the *approval* of the state assembly. We had a long discussion. To leave no room whatsoever for any doubt, I read out Article 3 of the Constitution:

Parliament may by law

(a) form a new State by separation of territory from any State or by uniting two or more States or parts of States or by uniting any territory to any part of any State;

(b) increase the area of any State;
(c) diminish the area of any State;
(d) alter the boundaries of any State
(e) alter the name of any State;

Provided that no Bill for the purpose shall be introduced in either House of Parliament except on the recommendation of the President and unless, where the proposal contained in the Bill affects the area, boundaries or name of any of the States, the Bill has been referred by the President to the Legislature of that State for expressing its views thereon within such period as may be specified in the reference or within such further period as the President may allow and the period so specified or allowed has expired.

The proviso was inserted through the Constitution (Fifth Amendment) Act, 1955 in order to put a time limit within which the states could express their views on any proposal for reorganization referred to them under Article 3. Constitutional scholars have been unanimous in their view that Article 3 (and Article 4) confers supreme and exclusive power on Parliament for creating new states by reorganization. In the words of the authoritative D.D. Basu, 'The law-making power under Article 3 (and Article 4) is paramount and is not subject to nor fettered by Article 246 and Lists II and III of the Seventh Schedule.'[56]

I also brought to the Chief Minister's attention four Supreme Court judgements—that my young aide, Muhammed Khan, was able to track down in minutes—that had upheld Parliament's supremacy in regard to the creation of new states. These were:

1. *Babulal Parate vs The State of Bombay and Another*; 28 August 1959
2. *Union of India vs Valluri Basavaiah Chaudhary, Etc.; Etc.;* May 1979
3. *ITC Limited vs Agriculture Produce Market Committee and Others;* 24 January 2002

---

[56]Basu, 2015.

4. *Mullaperiyar Environment Protection Forum vs Union of India and Others*; 27 February 2006

I also reminded the Chief Minister that the Acts that had bifurcated Bihar, Uttar Pradesh and Madhya Pradesh were challenged in the Supreme Court in 2002 in the *Pradeep Choudhury and Others vs Union of India Transfer Case (Civil)*. The Supreme Court had delivered its judgement on 5 May 2008 and held that 'consultations' with the state legislature were mandatory but that the legislature's recommendations were not binding on Parliament. However, the Supreme Court had held that 'consultations' would not mean 'concurrence'.

But I must admit that none of what I had to say on the Constitution had any impact on the Chief Minister.[57] He was convinced that the Government of India was completely in the wrong constitutionally, apart from being on a politically suicidal path. We agreed to disagree. He left with the promise that he would prepare a detailed response to each of the items in the GoM's terms of reference.

---

[57]I also handed over a note to him entitled 'Legal Position Regarding the Creation of a New State Under the Indian Constitution', that was prepared at my behest by the Home Ministry and the Law Ministry. In view of its continuing importance, the note is reproduced in Annexure 11.

6

Freezing Telangana

For decades, the geography of what might constitute Telangana was well-known. Undivided Andhra Pradesh had twenty-three districts of which ten constituted the Telangana region, broadly corresponding to the Telugu-speaking areas of the erstwhile princely state of Hyderabad. These were Adilabad, Khammam, Nizamabad, Mahabubnagar, Nalgonda, Warangal, Karimnagar, Medak and Hyderabad proper (from which a new district called Hyderabad [Rural] was carved out in 1978 and renamed Rangareddy a year later). Of these districts, Khammam was always considered a borderline case as it was created only in July 1953 and had included large areas of the East and West Godavari districts and some areas of the Krishna district from coastal Andhra (Map 5).

The GoM kept this in mind and started operating on the basis of Telangana having these ten districts. However, during its deliberations, a new idea emerged—that of Rayala-Telangana, comprising the ten districts of Telangana plus the districts of Anantapur and Kurnool from the Rayalaseema region.[58] There were many proponents of this idea.

---

[58] The four districts of Rayalaseema—namely, Anantapur, Cuddapah, Chittoor and Kurnool—were ceded by the Nizam of Hyderabad to the East India Company in October 1800.

MAP 5: KURNOOL AND ANANTAPUR IN RELATION TO TELANGANA

Note: Map not to scale

Asaduddin Owaisi of the AIMIM championed Rayala-Telangana on the grounds that it would strengthen secular politics and would be an effective foil to the Rashtriya Swayamsevak Sangh (RSS) in Telangana—an argument that appealed to the GoM greatly. Congress leaders from these two districts advocated it on the grounds of administrative convenience. These leaders—of whom N. Raghuveera Reddy and A. Venkatarami Reddy from Anantapur and Kotla Surya Prakash Reddy from Kurnool were the most prominent—met me with resolutions (all identical!) from around 1,600 gram panchayats from their districts favouring the merger with Telangana. They also made the point that if Rayala-Telangana were to be proposed in the Bill to be sent to the assembly for its consideration, we would be assured of the support of twenty-eight MLAs from these two districts, thereby increasing the support for bifurcation in that forum. Yet another argument given was that by attaching Anantapur and Kurnool to Telangana, the MLA and MP strength of the new states would be equal.

I brought these facts to the attention of the GoM, which spent some time discussing their pros and cons. Ultimately, it was felt that the inclusion of two new districts would raise a whole new set of issues. It would also provide fodder for further agitations in Telangana. In fact, the TRS, on getting wind of the GoM's deliberations, had already started protesting stridently against Rayala-Telangana.

My own feeling was that Rayala-Telangana had merit particularly from the point of view of minimizing disputes related to the sharing of the Krishna River waters. But I also felt that the idea came too late in the day for it to have any chance of being discussed coolly and of having a larger consensus built around it. It is true that the Srikrishna Committee had considered this option in 2010 but the idea had not gathered any worthwhile momentum. I was able to keep it alive till 4 December and, in fact, got two Bills prepared—one with a ten-district Telangana and another with a twelve-district Telangana. But I was unable to carry the day as the overwhelming opinion in the party, the government and the GoM favoured a Telangana with the original ten districts.

7
The Tussle for Hyderabad

Hyderabad was the main bone of contention during the bifurcation process. It generated all the political heat. The Telangana camp wanted Hyderabad lock, stock and barrel. The Seemandhra camp—still pleading with the GoM not to go ahead with the bifurcation—wanted Hyderabad to be a union territory like Chandigarh, if not permanently then at least for a period of ten years. The reason for the Hyderabad-fixation was no mystery. The Hyderabad Metropolitan Development Authority (HMDA) area generated close to half of the undivided state's own revenues.[59]

An overwhelming bulk of the investment that had taken place in Andhra Pradesh since the mid-1950s had been in and around Hyderabad, largely because of the easy availability of land—even though the perception was that the people of Telangana had not gained much from these investments. The Government of India's own investment in both civilian and defence research and development was in Hyderabad. Many public sector companies had been established in this area. Entrepreneurs from coastal Andhra had made huge investments in education, health and real estate. Hyderabad was the centre of the Telugu film industry, which was again largely the creation of people

---

[59]That is, the revenues available to the state on its own without any transfers from the central government.

from coastal Andhra. Between 1996 and 2003, Chandrababu Naidu had put Hyderabad on the IT map of India and the world, something that was skilfully carried forward and given further impetus by YSR.

The CWC resolution of 30 July 2013 had actually ruled out the possibility of union territory status for Hyderabad. But I felt that our ministerial colleagues from Seemandhra needed to be given the satisfaction that they were been heard and, as such, saw no harm in revisiting the issue.

There were a number of factors militating against Hyderabad being made a union territory. The Srikrishna Committee itself had studied this option and had not been terribly enthusiastic about it. The most important argument was that Hyderabad lay at the geographical core of Telangana. Besides, historically and culturally, Hyderabad was inextricably linked to Telangana. It had been at the centre of the Telangana movement since the 1960s.

Telangana without Hyderabad would really not amount to much. Indeed the entire fight between Telangana and Seemandhra boiled down to a fight over Hyderabad. Hyderabad with union territory status would never have been acceptable to the agitationists from Telangana. In fact, Congress and TDP MPs from Telangana, as well as political parties like the TRS, BJP and AIMIM, were firmly opposed to a Chandigarh-like status to Hyderabad on the grounds that there was no geographical contiguity between Hyderabad and Seemandhra. The geographical position of Chandigarh vis-à-vis Punjab and Haryana was completely unlike that of Hyderabad in relation to Seemandhra and Telangana as a glance at the respective maps would immediately reveal (maps 6A and 6B).

But which Hyderabad should be the common capital? Union ministers from Seemandhra, having seen the writing on the wall as far as the union territory issue was concerned, then argued that the HMDA area should be designated as the common capital. This covered something like 7,100 square kilometres and spanned five Telangana districts. There was no chance of this proposal being accepted but the GoM did consider it. The TRS argued for the Hyderabad Revenue District, if at all, as the common capital area. This covered some 217 square kilometres. This too was debated briefly. Ultimately, the

MAP 6A: CHANDIGARH IN RELATION TO PUNJAB AND HARYANA

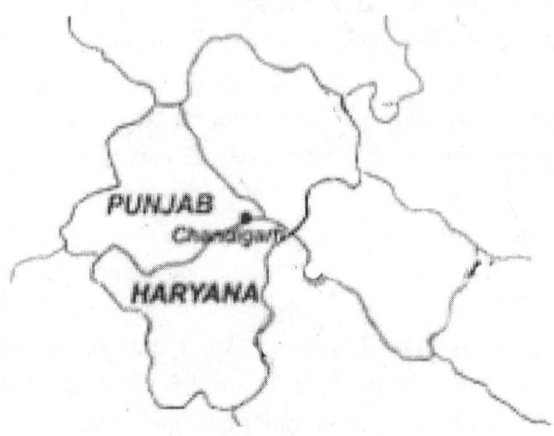

MAP 6B: HYDERABAD IN RELATION TO TELANGANA AND SEEMANDHRA

Note: Map not to scale

GoM felt that fairness demanded that the Greater Hyderabad Municipal Corporation (GHMC) area be designated as the common capital zone. This spread across about 625 square kilometres that had been increased to about 923 square kilometres in September 2013.

At one stage, I proposed to the GoM that we set up an independent committee to suggest the distribution of revenues from Hyderabad between the two new states for a period of ten years at least. If not a committee, then perhaps we could mandate the Fourteenth Finance Commission to perform this task. But this proposal did not survive for too long as the Finance Minister said that it would not be constitutionally sustainable. That was that.

Another idea which was discussed for some time in the GoM but was also shot down, was that of a common capital governance council. My main aim was to have a structure that would evoke the widest-possible confidence given the prolonged period of strife in the city. The council was meant to be a temporary body subject to review after five years. The governor was envisaged as the chairperson of the council that would also have as members the two chief ministers and key civil and police officials from both states and the central government. The council would be responsible for general oversight, review and coordination in matters relating to internal security, public order and the safety of all residents in the common capital area.

The Home Minister lauded the sentiments that prompted the proposal but did not think it to be practical at all. The idea didn't get Home Secretary Anil Goswami's support on the grounds that this would simply not be acceptable to the Telangana government once that state came into being. He was right. Besides, both the Home Minister (as a former Chief Minister) and the Home Secretary felt that the move would not stand the test of legality. They had a strong case. The Law Ministry also gave its opinion that such a coordination council would violate List II of the Seventh Schedule of the Constitution dealing with the powers of the states. I didn't, therefore, push my idea too much. But I thought it was worth a try.

8
A New Capital for a New Andhra Pradesh

When the GoM met with Union ministers from Seemandhra, it received varied suggestions for the location of the new capital. One suggestion favoured Kurnool which had been the capital of Andhra between 1953 and 1956. Another suggestion supported Visakhapatnam which was Seemandhra's largest city as well as a major investment destination. Voices were raised for Tirupati and Vijayawada too. The Home Minister and I felt that if the GoM was to make a specific recommendation on the capital, new complications would arise and fresh protests would erupt. So we decided on the safest and time-tested course of having an expert committee study the alternatives and make recommendations.

I was keen that we get the best experts on this committee. When Rajiv Sharma, an Additional Secretary in the Ministry of Home Affairs and one of the two officers who formed the core of the GoM's secretariat, suggested the name of K.C. Sivaramakrishnan as Chairman of this committee, I jumped at the idea and called him up then and there. He had been a distinguished administrator who had many years of experience in urban planning and development in West Bengal, the central government and the World Bank. As Secretary in the Ministry of Urban Development at the centre, he was responsible for drafting what became the 74th Amendment to the Constitution dealing with urban local bodies. I had known him well personally for years. In fact, he had contacted me of his own accord when the GoM was announced and sent a detailed note suggesting a structure to enable Hyderabad to function as a shared capital. That note had been circulated at the first meeting of the GoM but its suggestions were found to be politically impractical since its starting point—that the HMDA area would be the common capital zone—had been rejected by the GoM right at the outset.

Sivaramakrishnan readily accepted my request to chair the new capital selection committee. He also felt that the other people I had identified as members were first-rate. With that concurrence, I then got in touch with each of them and the committee was formed. The terms of reference were drawn up and the committee was notified on 28 March 2013; it was given time till 31 August 2013 to submit its report. The only substantive point I made to Sivaramakrishnan in my one and only meeting with him on this subject was that his committee should look at dispersing the location of functions and institutions so that the Hyderabad experience did not repeat itself in the new state. In this context, I reminded him that when the new state of Andhra was created in October 1953, the capital was in Kurnool and the High Court was in Guntur in the coastal area. Even today, Bhopal is the capital of Madhya Pradesh while the Madhya Pradesh High Court is located in Jabalpur. My suggestion to him was also that the committee could think of different 'clusters' for industry, education and administration across the new state of Andhra Pradesh.

One particular demand made by Seemandhra ministers and MPs caused me considerable anguish. They asked for the denotification of 50,000 hectares of forest land for the purpose of building the new capital. As Minister of Environment and Forests during 2009–11, I had adopted a tough policy on the diversion of forest lands, and what was being suggested went against all that I stood for. It took some time to reconcile myself to this demand but I was able to ensure that the denotification would only be for 'degraded' forest land, that is, where the quality of existing forest cover was very poor. I was also able to ensure that while we agreed to denotify, we did not specify how much forest land would be so denotified.

Demands were made by our Seemandhra colleagues that the

central government should fund the cost of creating the new capital. I was entirely in agreement with this sentiment as was the Home Minister, and we made sure that this commitment was reflected in the legislation. Thus, Section 94(3) of the final law that was passed said, 'The Central Government shall provide special financial support for the creation of essential facilities in the new capital of the successor state of Andhra Pradesh including the Raj Bhawan, High Court, Government Secretariat, Legislative Assembly, Legislative Council, and such other essential infrastructure.'

9
Two States, One Governor

Knowing the passions that had been aroused on the bifurcation issue but also acutely conscious of the commonalities that bound Telangana and Seemandhra, I felt that it was absolutely necessary to create institutions that would keep the two successor states together. I put forward the idea of a common governor to the GoM—and it readily saw merit in it. Both the Home Minister and the Finance Minister felt that the GoM should make an explicit recommendation to this effect and incorporate it in the legislation.

But what would be the role of the governor? The GoM believed that the governor would have a crucial role at least in the first decade, especially if there were to be a common capital. I argued that even if the capital were not common, it made sense to have a common governor for ten years because he, along with the centre, would ensure that the bifurcation would be effected in a relatively smooth manner.[60] Ultimately, of course, everything depended on the two chief ministers but I felt that there had to be a mechanism that would facilitate

---

[60]In this, I had also been influenced by B.K. Nehru's memoirs (1997) in which he had written about how as Governor of Assam and Nagaland he had advocated a common governor for Meghalaya, Manipur and Tripura which had been made full states of the Indian Union by the North-Eastern Areas (Reorganisation) Act, 1971. Indeed, he had functioned as one for two years. In Chapter 1, I have also highlighted Jawaharlal Nehru's own preference for a common governor for Andhra and Madras in 1953.

cooperation between them on a regular basis. Gone were the days when two chief ministers like N. Sanjiva Reddy of Andhra Pradesh and K. Kamaraj of Madras could resolve territorial disputes between their states (as they had done in the late 1950s). I also felt that the Home Minister could not always be expected to intervene to settle day-to-day disputes between the two states.

Jaipal Reddy, a senior ministerial colleague and an ardent Telangana advocate (though he had earlier been a strong champion of a united Andhra Pradesh), met the Home Minister and me on 27 November 2013. He drew our attention to Article 371-H of the Constitution which relates to the role of the governor in the state of Arunachal Pradesh. His suggestion was that we could use this as a model to define the role of the common governor. I pointed out to him that that article had been incorporated into the Constitution through a constitutional amendment because it had been contemplated *after* the state of Arunachal Pradesh had been formed (in February 1987) whereas in the case of Telangana the new state was yet to be created. But I thought Jaipal Reddy had given us a possible solution and had suggested something that the GoM could usefully consider.

At the next meeting of the GoM I mentioned his suggestion and added my caveat as well. As soon as I had finished, the Finance Minister—the legal eagle eye that he is—said, 'What is the problem, we can incorporate this transitional provision in the Reorganisation Bill itself?' I was not entirely sure and when I queried the Finance Minister further, he replied, 'according to Article 4(2) of the Constitution, no such law (making special provisions for the role of the common governor) shall be deemed to be an amendment to the Constitution.' To settle the issue in his inimitable style, the Finance Minister straightaway dictated what came to be Section 8 in the Andhra Pradesh Reorganisation Act, 2014. The Law Ministry did not tamper with his language much. Section 8 reads thus:

> (1) On and from the appointed day, for the purposes of administration of the common capital area, the Governor shall have special responsibility for the security of life, liberty and property of all those who reside in the area.

(2) In particular, the responsibility of the Governor shall extend to matters such as law and order, internal security and security of vital installations, and management and allocation of Government buildings in the common capital area.

(3) In discharge of the functions, the Governor shall, after consulting the Council of Ministers of the State of Telangana, exercise his individual judgement as to the action to be taken: Provided that if any question arises whether any matter is or is not a matter as respects which the Governor is under this sub-section required to act in the exercise of his individual judgement, the decision of the Governor in his discretion shall be final, and the validity of anything done by the Governor shall not be called in question on the ground that he ought or ought not to have acted in the exercise of his individual judgement.

(4) The Governor shall be assisted by two advisors to be appointed by the Central Government.

I was fully aware that this proposition would be controversial even though the role of the governor did not extend to revenue, municipal and land administration. Furthermore, day-to-day law and order would continue to be the responsibility of the government of Telangana in the common capital area. But all of us were convinced that there should be a common governor until such a time as the capital remained common and that his functions should be enshrined in the legislation itself.

Over and above this, I informed the GoM that the Ministry of Home Affairs should issue a directive to both states, detailing in writing the functions of the governor and the manner in which he would exercise these functions. This would spell out the implications of what we had in mind and leave nothing to doubt.

The GoM agreed but said that such a directive could be issued only after the two states had come into being. I did not want to argue because, strictly speaking, the GoM was right. However, my view was that if such a directive were to be issued immediately after Parliament had approved the reorganization legislation, there would be far greater clarity about what exactly the GoM had in mind. I discussed the contents of this directive with the Home Minister and his colleagues separately and gave them a draft of what I was proposing.

As it turned out, the Ministry of Home Affairs issued a draft three-page office memorandum titled 'Special Responsibility of the Governor of Telangana' on 4 June 2014, nine days after the new government led by Narendra Modi assumed office and Rajnath Singh had replaced Sushilkumar Shinde as Home Minister. I was gratified that the OM was virtually what had been finalized during Shinde's last days in North Block. It was extraordinarily detailed and such an 'advisory' was being issued perhaps for the very first time. It laid out in clear terms, as far as the common capital area was concerned, the powers of the governor, the state government (that of Telangana) and the police administration.

The OM was signed by S. Suresh Kumar, Joint Secretary in the Ministry of Home Affairs and was addressed, among others, to Rajiv Sharma, Chief Secretary to the government of Telangana (Annexure 12). I found this hilarious as Sharma had been Kumar's immediate boss till about a month earlier when he was still Additional Secretary in the Ministry of Home Affairs. Kumar, originally from Andhra Pradesh, was an officer of the West Bengal cadre of the IAS. Sharma, originally from Uttar Pradesh, was an officer of the (undivided) Andhra Pradesh cadre. The two of them comprised the secretariat of the GoM. The three of us had actually discussed the feasibility of issuing such an OM sometime in April 2014 and now one was sending it to the other in his new assignment! To be fair, both of them were of the view that such a directive would simply not be acceptable to the government of Telangana, but I was insistent. They were proven right. The state rejected the contents of the OM straightaway. That was that.

There were more weighty reasons that prompted me to push for this detailed communication. Put simply, the man who would be the first common governor, E.S.L. Narasimhan (a former Director of the Intelligence Bureau) himself wanted greater clarity about his precise role and the scope of his jurisdiction. He had, in fact, spoken to me and also sent the Home Minister a seven-page communication asking for an 'advisory' from the central government on how the governor should be executing the mandate of Section 8 of the Andhra Pradesh Reorganisation Act, 2014.

Why was this elaborate detailing of the role of the governor needed? Why was a special role for the governor being thought of in the first place? I must say that the main reason for this was the tension generated in Hyderabad by the highly provocative statements attributed to KCR and other TRS leaders. The GoM was inundated with messages that it must take note of what was being said against those from Seemandhra. There were grave apprehensions over calls by Telangana leaders and protagonists—like 'Telangana *jago aur Andhrawala bhago*' ('Wake up Telangana and Andhrawalas go away') and 'Hyderabad *sirf hamara*' ('Hyderabad is ours only'). The Telangana Employees Joint Action Committee had been saying that they had identified the Seemandhra-origin employees in Hyderabad who were participating in the Samaikya Andhra agitation and they would be 'taken care of' once Telangana state was created.

In fact, at the GoM meeting of 12 November 2013, both the Home Minister and the Finance Minister made their displeasure known to the TRS leaders, including KCR himself. It was in the background of the fear generated by KCR's vitriolic statements (some of which he disowned and repudiated though) that the GoM was virtually forced to think 'out-of-the-box' as far as the role of the governor was concerned. The GoM felt that it was its duty to instil confidence in all those living in Hyderabad, especially in those who hailed from the coastal districts of the state and had begun to feel insecure and threatened.

10

Internal Security Concerns

One major goal of the GoM was to ensure that bifurcation did not weaken the capacity of the new states to deal with the Maoist/Naxalite challenge. Seven of the ten districts of Telangana and eight of the thirteen districts in Seemandhra had been designated as 'LWE-affected' by the Ministry of Home Affairs, with LWE standing for left-wing extremism. But the situation varied, with Warangal, Khammam and Karimnagar districts in Telangana and Visakhapatnam district in Seemandhra being the most seriously impacted. We recognized the tremendous success that Andhra Pradesh had achieved over the past two decades through an intelligent mix of tough police action and sensitive developmental interventions in the disturbed areas. Indeed, what Andhra Pradesh had accomplished was being held out as a model to other similarly affected states like Chhattisgarh, Jharkhand and Odisha.

I had been actively involved, first as Minister of Environment and Forests and later as Minister of Rural Development, in shaping policies and special programmes in the LWE-affected districts. I had travelled extensively in these areas and had been advocating the 'Andhra' approach to fighting the Maoist cadres.[61] The team I hand-picked to

---

[61] This has been detailed extensively in my Sardar Patel Memorial Lecture 'From Tirupati to Pashupati: Some Reflections on the Maoist Issue', organized by Prasar Bharati at the Nehru Memorial Museum & Library, 11 October 2011. The terms Maoist and Naxalite are used interchangeably.

work with me on development issues in the LWE-affected districts consisted of officers who had earlier been abducted by Naxal cadres. My private secretary, Vineel Krishna—originally from Hyderabad and an Odisha cadre IAS officer—had been abducted by Maoist cadres in Malkangiri district of Odisha in February 2011 and kept hostage for ten days. The other two officers, joint secretaries from the Andhra Pradesh cadre—T. Vijay Kumar and R. Subramanyam—had been kidnapped and held hostage for three days by the Peoples' War Group (PWG) in East Godavari district of the state in December 1987. Our combined efforts, especially in Jharkhand, had evoked much positive comment. This has now popularly come to be known as the Saranda model that combines effective security and developmental interventions—Saranda being the forest area of Paschimi Singhbhum district of that state.

In the second meeting of the GoM, we had a detailed discussion on this subject. K. Vijay Kumar—an outstanding police officer who had made headlines earlier by apprehending the sandalwood smuggler Veerappan—was called in to share his views. I had worked closely with him in Jharkhand and elsewhere when he had been Director General of the Central Reserve Police Force (CRPF); he had gone on to become an advisor in the Home Ministry. His opinion was that bifurcation should be such that the two states were equipped with enhanced capabilities to ensure that Maoist activities did not get fresh impetus.

In addition, the GoM asked the Intelligence Bureau for its assessment of internal security issues arising out of the creation of two states. It received the Intelligence Bureau's five-page note on 17 October 2013. That very day, the Ministry of Home Affairs, through its Naxal Management Division, also provided a written nine-page assessment of the LWE situation in Andhra Pradesh. Apart from the issues of jihadi terrorism and coastal security, the IB report highlighted the insecurity that had gripped large sections of the population in Hyderabad because of the rhetoric used by Telangana leaders and their supporters.

Based on my discussions with K. Vijay Kumar and the two notes we had received, the GoM made some specific recommendations that included the following:

- The Government of India shall help the successor state of Telangana in raising six India Reserve Battalions and also deploy another unit of the Rapid Action Force[62] in Hyderabad.
- The Greyhounds Training Centre[63] in Hyderabad shall function as a common training centre for the two successor states for a period of three years. During this period, the centre shall be under the administrative control of, and be financed by, the Ministry of Home Affairs, Government of India. During this period of three years, the Government of India shall assist the successor state of Andhra Pradesh in setting up a similar state-of-the-art training centre at a suitable location in the state. At the end of three years, the Greyhound Training Centre shall revert to the successor state of Telangana.
- The Government of India will financially assist both the successor states in setting up new operational hubs for Greyhounds at suitable locations.
- The existing Greyhounds and OCTOPUS[64] forces shall be distributed between the two states after obtaining options from the personnel. Each of these forces, after the bifurcation, shall function under the respective DGPs (director generals of police) of the two successor states.
- If need be, the Government of India shall deploy additional centrally-administered police forces in both the successor states.

---

[62] A special police force created by the Government of India in 1991 to deal with communal violence.

[63] Greyhounds is an elite police force created by the undivided state of Andhra Pradesh in 1989 to deal with the Maoist challenge.

[64] OCTOPUS—Organisation for Counter Terrorist Operations—is a specialized police force created in 2007 by the undivided state of Andhra Pradesh to deal with jihadi terrorism.

II

Managing Water Resources

In its report of March 1955, the SRC had pointed out that one important factor for the formation of Vishalandhra 'will be that the development of the Krishna and Godavari rivers will be brought under unified control. The Krishna and the Godavari projects rank amongst the most ambitious in India. They have been formulated after prolonged period of inactivity, during which, for various technical and administrative reasons, only anicuts in the delta areas have been built. If one independent political jurisdiction, namely that of Telangana, can be implemented, the formulation and implementation of plans in the eastern areas in these two great river basins will be greatly expedited'. The Nagarjuna Sagar Dam, for which Jawaharlal Nehru had laid the foundation stone on 10 December 1955, was one beneficiary of this unified control and it got completed in 1967. It had transformed the state.

With my knowledge of the politics of the state, it was abundantly clear to me that the sharing of the Krishna River waters was going to be perhaps the most contentious issue. This river starts in Maharashtra, flows through Karnataka, gets into Telangana, and joins the Bay of Bengal at Hamsaladeevi in the Krishna district of Seemandhra.[65]

---

[65]I still vividly recall sitting next to V. S. Sampath, who was then Finance Secretary in Andhra Pradesh, at C.V.S.K. Sarma's presentation on development of water resources to the Prime Minister at Raj Bhavan in August 2004. I asked Sampath, who later became Chief Election Commissioner, why he thought the Krishna projects had been

Godavari, too—a river that begins in Maharashtra, flows through Telangana and joins the Bay of Bengal at Narsapuram in the West Godavari district of Seemandhra—would pose major problems. But Krishna was the crux.

Historically, the maximum grievances in the Telangana region have related to the Krishna waters and for long the complaint had been that the coastal districts had benefitted disproportionately and Telangana had suffered as a result. Soon after becoming Chief Minister, in 2005, YSR had started a mega Jalayagnam—this was a hugely ambitious programme to expand irrigation facilities all over the state. But Telangana protagonists had criticized it for neglecting the demands of their region.

The Krishna Water Disputes Tribunal-I had been set up in 1969 and had allocated water to the three riparian states of Maharashtra, Karnataka and Andhra Pradesh. In August 2003 a Krishna Waters Disputes Tribunal-II had been set up. This second tribunal had submitted its report in December 2010 but its recommendations could not be notified because Andhra Pradesh went to the Supreme Court and obtained a stay.

While granting the stay in September 2011, the Supreme Court directed the tribunal to review its recommendations in the light of the petitions received against them and submit a report to the Government of India. It however ruled that the recommendations should not be notified. Accordingly, the tribunal submitted its revised recommendations in November 2013 when the GoM meetings were taking place. This report had not anticipated the creation of a fourth riparian state of Telangana. Hence, the term of the tribunal had necessarily to be extended so as to get a recommendation for the allocation of water for the two new states out of the award recommended for the undivided state of Andhra Pradesh. I discussed this with the officers of the state government who were dealing with water resources and based on their advice, the GoM accordingly incorporated Section 89 in its

---

implemented so extensively but projects on the Godavari seemed to have lagged. He smiled and answered cryptically: 'Sir, K.L. Rao'—a humourous allusion to the influence that this great engineer had at the national level as MP between 1961 and 1977 and as Union Minister of Irrigation between 1963 and 1973.

legislation which reads thus:

> (1) The term of the Krishna Water Disputes Tribunal shall be extended with the following terms of reference, namely:
> (a) shall make project-wise specific allocation, if such allocation have not been made by a Tribunal constituted under the Inter-State River Disputes Act, 1956;
> (b) shall determine an operational protocol for project-wise release of water in the event of deficit flows.

This was the relatively easy and straightforward part. What was going to be more problematic and complicated was the management of the vast assets already created on the Krishna (Map 7) as well as the projects under implementation.

I studied the Acts that had earlier bifurcated Bihar, Madhya Pradesh and Uttar Pradesh to see whether they could guide the GoM. They were not of any help at all because the language used was very general; furthermore, water was not as emotive an issue in these three cases as it was in Andhra Pradesh. It was clear that what was being asked of us was completely new thinking.

What I was clear about from the outset was that whatever needed to be done to manage the bifurcation of water resource-related assets peacefully and properly had to be enshrined in the Reorganisation Law itself. I had four officers helping me out—Aditya Nath Das, who was Principal Secretary, Water Resources, in the state; K. Raju, who had served in the state in various capacities and was then in the National Advisory Council; Rajiv Sharma; and Vineel Krishna. I also asked the Chief Minister to send us a detailed note on the water resources issue.

I must have spent all of October on this issue alone. I knew it was enormously complicated but by early November felt confident that we had something that could work, provided of course that the two new states cooperated to make it work. On 4 November 2013, in keeping with a promise I had made to him earlier, I sent the Home Minister a detailed letter making specific proposals on how best to manage water resources between the two states (Annexure 13).

The challenges were many, and issues of day-to-day management were involved. While these concerns were of a technical nature, I

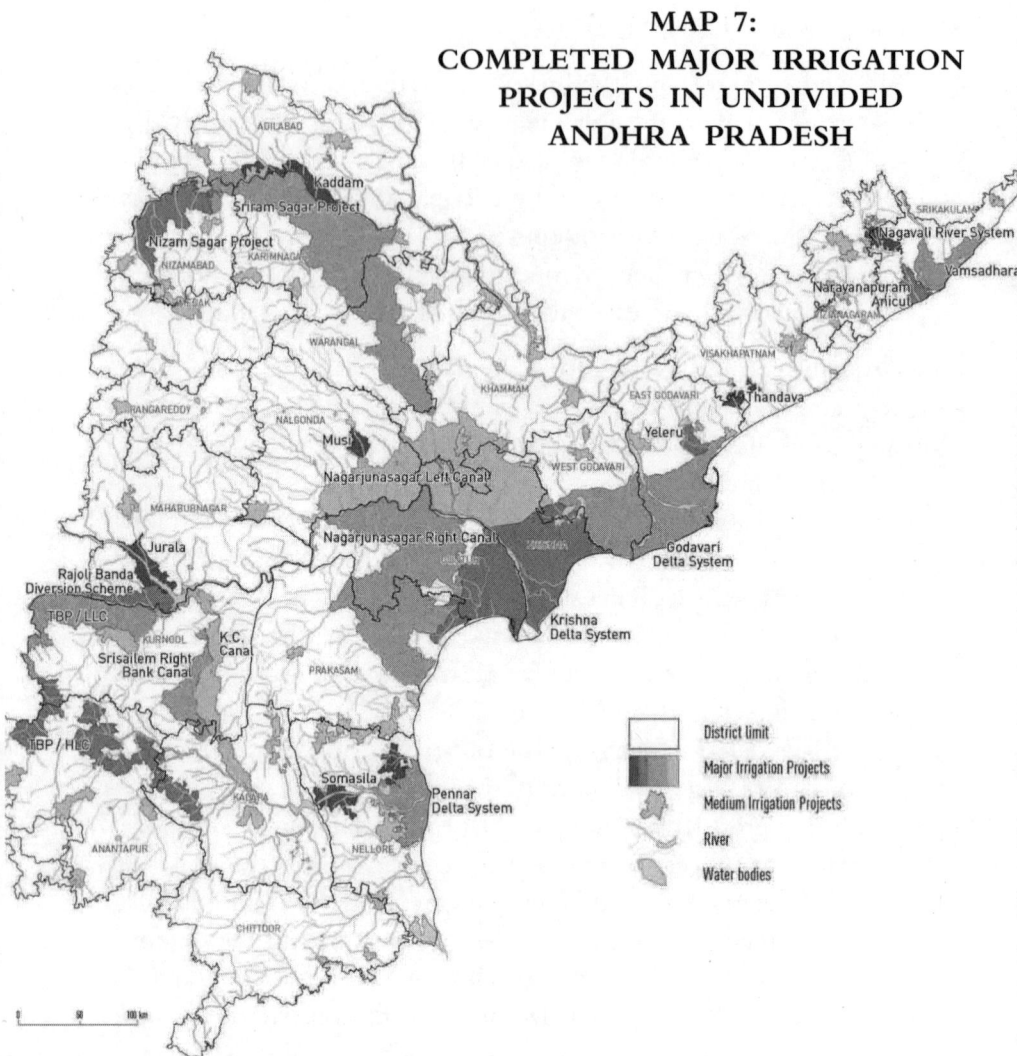

Source: Government of Andhra Pradesh

Note: Map not to scale

realized that they needed political direction since in the undivided state whenever a problem arose that involved different regions, the Chief Minister stepped in and took the final decision. That is why I first proposed to the Home Minister that an apex council on the Krishna and Godavari river waters be set up under the chairmanship of the Union Minister of Water Resources. This council, which would also have the two chief minsters and others as members, would oversee the functioning of technical agencies, sanction proposals for new projects and provide a forum for the amicable resolution of disputes as and when they arose.

Under this political body, I then proposed that the central government create a Krishna River board and a Godavari River board with the headquarters of the former in the successor state of Andhra Pradesh and of the latter in Telangana. These boards would be autonomous institutions under the administrative control of the Ministry of Water Resources and were to be primarily engineering organizations that would operate and maintain all the assets created (or to be created) on these two rivers. In my scheme of things, the boards would ensure that awards already made (or to be made) by the tribunals would be implemented seamlessly. While the individual states would execute ongoing and future projects, the respective boards would take over the management of the reservoirs after the completion of the projects.

So this was the institutional mechanism—a political body and a technical body. But that still left open the question of rules and protocols that would govern the day-to-day operations which, in many ways, was the crux. Thus was born the idea of listing out the principles to govern the functioning of this two-tiered structure so that there would be no room for ambiguity later.

The letter to the Home Minister was excruciatingly detailed, something that did not escape his comment when he first received it. It had to be so because I wanted to deal with all eventualities in the Reorganisation Law itself. The letter also made evident the strong interventionist role I had envisaged for the Government of India. I was quizzed about this in the GoM—which appeared a bit uncomfortable with my proposals to begin with—on the grounds that they may be seen as exceeding the limits imposed on the centre's role in our Constitution. But I pointed out that entry 56 in List I of the Seventh Schedule of the Constitution that enumerated the jurisdiction of the Union government read, 'Regulation and development of inter-

State rivers and river valleys to the extent to which such regulation and development under the control of the Union is declared by Parliament by law to be expedient in the public interest'. In my view, an interventionist role for the central government was essential given the huge controversies that had always surrounded the sharing of water resources and its equitable distribution across the state. There was also, I have to admit, a recognition that the successor state of Andhra Pradesh would need safeguards as it would be a downstream riparian vis-à-vis Telangana. I was gratified that the letter was, almost to the last word, to form the basis of Sections 84-88 of the Andhra Pradesh Reorganisation Act, 2014.

After the Reorganisation Bill, as drafted by the GoM, was made public in early December, I received a number of representations that certain irrigation projects which were coming up on the Krishna River for the benefit of the Rayalaseema region could be affected by bifurcation. Venkaiah Naidu also spoke to me about this matter. I was convinced that we had taken care of such concerns but to make things abundantly clear and to give the senior BJP leader an opportunity to claim some credit—so very essential in the process of consensus-building—a new para was added to the Eleventh Schedule of the Reorganisation Law which read as follows:

10. The following irrigation projects which are under construction shall be completed as per the plan notified by the existing state of Andhra Pradesh and the water sharing arrangement shall continue as such:
    (i)   Handri Neeva
    (ii) Telugu Ganga
    (iii) Galeru Nagari
    (iv) Veligonda
    (v)   Kalwakurthy
    (vi) Nettempadu

While I was Minister of State for Power (April 2008 to February 2009) I had been impressed by the design and functioning of the Bhakra Beas Management Board (BBMB), which had representatives from the four states of Punjab, Haryana, Rajasthan and Himachal Pradesh. It was my experience with the BBMB that was at the back of my mind while suggesting institutional arrangements for the management of the Krishna and Godavari rivers. The main difference was that while the BBMB was under the administrative control of the Ministry of Power, my suggestion to the Home Minister was to bring similar boards for the Krishna and Godavari under the administrative control of the Ministry of Water Resources. This was with the understanding that irrigation was the main purpose of the projects on these two rivers.

12

The Polavaram Saga

The Polavaram multi-purpose project came to acquire iconic status for political leaders from Seemandhra. The foundation stone for this prestigious project had been laid by the then Chief Minister of Andhra Pradesh, T. Anjaiah, way back in February 1980. Just as Telangana protagonists insisted on full control over Hyderabad, those from Seemandhra were adamant that the Polavaram project should be declared a 'national project', which would mean that 90 per cent of the project costs would be funded by the Government of India.

The attractiveness of the Polavaram project from different points of view was never in doubt. By harnessing the waters of the Godavari, it would (*i*) bring an additional 7 lakh acres in the districts of East Godavari and West Godavari under assured irrigation; (*ii*) transfer around 80 tmc[66] of water to the Krishna basin which would, as a consequence, augment the water availability there and benefit farmers in both Telangana and Seemandhra; (*iii*) provide around 24 tmc of drinking water to Visakhapatnam city and adjacent areas; and (*iv*) have a power generating capacity of about 960 megawatts which would be substantial. It is no wonder that all ministers from Seemandhra were staunch advocates of the Polavaram project.

---

[66]tmc is a unit of measurement with reference to the volume of water in a reservoir or river flow. It is equivalent to a thousand million cubic feet.

The project had been given environmental clearance by the Ministry of Environment and Forests way back on 25 October 2005. But in January 2009 it was discovered that the project included the construction of embankments on the rivers Sabari and Sileru to avoid land submergence in the Malkangiri district of Odisha and the Dantewada district of Chhattisgarh. This aspect had not been considered at the time of granting environmental clearance. Accordingly, to ensure full adherence to the law, the Ministry of Environment and Forests asked the Andhra Pradesh government to conduct public hearings in the other two states as well. This communication went out on 9 March 2009, some three months before I took charge of the Ministry of Environment and Forests.

Sometime in October 2010, the Chief Ministers of Chhattisgarh and Odisha mentioned to me that work on the Polavaram Dam was continuing even though it had not got full environmental clearance. On checking, I discovered that the Andhra Pradesh government had *not* yet complied with the March 2009 instructions even though almost eighteen months had elapsed. Therefore, I asked my officers to issue an official letter to the state asking why a show cause notice should not be formally issued under Section 5 of the Environment (Protection) Act, 1986 as work on the dam was continuing without getting the original environmental clearance amended for the additional works like embankments and drainage sluices. This letter was issued on 1 November 2010.

There was an instant reaction from the Chief Minister and his colleagues. How could a Congress minister at the centre, and that too one representing Andhra Pradesh, threaten to issue a show cause notice to a Congress state government? To them, this was not just blasphemy but betrayal. I explained to them the legal requirements and that I simply could not make any exception. The government of Andhra Pradesh told me that they had been making requests to the other two states to conduct statutory public hearings but there had been no response from them. I then promised to use my good offices to get Chhattisgarh and Odisha to have these public hearings conducted—an offer I reiterated in the Rajya Sabha a few months later as the following letter to the two Chief Ministers, Raman Singh

(Chhattisgarh) and Naveen Patnaik (Odisha), would show:

4th March 2011

This afternoon, Shri M. Venkaiah Naidu, MP raised the Polavaram project issue in the Rajya Sabha. During the course of my reply to his question, I mentioned that one of the key conditions governing both the environmental and forest clearance for the project is that there will be no submergence in Chhattisgarh and Orissa. The Government of Andhra Pradesh has proposed to build protective embankments on the Sabari and Sileru in Chhattisgarh and Orissa at a cost of about Rs 620 crore. However, I understand that the public hearing requirement before this construction can be taken up in Dantewada district in Chhattisgarh and Malkangiri in Orissa has not been met so far even after almost two years have elapsed.

I assured the Hon'ble Members Shri Venkaiah Naidu and Shri Mysura Reddy that I would convene a tripartite meeting involving Andhra Pradesh, Orissa and Chhattisgarh soon to see how the conduct of public hearing can be expedited in Orissa and Chhattisgarh which is a statutory requirement. I am told the Government of Andhra Pradesh had already made a request to the two State Pollution Control Boards for conduct of the statutory public hearing but there has been no response from them so far.

Since I have made a commitment on the floor of the House and I have stressed the need to implement the Polavaram project with the full cooperation of Orissa and Chhattisgarh, I would request for your cooperation in the matter to facilitate conduct of public hearings in Orissa and Chhattisgarh soon.

There was another issue that bothered me a great deal. The Polavaram project would end up displacing around 50,000 families (mostly tribal communities) in Khammam district. Andhra Pradesh had announced a progressive Rehabilitation and Resettlement (R&R) policy in 2005, but I could not forget the fact that the nation's track record in this regard had been disappointing, to say the least. A new concern had arisen with the passage of what is popularly called the

Forest Rights Act, 2006 by Parliament.[67] After becoming Minister of Environment and Forests, I had announced that projects in forest areas could proceed only after the ownership rights of tribals and other communities had been settled under the provisions of this law. In this connection, I had written to the Chief Minister of Andhra Pradesh K. Rosaiah:

> 22nd November 2010
>
> I have received a number of letters from different activist groups saying that the Andhra Pradesh Government has misrepresented facts regarding settlements of rights under Forests Rights Act, 2006 on the Polavaram project. These complaints have come to me from Kotarugommu village in Bhadrachalam division of Khammam district and from Gommukottagudem village also of the Bhadrachalam division of Khammam district. I have been informed that there are other complaints also, as for example from Mulagalagudem village in Polavaram Mandal of West Godavari district.
>
> The matter that has been made available to me clearly seems to indicate that the claims of local tribal communities do not seem to have been settled. This is a very serious matter. I have asked my colleagues in the MoE&F to examine the various representations that I have received and take the necessary follow-up action. Meanwhile, I thought I should bring this matter to your personal attention as well.

My position on the Polavaram project did not earn me any friends in my own party but I gathered support in unlikely quarters. One day, a young woman who said she was running an environmental NGO in Hyderabad, came to see me. Very soon, I discovered that she was the daughter of KCR. Kavitha and I became good friends and this friendship has survived political vicissitudes.

But all that was in the past. Now in the GoM I had necessarily to play a different role. The CWC resolution of 30 July 2013 and

---

[67]The law was formally known as the Scheduled Tribes and Other Traditional Forest Dwellers (Recognition of Forest Rights) Act, 2006.

the Cabinet decision of 3 October 2013 had committed to Polavaram being declared a 'national project'. Seemandhra representatives who met the GoM formally and informally were united in their demand that the GoM not reopen this issue and enshrine this commitment in the Reorganisation Law. My colleagues were apprehensive of what I would do given my past position on the Polavaram issue. I realized this was not the occasion or the forum to voice my concerns. It was a dilemma but I realized that I had to make a nuanced departure from my previous stance

I kept quiet knowing that in many ways what Hyderabad was to Telangana, Polavaram was to Seemandhra. I also realized that the GoM needed to do something 'extra' for Seemandhra given that Hyderabad was to be in Telangana. That is why I got the GoM to agree to not only retain Polavaram as a 'national project' but also have it executed entirely by the centre after obtaining all the necessary environmental and forest clearances and meeting all R&R norms. Keenly aware that Telangana would make it very difficult for the project to be implemented, the GoM incorporated a provision in the Reorganisation Law which said that all clearances would be 'deemed' to have been given by the new state of Telangana.

Polavaram presented another special problem. The submergence was almost entirely in the Khammam district of Telangana while the benefits would flow largely to the coastal districts. Seemandhra leaders argued that the entire area of submergence which fell in the Bhadrachalam division of Khamman district should be transferred to the East Godavari district of which it was originally a part before 1959 (actually prior to 1959, the larger Bhadrachalam revenue division was part of the East Godavari district). If the Bhadrachalam revenue division had been made part of Khammam district from 30 November 1959, it was on grounds of geographical contiguity and administrative convenience. Hence, Seemandhra leaders were, as they kept saying, only asking for a restoration of the pre-1959 status.

The GoM deliberated at some length on the matter of re-transferring the entire Bhadrachalam revenue division back from Khammam district to East Godavari district. I supported the Seemandhra position but, on balance, the GoM decided against making any recommendation regarding this matter because it was apprehensive about agitations in Bhadrachalam and in Khammam district if this were done. Besides, Congress leaders from this area were stoutly opposed to the move. That is why the Reorganisation Law that was sent to the state assembly for its consideration on 7 December 2013 had no provision for the transfer of the submerged area from Telangana to the new state of Andhra Pradesh.

All of December 2013 and January 2014, Seemandhra leaders kept protesting to the GoM that grave injustice had been done to the proposed new state of Andhra Pradesh because of the GoM's reluctance to take a clear stand on the transfer of the submerged area. They believed that with the submerged area being within Telangana, the Polavaram project would be a non-starter from day one. After meeting them as well as a number of farmer delegations from the coastal districts, I was persuaded that the GoM should revisit its stand on this subject. Accordingly, I urged it to agree to the transfer of all seven mandals[68] of Khammam district in their entirety (submerged villages plus villages that would not get submerged) to East Godavari district. The Cabinet gave its approval to this proposal on 7 February 2014.

Then all hell broke loose in Telangana. There were strong protests at this decision and another agitation loomed large on the horizon. Delegations from Khammam district now descended on me saying that they would stop this wholesale transfer at all costs as there would be no accessibility to Bhadrachalam town. In addition, they complained that two crucial irrigation initiatives on the Godavari in Khammam district (the Indira Sagar lift irrigation project and the Rajiv Sagar lift irrigation project) and the Upper Sileru hydroelectric project would end up in Seemandhra.

The Home Minister, too, asked me to find some way out. After meeting the Telangana protagonists, I now came forward with a different proposal for the GoM—only the submerged villages in the seven mandals of Khammam district would be transferred to the East Godavari

---

[68] Mandals were created by NTR in his first tenure as the intermediate level of administration between a group of villages (gram panchayats) and a district. In other states, this would be called a 'block'. Around twenty gram panchayats constitute a mandal.

district, leaving the unsubmerged villages undisturbed. I thought this would be a good compromise. I went back to the GoM which promptly approved the new proposal and the Cabinet gave the go-ahead to it on 12 February.

Parliament was to convene very soon and I thought we had resolved all contentious issues. But I was mistaken because on the very night of 12 February, Seemandhra was up in arms against the Cabinet decision to transfer only the submerged villages. First Telangana had objected and now Seemandhra was protesting on the grounds that the Sileru hydroelectric project would be lost to Telangana, isolated enclaves would be created in Maoist-affected areas and there would be no 'scheduled area' lands (that is, lands in tribal areas declared 'scheduled' by the Constitution) in which R&R could take place.

So I went back to the drawing board and started meeting representatives of Telangana and Seemandhra once again to figure out a mutually acceptable formula. This was the third such attempt in a matter of less than a week. There was no way that a solution, even if found, could be incorporated in the Bill that was going to be presented in Parliament. It would have to await an ordinance thereafter, if at all.

Having burnt my fingers twice, I was extremely pessimistic about coming up with a solution that would be acceptable. I made my frustration pretty evident but I was exhorted by both Telangana and Seemandhra spokespersons not to give up at this very last stage. I said I could continue if both sides showed some flexibility. Finally, after almost two weeks of further discussion, with a scrutiny of maps at the minutest level, we arrived at a formula that satisfied both sides.

Telangana was happy that accessibility to Bhadrachalam was ensured and the completion of the Rajiv Sagar and Indira Sagar projects would not be hampered in any way. Seemandhra was happy that the Sileru project would be in the new state of Andhra Pradesh, administrative boundaries would be contiguous and there would be sufficient 'scheduled area' land for the R&R of displaced tribal communities.

I now found myself in an altogether embarrassing position. I had taken a proposal to the GoM and the Cabinet on 7 February and got it approved only to find that it was unacceptable to one of the two sides. I had then gone back to the GoM and the Cabinet on

12 February with a second proposal and got that approved only to find it rejected by the other side. Now I had a third proposal that I was taking to the GoM and the Cabinet. My Cabinet colleagues were not amused.

This new proposal for which I had secured the consent of both the Telangana and Seemandhra representatives was approved by the GoM and the Cabinet on 1 March 2014. Now only an ordinance could be issued and that too after a new government assumed office. Elections having been announced, the President was extremely reluctant to approve the ordinance for issue. As it turned out, the ordinance was finally issued on 28 May 2014, two days after the Narendra Modi government had assumed office. The new Home Minister, Rajnath Singh, had spoken to me after he had been sworn in on 26 May 2014 and I impressed upon him the extreme urgency of having the ordinance issued before the formation of Telangana itself. I told him that issuing the ordinance after the Telangana assembly had been constituted would be virtually impossible. I am glad he saw the political point in the urgency right away.

I should mention one interesting aspect of the Polavaram debate. At the outset, I had made it clear that, in keeping with the sentiments expressed by representatives of Telangana, the famous Sree Seetha Ramachandra Swamy Temple in Bhadrachalam town would remain with Telangana. This shrine had been built in the late seventeenth century at a time when Bhadrachalam had been part of the Qutb Shahi empire that ruled from Golconda. Thereafter, successive nizams of the Asaf Jahi dynasty ruling from Hyderabad made regular contributions and maintained close links to the temple. One leader of Telangana half-jokingly told me that Seemandhra could not have both the Tirupati Temple and the Bhadrachalam Temple. We could now find a powerful historical precedent for making sure that this did not happen and sources of salvation were equally distributed, thanks to the broadmindedness of the Nizam. That was as good a reason as any for me to recommend to the GoM that Telangana retain control over it after bifurcation even if areas around Bhadrachalam were to be transferred to East Godavari district for facilitating the implementation of the Polavaram project.

My Polavaram story was not done on 1 March with the Cabinet

approval of the ordinance for the transfer of part of Bhadrachalam mandal to the East Godavari district. The ordinance, finally issued on 28 May, had still to be converted into law and made part of the Andhra Pradesh Reorganisation Act, 2014. The Lok Sabha gave its approval on 12 July 2014 and the ordinance was taken up in the Rajya Sabha two days later. I was once again forced to go over the Polavaram saga and the various compromises that had taken place regarding the transfer of submerged areas from Khammam to East Godavari.

I was repeatedly interrupted by my own party colleagues from Telangana as also by the lone TRS MP in the Rajya Sabha who happened to be an ex-Congressman. They vociferously opposed the Polavaram project. I allowed them to have their say but persisted with my arguments in its favour. Ironically, the TDP MPs from Seemandhra who had opposed the bifurcation just three months ago in the Rajya Sabha were now appreciative of my stance. In his closing speech, Home Minister Rajnath Singh was gracious enough to acknowledge that the new government was only implementing what the predecessor regime had already decided. He was also large-hearted in saying that my opening speech, was very 'healthy' for democracy and praised it. Alas, this was to be one of the rarest of rare moments when bipartisanship was on full display (Annexure 14).

13

Education and Article 371-D

I knew that along with water, education would be another contentious issue for the GoM to grapple with. When the GoM had asked the central ministries for their suggestions, the Ministry of Human Resource Development had responded by simply listing out the new institutions—like Indian Institute of Technology (IIT), central university, Indian Institute of Management (IIM)—that they would propose for establishment in the successor state of Andhra Pradesh. I was not very happy with this and wrote to Home Minister Sushilkumar Shinde accordingly.

6th November 2013

1. I have just seen a note sent by the Ministry of Human Resource Development (MHRD) to the Group of Ministers (GoM) on Telangana.
2. I find that the MHRD note is very limited in its scope and confines itself to the creation of new national level institutions which are under the control of the MHRD presently. All that the note says is that new institutions have to be created in the successor State of Andhra Pradesh following bifurcation since all these national-level institutions presently are located in Hyderabad. The only thing that the MHRD note does is to indicate the additional resources required during the 12th

Plan period to create new institutions and that too other than in the fields of health, law and agriculture.

3. To my mind, issues relating to educational opportunities as a result of bifurcation have not been addressed at all in this MHRD note. Higher educational institutions run by the State Government presently fall into two categories—government-owned and private. In each of these two categories there is a formula that is applied for the domicile and non-domicile students which ensures opportunities for students from all parts of the State. The government-owned institutions are indeed spread across the State but the reputed and most-sought after institutions are clustered around Hyderabad. Private institutions also are concentrated mostly around Hyderabad.

4. There are two options before the GoM. The first option is to freeze the existing quotas for a period of 5 or 10 years and incorporate that in the Reorganisation Bill. The second option is to ask the MHRD to work out a new formula in consultation with the State Government and other stakeholders. The GoM must ensure that the youth from outside Telangana are not deprived of opportunities in government-owned and private institutions which predominate in and around Hyderabad till such a time [that] reputed institutions develop elsewhere in the districts outside Telangana.

The GoM considered my letter. I made a forceful plea that the existing system should be retained and all existing quotas be frozen for a specified period. Thus, Section 95 got incorporated in the Andhra Pradesh Reorganisation Bill 2013 which read as follows:

> In order to ensure equal opportunities for quality higher education to all students in the successor states, the existing admission quotas in all government or private, aided or unaided, institutions of higher, technical and medical education in so far as it is provided under Article 371-D of the Constitution, shall continue for a period not exceeding ten years during which the existing common admission process shall continue.

The last part was a very important addition—the existing common admission process would continue for a decade. There was some hesitation on providing for such a long period, and some GoM members argued for a five-year limit. But the Home Minister backed me fully when I insisted on ten years. This was objected to by some Telangana protagonists, but I insisted that this addition was essential so as not to dash the aspirations of lakhs of young boys and girls who had got used to a particular system for many years and would find it traumatic to have that change following bifurcation. As in the case of water, I felt particularly happy at what the GoM had done. Again, as in the case of water, we had absolutely no precedent to go by and had necessarily to break new ground.

◆

Article 371-D, dealing with public employment and education in Andhra Pradesh, had been inserted into the Constitution through the 32nd Amendment and had become effective from 1 July 1974. The background to it has been described earlier in Chapter 1. It had come about against the backdrop of agitations that had rocked the state, first by the Telangana agitationists for a separate Telangana state and thereafter by the Jai Andhra agitationists in the coastal districts for creating a new state for them minus Telangana.

The GoM had to grapple with a basic issue—what would happen to Article 371-D after bifurcation? Different views were expressed, and the Andhra Pradesh Chief Minister and Seemandhra ministers insisted that it would need to be amended. The attorney general (AG) was asked for his opinion. His views caused some consternation in the GoM since he said that a fresh constitutional amendment may be required to preserve the special provisions after bifurcation. When the matter came up in the GoM, the Finance Minister was of the firm view that there was no need to amend Article 371-D.

Chidambaram called for a copy of the Constitution, and drew our attention to Article 371-B entitled 'Special Provisions with respect to the State of Assam', which had been inserted by the 22nd Amendment in 1969. He went on to point out that when Meghalaya had been carved out of Assam as a separate state by the North-Eastern Areas (Reorganisation Act), 1971, without affecting the nomenclature of Assam state, the Reorganisation Act had been passed by Parliament in exercise of its supreme powers under Articles 3 and 4, without disturbing the textual provisions of Article 371-B. He also recalled—and his recollection turned out to be right when we checked immediately—that the original Article 371 of the Constitution referred to 'Special Provisions with Respect to the State of Bombay' but after Parliament had passed the Bombay Reorganisation Act, 1960, the words 'The State of Bombay' in Article 371 (2) had been replaced by 'the State of Maharashtra and Gujarat'. In any case, the Finance Minister said that, in view of previous Supreme Court judgements, amendments or alterations—if they needed to be done in Article 371-D—would not require the procedure of amendment under Article 368 of the Constitution.

The GoM heaved a sigh of relief. The Finance Minister, a top lawyer himself, had provided it with clinching and decisive arguments to counter the AG's views. Naturally, these arguments found their place in the GoM's final report.

The crucial meeting of the Congress Working Committee when it was decided to bifurcate Andhra Pradesh to create Telangana, 30 July 2013.

Meeting of the Group of Ministers, 7 November 2013.
Only A.K. Antony is not seen in the photo.

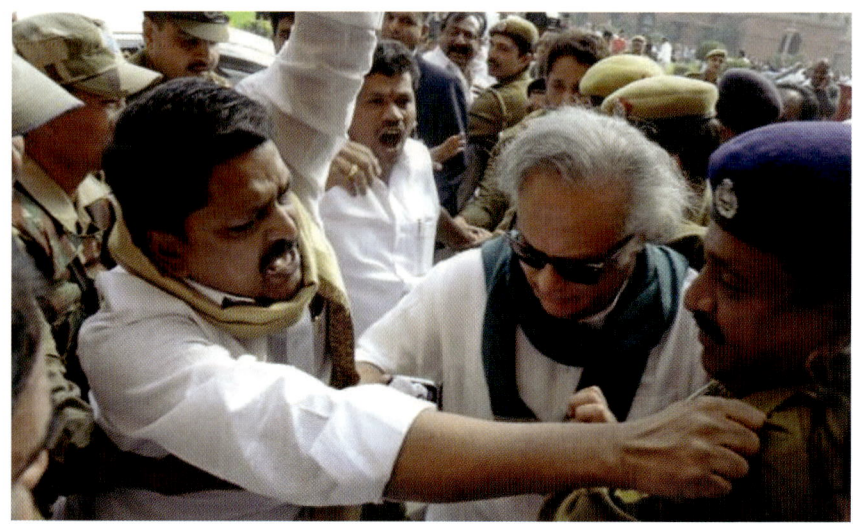

TDP MLAs protesting outside the Home Ministry,
18 November 2013.

Meeting of the Group of Ministers on 18 November 2013. Author in discussion with V. Narayanasamy. Sushilkumar Shinde, Ghulam Nabi Azad and Veerappa Moily are also present.

Union ministers from Seemandhra coming out of the Ministry of Home Affairs after meeting the GoM, 18 November 2013.

Members of the Group of Ministers meet Kiran Kumar Reddy, Chief Minister of Andhra Pradesh, 18 November 2013.

The *India Today* awards function. The Chief Minister of Andhra Pradesh gets the award for the best governed state, 20 December 2013.

Congress MPs from the Telangana region agitating at the entrance to Parliament House, 12 February 2014.

Speaker of the Lok Sabha Meira Kumar running out after the pepper spray incident of 13 February 2014.

'Jairam Manhandles Hanumantha Rao', 13 February 2014.

Members in the Rajya Sabha protesting, 20 February 2014.

Congress MPs from the Telangana region celebrating after the Rajya Sabha vote, 20 February 2014.

Hyderabad vs Karnataka Ranji Trophy Final, 1975-76. In the photo are Brijesh Patel, B.S. Chandrasekhar, G.R. Viswanath, M.L. Jaisimha, Mansur Ali Khan Pataudi, E.A.S. Prasanna, Abid Ali, Abbas Ali Baig and S.M.H. Kirmani (V. Ramnarayan is standing fifth from left).

14

Economic and Financial Matters

During its deliberations, representatives from both Telangana and Seemandhra kept highlighting specific development projects that the Government of India should support in their respective states. Initially, the GoM believed this was outside its purview and that it was for individual ministries of the Government of India to decide the feasibility of these projects. But given Seemandhara's extreme hostility to the idea of bifurcation, I felt that if we were to include specific projects in the Reorganisation Bill itself, we may be able to enhance our credibility as objective arbiters. Legislative sanction would send, in my view, a more powerful signal than a mere statement of executive intent.

My view was that the Telangana protagonists were not only getting a separate state of Telangana but also complete financial control over Hyderabad. In addition, when we were discussing apportioning of assets and liabilities in the GoM, I had argued that the 51 per cent stake of the undivided government of Andhra Pradesh in Singareni Collieries should belong to the government of Telangana as the coal mines would be in that state when it got formed (the balance would continue to be with the Government of India). Thus, it was essential that we do something substantive to 'compensate' Seemandhra.

It was against this background that the Thirteenth Schedule got added to the Bill giving Parliament's sanctity to specific government projects in Seemandhra in the areas of education, industry and infrastructure. While the GoM did add some commitments for Telangana—like a power plant and a steel factory—for the most part the Thirteenth Schedule was for Seemandhra. The Seemandhra projects included in the schedule were:

Education

1. The Government of India shall take steps to establish institutions of national importance in the 12th and 13th Plan periods in the successor state of Andhra Pradesh. This would include one IIT, one National Institute of Technology (NIT), one IIM, one Indian Institute of Science Education and Research (IISER), one central university, one petroleum university, one agricultural university and one Indian Institute of Information Technology (IIIT).
2. The Government of India shall establish one AIIMS-type super-speciality hospital-cum-teaching institution in the successor state of Andhra Pradesh.
3. The Government of India shall establish a tribal university in the state of Andhra Pradesh.
4. The Government of India shall establish the National Institute of Disaster Management in the successor state of Andhra Pradesh.

Infrastructure

1. The Government of India shall develop a new major port at Dugarajapatnam in the successor state of Andhra Pradesh to be completed in phases with Phase I by end-2018.
2. SAIL shall, within six months from the appointed day, examine the feasibility of establishing an integrated steel plant in YSR district of the successor state of Andhra Pradesh.
3. Indian Oil Corporation (IOC) or Hindustan Petroleum Corporation Limited (HPCL) shall, within six months from the appointed day, examine the feasibility of establishing a

greenfield crude oil refinery and petrochemical complex in the successor state of Andhra Pradesh and take an expeditious decision thereon;
4. The Government of India shall, within six months from the appointed day, examine the feasibility of establishing a Vizag-Chennai Industrial Corridor along the lines of Delhi-Mumbai Industrial Corridor and take within such period an expeditious decision thereon;
5. The Government of India shall, within six months from the appointed day, examine the feasibility of expanding the existing Visakhapatnam, Vijayawada and Tirupati airports to international standards and take an expeditious decision thereon;
6. Indian Railways shall, within six months from the appointed day, examine establishing a new railway zone in the successor state of Andhra Pradesh and take an expeditious decision thereon;
7. The central government shall take measures to establish rapid rail and road connectivity from the new capital of the successor state of Andhra Pradesh to Hyderabad and other important cities of Telangana;
8. The Government of India shall examine the feasibility of a metro rail facility in Visakhapatnam and Vijayawada-Guntur-Tenali Metropolitan Urban Development Authority within a period of one year from the appointed day and take an expeditious decision thereon.

There was criticism from Seemandhra ministers and MPs that the GoM had not done adequate justice to their concerns regarding the resource base of the new state of Andhra Pradesh. The GoM reconsidered the issue and inserted what became Section 46 of the Act. This section said that the 'President shall make a reference to the Fourteenth Finance Commission to take into account the resources available to the successor States and make separate awards for each of the successor States'. That was the very least that needed to be done. The Chairman of the Fourteenth Finance Commission was the redoubtable Y.V. Reddy who I had known and worked with for over two decades. He was an IAS officer of the Andhra Pradesh cadre and had retired as Governor of the Reserve Bank of India. He knew the financial issues surrounding the bifurcation better than anybody else. But in one of the meetings of the GoM, it had been mentioned that he was a little uneasy with the terms of reference being expanded at this late stage when the commission had almost completed its work. That was the reason why I had made it a point to call on him on 5 February 2014 and get him on board.

The GoM added two new sub-sections keeping in mind the sentiments of the Seemandhra representatives. These became sections 46 (2) and 46 (3) of the Andhra Pradesh Reorganization Act, 2014 which read thus:

> (2) Notwithstanding anything in sub-section (1), the Central Government, may, having regard to the resources available to the successor State of Andhra Pradesh, make appropriate grants and also ensure that adequate benefits and incentives in the form of special development package are given to the backward areas of that State.
> (3) The Central Government shall, while considering the special development package for the successor state of Andhra Pradesh, provide adequate incentives, in particular for Rayalaseema and north coastal regions of that State.

As far as the division of assets and liabilities were concerned, I came up with a simple rule which I communicated to the Home Minister in the very first meeting of the GoM, 'Let us simply accept whatever the Finance Minister suggests'. The Home Minister smiled in agreement but did not fail to remark in Hindi, '*Yaar, pandit ho toh aisa!*' ('Buddy, if there is a learned man, this is he.') And that is exactly what happened. The reorganization of Bihar, Madhya Pradesh and Uttar Pradesh in 2000 had established firm principles for the distribution of assets and liabilities which were adopted by the GoM for Andhra Pradesh as well. This was the only time precedent was used. The principles were either location-based (as in the case of assets like power stations) or population-based (as in the case of pension payments).

15
The GoM Completes Its Main Task

The GoM had held its formal meetings on 11 and 19 October and also on 7, 21 and 27 November 2013. It interacted with the secretaries of the ministries and departments of the Government of India on 11 and 27 November 2013. The GoM met the representatives of the recognized political parties of Andhra Pradesh on 12 and 13 November 2013. All these parties submitted written representations on the terms of reference. The GoM also met the Union ministers from Telangana and Seemandhra on 18 November to hear their views. They submitted written responses to the GoM arguing their case—one for bifurcation and the other against it. The Seemandhra ministers also gave the GoM a detailed note on the special concessions and incentives that Seemandhra should get from the central government if at all the bifurcation was going to be pushed through. The GoM met separately with the Chief Minister of Andhra Pradesh that very day. In addition, it received over thousands of suggestions from the public on the issues given in its terms of reference.

The GoM finalized its report along with the draft Reorganisation Bill on 3 December 2013. While it had met formally five times, the Home Minister, his officials and I had been meeting daily for fifty-five days. I later calculated that during this period I must have spent, on an average, at least five hours daily on the GoM's business. I had also been meeting members of the GoM individually every now and then, apart from delegations from the state representing varying viewpoints. The GoM had been a collective exercise. But for various reasons, most of the burden of work had fallen on me and, in many ways, I had become its public face—the punching bag, as it was to turn out.

The Cabinet met on 5 December 2013. This meeting too, like the earlier one on 3 October 2013, was quite stormy with M.M. Pallam Raju and K.S. Rao once again arguing against the bifurcation of Andhra Pradesh with great vigour, and all others supporting the creation of Telangana (when asked individually for a second time in two months by the Prime Minister). Finally, the Cabinet approved the GoM's report as well as the draft legislation. The draft Bill was then sent by the President to the Andhra Pradesh legislature on 12 December 2013. The legislature was initially given time till 24 January 2014 to express its views. It asked for an extension of two months but the President, on the advice of the Government of India, permitted one extra week. What the assembly would do, given the distribution of 294 MLAs between Telangana and Seemandhra, was not in doubt—119 MLAs were from Telangana and 175 MLAs from Seemandhra. The extremely aggressive stance taken by the Chief Minister in defiance of what his party had decided and what the central government led by his own party had decided made it virtually certain that the Bill would be returned with a refusal.

The Andhra Pradesh Reorganisation Bill, 2013 was introduced both in the Andhra Pradesh legislative assembly and the legislative council on 16 December 2013. There was debate on the Bill in the assembly for twenty-three days during which eighty-four members spoke. But there were constant interruptions and unruly scenes. On 26 January 2014, the Chief Minister introduced a resolution in the assembly rejecting the Andhra Pradesh Reorganisation Bill, 2013. The resolution read thus:

> The House while rejecting the A.P. Reorganization Bill, 2013, resolves to request the President of India not to recommend the A.P. Reorganization Bill, 2013, for introduction in the Parliament as the Bill seeks to bifurcate the State of Andhra Pradesh without any reason/basis and without arriving at a consensus,

in utter disregard to the linguistic and cultural homogeneity and economic and administrative viability of both regions. The Bill also completely ignores the very basis of formation of the State of Andhra Pradesh, the first linguistic State created in Independent India.

On 30 January 2014, with Telangana MLAs abstaining, the Chief Minister's resolution was passed by a voice vote. The entire business had lasted ninety minutes. Similar scenes were witnessed in the council as well where a similar resolution was passed by voice vote.

The GoM met informally on the 4, 5 and 6 February 2014 to consider the communication received from the state legislature. We had received the two resolutions rejecting the Andhra Pradesh Reorganisation Bill, 2013 along with numerous amendments suggested by the legislature. Each of these recommendations was examined by the officials assisting the GoM and me, with the work being divided amongst ourselves.

There were some important changes made in the Bill based on the feedback that we had received from various quarters, including Congress MPs from Telangana and Seemandhra. As I have explained in Chapter 12, the original Bill had not included the transfer of submerged areas of Khammam district of Telangana to the East Godavari district of the new Andhra Pradesh to facilitate the R&R work of the Polavaram project. The revised Bill made such a provision. In addition, a provision was made to create a Public Service Commission for Telangana under Article 315 of the Constitution and have the Union Public Service Commission (UPSC) fill the gap till such a time that the state-level body came into being.

I made another crucial change to the Bill in response to suggestions that had been received. The Bill sent to the state legislature had a provision that said that the present admission system and quotas in higher education 'shall continue for a period not exceeding ten years'. This gave rise to the fear that access could be curtailed by the new Telangana government before the period of ten years was over. Hence, this was changed to 'shall continue as such for a period of ten years'. This was more than an exercise in the creative use of the English language. It would have profound implications for the future of lakhs of young men and women of the entire state and that is why I was very particular that the change be made.

A number of delegations from Rayalaseema met me. Venkaiah Naidu also spoke to me about irrigation projects coming up on the Krishna River for the benefit of the Rayalaseema region that could be affected by the bifurcation. I went across to his residence and explained to him, as I did to the delegations that Congress MPs and MLAs had led, that these concerns were misplaced and that the Bill fully protected these projects. However, as a measure of abundant caution and to leave no room for further conflict, I agreed to specify individual projects in the Eleventh Schedule of the Bill and incorporate a provision that said that they 'shall be completed as per the plan notified by the existing state of Andhra Pradesh and the water sharing arrangement shall continue as such'. These projects were Handri Neeva, Telugu Ganga, Galeru Nagari, Veligonda, Kalwakurthy and Nettempadu. We had come full circle as this is exactly what I had suggested to the GoM in my letter to the Home Minister (Annexure 13). Then, after some discussion, the GoM had come to the conclusion that there was no need to specify individual projects. Now we ended up doing precisely that.

Another very important issue that I took up during these informal meetings of the GoM related to 'appointed day' and 'notified date'. There was considerable confusion about these two concepts amongst political parties and in the media. I felt it was imperative to bring clarity immediately. 'Notified date' meant the date when the Reorganisation Act would get published in the Gazette of India after receiving the approval of Parliament as well as of the President of India. 'Appointed day' meant the date when the new state would come into being, that is, the day the chief minister would get sworn in. Telangana wanted the appointed day to be immediately after the notified date. But I was not in favour of this and informed the GoM that it would take at least four to six months to complete all the preparatory work to make the bifurcation relatively smooth and less contentious.

The GoM asked for a precedent in this matter and when told that in the case of Uttarakhand, Jharkhand and Chhattisgarh, the gap between the notified date and the appointed day was three months, it decided to adopt the same period for Telangana. I was not entirely happy even though I was aware that by 16 May 2014, the MLAs of both states would be declared elected and the chief ministers would also become known. They would naturally want to take over at the earliest and therefore the GoM's three-month gap between the notified date and appointed day did make eminent political sense. But I certainly wished we could have taken another three months to complete the homework required in a more comprehensive manner.

The Cabinet met on 7 February 2014 to give its nod to the revised Bill that would be placed before Parliament a few days later. This was the third Cabinet meeting in four months on the bifurcation issue. At this meeting, M.M. Pallam Raju and K.S. Rao argued for a special economic package for Seemandhra and also for the speedy execution of the Polavaram project with R&R being facilitated by the central government. We were literally racing against time since the Lok Sabha elections would soon be announced and my mandate from the Home Minister was to ensure everything got done prior to that.

III
HIGH DRAMA AND AFTER

16

The Lok Sabha Drama, Act I

The Prime Minister hosted a lunch for BJP leaders on 12 February 2014 to get their cooperation in Parliament for passing the Andhra Pradesh Reorganisation Bill, 2014. The leaders assured him of their party's support but wanted the Congress floor managers to ensure that Parliament functioned smoothly and that there were no disturbances in either House of Parliament. The Congress had already taken some steps in this direction. The previous day it had expelled six of its own MPs from Seemandhra, who had given notice for a no-confidence motion against their own government. These MPs—Sabbam Hari, G.V. Harsha Kumar, V. Aruna Kumar, Lagadapati Rajagopal, R. Sambasiva Rao and A. Sai Prathap—were vocally and resolutely opposed to the bifurcation of the state.

At two minutes past noon on 13 February 2014, the Home Minister rose to finally introduce the Andhra Pradesh Reorganisation Bill, 2014. As he was doing so, Lagadapati Rajagopal, the Vijayawada industrialist-MP rushed into the well of the House and started releasing pepper spray from a can he produced from his jacket pocket. I was mortified as he and I had been in conversation for quite some time before the House assembled. We had had coffee together in the Central Hall of Parliament and he had told me that he would be protesting. But never once had I imagined what form this protest would take. There was all-round shock and consternation. Instantaneously, the spray began to have its effect and many MPs, including myself, started feeling sick, sensing deep irritation in the eyes and throat. As he was running around, another MP, Modugula Venugopala Reddy of the TDP, broke the glass and microphone on the table of the Lok Sabha Secretary-General. Within five minutes of the Home Minister getting up, the Lok Sabha was adjourned and the MPs affected by the pepper spray were taken away in ambulances.

What had happened was indeed unprecedented and had undoubtedly diminished all of us. The members had every democratic right to protest. But the manner of this protest had crossed all limits. The Speaker reconvened the Lok Sabha after an hour and announced the suspension of sixteen Seemandhra MPs—ten from the Congress, four from the TDP and two from the YSR Congress Party. But all of us were still dazed by what had happened and what we had seen. I was shaken up and felt that the Bill was going nowhere now. There was the added controversy about whether the Bill could be considered as having been introduced, given the unprecedented fracas in the Lok Sabha.

Later that evening, the Home Minister, Parliamentary Affairs Minister Kamal Nath and Law Minister Kapil Sibal said that the Bill had been introduced, but the Leader of the Opposition Sushma Swaraj insisted that the Bill had not been tabled. The BJP leader was also sore that the Bill had not been listed on the agenda of the day that had been circulated the previous night and that normal procedures had been given the go-by in the haste to get the Bill through. This was, of course, contested by Kamal Nath who took the line that the Speaker had the discretion to decide on the order of the agenda to be followed for the day.

15 February was a Friday—a day when government bills are normally not taken up. The next two days were holidays. Thus, any further action would have to be taken on 17 February. But that was the day Finance Minister P. Chidambaram was to present the Interim Budget for 2014–15. Thus, the Bill had to be put on hold till at least 18 February. I was pretty cut up about what had happened in the Lok Sabha on 13 February and gave vent to my frustration in a television interview to Karan Thapar on CNN-IBN on 16 February,

which was reported widely in the newspapers the next day. *The Hindu* reported it thus:

We Cannot Rush T-Bill, Says Jairam Ramesh

Jairam Ramesh, member of the Group of Ministers on the issue said that the government should not rush into it amid 'cacophony'. 'My personal belief is that such an important piece of legislation must be debated and discussed and not pushed through in din. We shouldn't have any unilateral initiative in the House. We have to bring the BJP on board. We should try and create a larger consensus beyond [the] BJP as well. We have four days left. I hope we can get it done,' he said during a television interview.[69]

---

[69]Quoted in Reddy, 2014.

17

The Lok Sabha Drama, Act II

As scheduled, Finance Minister P. Chidambaram presented the Interim Budget for 2014–15 on 17 February 2014. After this had been done, the Home Minister and I went across to L.K. Advani's room where Sushma Swaraj, Arun Jaitley and M. Venkaiah Naidu were present. The Home Minister had sought this meeting in order to bring them on board for the introduction of the Reorganisation Bill the next day. The meeting lasted for about forty minutes. Venkaiah Naidu said that we ought to protect the interests of Seemandhra and that the Congress must get its house in order to ensure that the Bill passed smoothly. Jaitley said that a constitutional amendment would be needed to ensure that the governor could function in the manner envisaged in the Bill. The Home Minister asked me to respond to these points, which I did.

After the meeting ended, I emailed Jaitley a two-pager on the concern he had expressed.

Note on Provision of Governor

The Andhra Pradesh Reorganisation Bill to create a separate state of Telangana is being brought under Article 3 of the Constitution. Under Section 8.1 of the Bill, the Governor shall have special responsibility for the security of life, liberty and property of all those who are residing in the common capital of Hyderabad.

In doing so, it has been clearly provided that the Governor shall, in the discharge of these functions, consult the Council of Ministers in the State of Telangana and then exercise his individual judgement on the action to be taken. So it is not the case that the Governor has been given any independent powers.

There is a similar provision under Article 371-H of the Constitution regarding the State of Arunachal Pradesh in view of the special circumstances of that State. This provision was actually incorporated in the Constitution through Constitutional Amendment because it was contemplated after the State of Arunachal Pradesh was formed.

In case of Telangana, the State is yet to be formed and considering the special circumstances prevailing there and the concerns of people regarding law and order and the security and safety of the residents, it is considered necessary to incorporate this provision as a special case.

In Arunachal Pradesh, this amendment was made subsequent to the formation of the State and hence a Constitutional amendment was necessary. In the case of Telangana, we are incorporating this transitional provision in the State Reorganization Bill itself. According to Article 4(2) of the Constitution, no such law shall be deemed to be an amendment to the Constitution for the purpose of Article 368 and according to Article 4(1) such a law may also contain such supplementary, incidental and consequential provisions, as Parliament may deem necessary. This provision has also been settled by the Hon'ble Supreme Court in Mullaperiyar Environmental Protection Forum v Union of India reported in 2006 and Babulal Parate v State of Bombay reported in 1960.

Therefore, this is a transitional provision and the same is being incorporated as a special case considering it to be necessary for the formation of the State of Telangana. It will be in force for a limited period of ten years until Hyderabad remains the common capital of both the States.

The next day, all of us were gearing up for the discussion on the Reorganisation Bill. At about 12:15 p.m., the Home Minister got up to take the Bill forward but the Lok Sabha had to be adjourned within two minutes because of the din. It reassembled at 12:45 p.m. but again within two minutes it was adjourned for a second time because of the high noise levels.

Thereafter, I sat in the Central Hall of Parliament wondering what the afternoon had in store for all of us. I was beginning to wonder whether the Bill would ever come up when, all of a sudden, I was told that the Home Minister would make a third attempt to get the Reorganization Bill going at 3 p.m. He did so and made a brief introductory speech. What had happened between 1 p.m. and 2:30 p.m. in the Speaker's chamber that enabled him to do so is unknown to me. All I know is that the Speaker, Kamal Nath and Sushma Swaraj met during that period and decided to write the script for what was to follow at 3 p.m., and thereafter.

But within a minute of the Home Minister beginning to speak, the live telecast went off mysteriously. It was to be explained later as a technical glitch, but nobody was convinced. Protests continued and there was complete chaos. Even though some Seemandhra MPs had been suspended, there were still others present to protest. Other parties, too, did not remain quiet. The Trinamool Congress (TMC) was upset with the manner in which the Bill was being brought forward. The lone member representing the Bodo Liberation Front was clamouring for a separate Bodoland to be carved out of Assam.

After the Home Minister's opening statement, Sushma Swaraj stood up to make her speech in support of the Bill. Most of what she had to say was drowned in the din, and all I could hear was her support for the bifurcation on behalf of the BJP. I also heard her saying in her inimitable language that while Congressmen could call Sonia Gandhi 'amma' (mother) for making Telangana possible, she (that is, Sushma Swaraj) could be considered the 'chinamma' of Telangana (loosely translated as aunt).

Right after her, Jaipal Reddy got up as the opening speaker on behalf of the Congress and, for a while, instead of speaking on Telangana, started criticising his own party colleagues from Seemandhra for their loud protests and for not allowing a proper debate to take place. This further incensed the protesters. Jaipal Reddy had to be persuaded to speak in a less confrontational manner and also to wind up quickly. Thankfully, he agreed.

After this, the Lok Sabha witnessed a free-for-all. Nobody could be heard. The Speaker announced that all speeches of members like Madhu Yakshi Goud, Suresh Shetkar, Ponnam Prabhakar and G. Vivekanand (all Congress MPs from Telangana) and of Panabaka Lakshmi and Botcha Jhansi Lakshmi (Congress MPs from Seemandhra) were to be taken as read. These members laid written copies of their speeches on the table of the House so that they could form part of the official proceedings.

Then the Speaker moved to have the Bill considered. Some members like Asaduddin Owaisi and Saugata Roy of the TMC were allowed to move their amendments, which were promptly put to the voice vote and negatived. In just over eighty minutes—at about 4:20 p.m.—the Andhra Pradesh Reorganisation Bill, 2014 had been considered and passed by the Lok Sabha. Telangana MPs, all of whom were from the Congress, were exultant. Ironically, KCR was not even present in the House. I went home, depressed at the manner in which the Bill had passed, but tried to keep my morale high because the battleground would shift to the Rajya Sabha two days later.

The next day, on 19 February, the Prime Minister called the Seemandhra MPs who had been wanting to see him after the Lok Sabha fracas. Once again, they made a pitch for Hyderabad to be declared a union territory. The Prime Minister gently explained to them for the umpteenth time that this would not be possible. Then, they demanded that the new state be accorded 'special category status' for purposes of receiving financial assistance from the centre. The Prime Minister asked me to speak to the Finance Minister and see whether we could agree to this request. I then met the Finance Minister whose response was that this would immediately lead to a clamour for a similar dispensation from other states like Bihar, Odisha and Jharkhand which had been, in any case, making such a demand for quite some time.[70]

---

[70]'Special category status' had been extended by the Planning Commission over the years to eleven states for the purposes of normal central assistance (that was provided to all states annually). 30 per cent of the total resources available for such assistance was earmarked for these eleven states which repaid only 10 per cent of the

I went back to the Prime Minister and requested him to call the Finance Minister and the Home Minister for a discussion on this 'special category status' issue. At this meeting, the Home Minister expressed his support while the Finance Minister reiterated his arguments as any Finance Minister would have done. The Prime Minister asked me for my views. I told him that he himself had been Deputy Chairman of the Planning Commission and a finance minister as well. He knew the intricacies of the subject better than anyone else. But this was not the time for a technical discussion but a time for a political decision. Seemandhra had 'lost' the revenues generated in Hyderabad and 'special category status' for a limited period would be a good gesture on our part.

The Home Minister and I then met Arun Jaitley and Venkaiah Naidu. Jaitley again raised some questions about the role of the governor and Venkaiah Naidu spoke of a special package for Seemandhra. I responded to their queries and said that the Prime Minister would be making a special intervention in the Rajya Sabha the next day and, if they insisted, the contents of that intervention could be shared with them once it was finalized.

After this, the Prime Minister called Jaitley and Naidu into his room in Parliament House and with the Home Minister and me present, asked for their support in getting the Bill through smoothly in the Rajya Sabha. Venkaiah Naidu insisted that the Prime Minister make an intervention to assuage the hurt sentiments of Seemandhra, and Manmohan Singh replied that he would be doing so.

After they had left, the Prime Minister asked me to put together his speech. That night, I sent him a six-point announcement that he could make in the Rajya Sabha the next day. He asked me to show this six-point announcement to the BJP leaders, which I did. Venkaiah Naidu insisted that the Prime Minister speak in the debate, and I

---

amount, with 90 per cent being a grant. The non-special category states got assistance on the basis of 70 per cent loan and 30 per cent grant. The eleven states—each with distinctive economic, physical, geographical and strategic characteristics—were Assam, Arunachal Pradesh, Mizoram, Manipur, Meghalaya, Nagaland, Tripura, Sikkim, Himachal Pradesh, Jammu and Kashmir, and Uttarakhand. These states also enjoyed special advantages as far as externally-aided projects were concerned.

reassured him that Manmohan Singh had every intention of doing so.

Earlier that very day, news came that the Andhra Pradesh Chief Minister, Kiran Kumar Reddy, had submitted his resignation protesting the Lok Sabha's green signal to the creation of Telangana. He had hyper-aggressively opposed the bifurcation, defying his party leadership. He had no ministerial experience when he had been catapulted to the chief minister's post on 25 November 2010. But he was a quick learner and had enormous energy. However, the bifurcation issue simply overwhelmed him.

18

The Rajya Sabha Drama

After some initial hiccups, the Andhra Pradesh Reorganisation Bill, 2014 was taken up for debate in the Rajya Sabha on 20 February. Compared to what had happened two days earlier in the Lok Sabha, the Rajya Sabha debate was not as chaotic. But it was acrimonious with two Congress and two TDP MPs from Seemandhra waving placards and protesting from the well of the House. This went on for about two hours, but finally the debate started at about 4:45 p.m. with Venkaiah Naidu as the first speaker.

He, of course, supported the creation of Telangana but was very critical of the way in which the Congress party and the government had handled the entire issue. He felt that injustice was being done to the people of Seemandhra. He also gave notice that he would be moving three or four amendments. My heart sank when I heard this. If these amendments were to pass, the government would be in a serious bind and we would have to go back to the Lok Sabha for approval. And there was no time for that. After Venkaiah Naidu finished speaking, I went across to where Arun Jaitley was sitting and pleaded that these amendments not be pressed. Venkaiah Naidu joined the conversation and told me that if I offered a convincing explanation when he moved the amendments, he would be satisfied.

The Congress' opening speaker was the film star-turned politician, Chiranjeevi.[71] I was sitting next to him and thumped the desk as he rose to speak. But in less than two minutes I slumped in despondency. I had requested our leadership in the Rajya Sabha to field him as our first speaker because of his unique standing in Andhra Pradesh and also because he was from Seemandhra. However, he chose to oppose the bifurcation in no uncertain terms. The opposition, especially the BJP, was loving every minute of Chiranjeevi's speech and was egging him on. Chiranjeevi did not disappoint our critics and it was, I have to admit, agonizing to listen to him criticize his own party and the government in which he was a minister.

Despite constant interruptions, the debate went on with some speakers making very good speeches. Sitaram Yechury, although strongly opposed to the bifurcation and critical of the Congress, made a forceful intervention. The Leader of the Opposition, Arun Jaitley, raised concerns regarding the role that was being assigned to the governor in the Bill. His point was that this was contrary to the federal scheme and would require a constitutional amendment. I had already made our position about this clear two days earlier in writing. I thought the matter had been settled as this point had not been raised by the BJP earlier in the Lok Sabha and I was beginning to wonder whether this was a deliberate stalling tactic on its part. Law Minister Kapil Sibal responded to the BJP leader at some length. Two top-flight lawyers were exchanging arguments and counter-arguments; this was Parliament at its debating best.

As had been agreed to earlier, the Prime Minister made a brief intervention to officially announce on the floor of the House the six-point package for Seemandhra, including the grant of special category status. The announcement went thus:

> First, for purposes of Central assistance, special category status will be extended to the successor state of Andhra Pradesh comprising 13 districts including the four districts of Rayalaseema and the

---

[71] I used to pull Chiranjeevi's leg frequently and urge him to do his 150th film soon as he seemed to have stopped one short for quite some time. He is expected to cross that milestone sometime in 2016 with the Telugu remake of the Tamil superhit, *Kaththi*.

three districts of north coastal Andhra for a period of five years. This will put the state's finances on a firmer footing.

Second, the Bill already stipulates that the Central government shall take appropriate fiscal measures, including the offer of tax incentives to the successor states in order to promote industrialisation and economic growth in both the states. These incentives will be along the lines extended to some other states.

Third, the Bill already provides for a special development package for the backward regions of the successor state of Andhra Pradesh, in particular for the districts of Rayalaseema and north coastal Andhra Pradesh. This development package will be on lines of the K-B-K (Koraput-Bolangir-Kalahandi) Special Plan in Odisha and the Bundelkhand special package in Madhya Pradesh and Uttar Pradesh.

Fourth, I would like to reassure the hon. Members that if any other further amendments are needed to facilitate smooth and full Rehabilitation and Resettlement (R&R) for the Polavaram project, they will be given effect to at the earliest. Our Government will execute the Polavaram project; let there be no doubt about it.

Fifth, the appointed day for the formation of the new State will be so fixed in relation to the notified date so as to enable preparatory work relating to personnel, finance and distribution of assets and liabilities to be completed satisfactorily.

Sixth, the resource gap that may arise in the successor state of Andhra Pradesh in the very first year, especially during the period between the appointed day and the acceptance of the Fourteenth Finance Commission recommendations by the Government of India, will be compensated in the Regular Union Budget for 2014/15.

Immediately after the Prime Minister's statement, there was a sharp exchange between the Home Minister and Venkaiah Naidu. I was being egged on by some of my colleagues to intervene but decided not to.

Mr. Deputy Chairman: Mr. Naidu, what do you want?
Shri M. Venkaiah Naidu: The Special Category Status, we wanted for ten years. The Prime Minister is saying 'five years'...

Shri Sushilkumar Shinde: The Special Category Status for Seemandhra is five years as the Prime Minister has announced. Shri M. Venkaiah Naidu: That should be ten years. That is the demand of the people.[72]

Earlier, the Home Minister had made a brief statement while moving the Bill for consideration and passing. Conscious of Seemandhra sentiments, I had inserted the following in his speech which he faithfully read out:

> We want to ensure that the economy of the successor state of Andhra Pradesh should continue to grow. Therefore, the Bill also contains our firm commitment to execute the Polavaram project as a national project by obtaining all necessary clearances including ensuring rehabilitation and resettlement.
>
> The Central Government shall provide a special development package for Rayalaseema and north coastal districts of the successor state of Andhra Pradesh.
>
> I wish to reiterate what I said in the Lok Sabha the day before—a special financial package will be given to Seemandhra. I would also assure the House that a Special Cell will be created immediately in the Planning Commission under the Deputy Chairman to address the developmental needs of the successor state of Andhra Pradesh.

The language used, particularly the word 'feasibility' in the Thirteenth Schedule, came in for criticism from Venkaiah Naidu in the debate. He said that the language was vague and was not definitive. I was forced to intervene to respond to his criticism thus:

> Shri Jairam Ramesh: Sir, the Government of India in the Thirteenth Schedule is absolutely crystal clear...(*interruptions*). When it says, 'the Government shall take steps' we have to take steps. We have to get [the] Planning Commission's approval, we have to get the Finance Ministry's approval...(*interruptions*). We have to get Cabinet approval.

---

[72] Ironically, when the Modi government came to power and Venkaiah Naidu became minister, the very concept of 'special category status' got abolished in early 2015.

Mr. Deputy Chairman: Government is continuous... (*interruptions*).

Shri Jairam Ramesh: Mr. Venkaiah Naidu has been a senior Cabinet minister. It is not 'may'. It says 'Government shall'... 'Government shall' means it is committed to it (*interruptions*).

Mr. Deputy Chairman: Venkaiahji, Government is continuous. Why do you worry?...(*interruptions*).

Shri Venkaiah Naidu: Sir, my point is about the wordings used. Hon. Minister, go through page no. 17. 'Infrastructure'—the words 'examined within six months'...(*interruptions*) could be examined and rejected, those can be the words....(*interruptions*).

Shri Jairam Ramesh: Sir, I will explain why...(*interruptions*). Where Government is taking the decision on its own the words are 'Government shall'...(*interruptions*). But there are certain projects implemented by public sector companies like the NTPC, the Steel Authority of India, the IOC...(*interruptions*). Now we don't want to decide on their behalf. That is why we have said...(*interruptions*).

Mr. Deputy Chairman: Venkaiahji is ready to accommodate you...(*interruptions*).

Shri Jairam Ramesh: Let me finish...(*interruptions*).

Mr. Deputy Chairman: It is okay. That is the assurance... (*interruptions*).

Shri Jairam Ramesh: Let me finish...(*interruptions*). I am sure you respect the autonomy of the PSUs, as much as we do.... (*interruptions*). We don't take decisions on behalf of the PSUs... (*interruptions*). The investment decision has to be taken by the Board of NTPC, by the Board of SAIL Authority, by the Board of IOC. That is why we have said that within a period of six months these companies will complete the feasibility study. Without a feasibility study, mega investments cannot take place... (*interruptions*). But where Government is taking the responsibility like IIT, like IIM and like AIIMS, we have said 'Government shall' do it. I request the hon. Member to see this distinction between [the] Government as an investor and public sector companies as investors...(*interruptions*).

Mr. Deputy Chairman: Okay, Mr. Venkaiah, so, you are not

pressing the Amendment now.

Shri M. Venkaiah Naidu: No, Sir.

Mr. Deputy Chairman: Now in light of the explanation given by the Minister, that is not being...

Shri Ravi Shankar Prasad: Mr. Jairam Ramesh, we hope you will persuade those public sector undertakings to expedite the process...(*interruptions*). Will you do that?...(*interruptions*).

Shri Jairam Ramesh: If we come back to power, we will do it...(*interruptions*).

Mr. Deputy Chairman: All right...(*interruptions*) that is a very positive assurance. So, you are not pressing the amendment, Mr. Naidu?

Shri M. Venkaiah Naidu: Sir, on the basis of his assurance and the hope that anyhow, we would be coming to power in another two months, I am not going further...(*interruptions*).

There was another issue which Venkaiah Naidu raised which required me to get up and speak:

Shri M. Venkaiah Naidu: Sir, the issue is till the Union Budget is presented, there will be a revenue gap for the state of Seemandhra. The Government told us that they will take care of that revenue gap...(*interruptions*) it is said that it will be taken care in the next Budget. In between what will happen to the state? What about money for salaries, about pensions and also interest payments? That is a very important issue. Sir, that is why I am insisting on this. Sir, in Clause 46, page 11, line 48, see the words 'areas of the State'. It shall be the responsibility of the Central Government to form an independent committee to assess the revenue deficit of the successor state of Andhra Pradesh and recommend non-Plan revenue grants, including but not limited to the revenue deficit grant which shall be charged from the Consolidated Fund as provided in Section 67(N) of this Act for a period of at least ten years. Till such time, in the first year, the Consolidated Fund should give an amount of Rs 10,000 crore. For that, I would like to hear the response of the Government. If they are giving a positive response, then...(*interruptions*).

Then followed a somewhat lengthy exchange between the Home Minister and Venkaiah Naidu, which clearly did not satisfy the latter who called on me to answer his doubts.

> Shri Jairam Ramesh: Sir, the concern expressed by the hon. Member is…(*interruptions*). There is a notified date and there is an appointed day…(*interruptions*). We have not fixed what the Appointed Day is…(*interruptions*). All what we have said is whatever the Appointed Day is, if there is a gap in the first year of the successor state of Andhra Pradesh, it will be compensated…(*interruptions*). What 'compensation' means is that if there is a gap it will be filled when the regular Budget is presented. That is what the 'compensation' means. The hon. Member knows that the Finance Bill has been passed. The process of the 'Interim Budget' is over. In the Interim Budget we cannot have provisions. That is why, we have made a gap between the notified date and the appointed day. In the case of Chhattisgarh, in the case of Jharkhand and in the case of Uttarakhand, the gap between the notified date and the appointed day was three months. It was three months….(*interruptions*). Now I am not saying whether it will be two months or three months or four months…(*interruptions*). But what the hon. Prime Minister has said is that the appointed day will be fixed in such a manner that this gap will not exist for the successor state of Andhra Pradesh…(*interruptions*).
>
> Mr. Deputy Chairman: Are you still pressing?…(*interruptions*). Are you still pressing?…(*interruptions*).
>
> Shri M. Venkaiah Naidu: Sir, I am giving a solution…(*interruptions*). That means, till such time the money can be made available from the combined State account…(*interruptions*). Is it so, Mr. Jairam Ramesh?…(*interruptions*).
>
> Shri Jairam Ramesh: Till the appointed day the state of Andhra Pradesh continues undivided. The appointed day means that there is a state of Telangana and there is a state of Andhra Pradesh…(*interruptions*).
>
> Mr. Deputy Chairman: Are you still pressing?…(*interruptions*).
>
> Shri M. Venkaiah Naidu: It's okay now…(*interruptions*).

That issue having been settled, two members of the Biju Janata Dal (BJD) proposed amendments disapproving of the Polavaram project. Venkaiah Naidu also moved an amendment to the effect that Polavaram was not just an irrigation project as mentioned in the legislation but actually a multi-purpose project.

> Shri Rabinarayan Mahapatra: I urge upon the Government that when several cases are pending and the matter is sub judice in the court, why the Government is pressing for that. The villagers of Odisha will suffer. What is the problem with the Government?... I want a specific answer.
>
> Mr. Deputy Chairman: Okay. Now, Mr. Jairam Ramesh will reply...(*interruptions*).
>
> Shri Jairam Ramesh: Let me explain the situation in relation to the amendments moved both by Mr. Venkaiah Naidu and the BJD members...(*interruptions*). The Polavaram project is a multi-purpose project...(*interruptions*). I want to assure Mr. Venkaiah Naidu that although the Bill says 'Polavaram Irrigation Project', it is a multi-purpose project providing drinking water to Visakhapatnam, irrigation water in the Godavari basin and transfer of water from [the] Godavari basin to [the] Krishna basin...(*interruptions*). So I want to reassure him that it is a multi-purpose project and Polavaram is declared as a national project which also includes power generation.. (*interruptions*) the Government of...(*interruptions*). Odisha and the-then Government of Madhya Pradesh had given their approval for the Polavaram project...(*interruptions*). Subsequently, because of the submergence of villages in Dantewada district of Chhattisgarh...(*interruptions*) and Malkangiri district of Odisha...(*interruptions*). Odisha and Chhattisgarh have gone to the Supreme Court on the Polavaram project...(*interruptions*)...there is no question about it. But the Government of India will take a stand and the Government of India is committed to implement the project...(*interruptions*) with full R&R for all the submerged villages and ensuring that all environment and all forest laws are fully enforced...(*interruptions*).
>
> Shri Rabinarayan Mohapatra: Sir, we are staging a walk-out.

Shri M. Venkaiah Naidu: Sir, I am not pressing. I am satisfied with the answer given by the hon. Minister...(*interruptions*).

Finally, at around 9 p.m. on 20 February, the Rajya Sabha passed the Andhra Pradesh Reorganisation Bill, 2014. There had been tense moments that had often required me to cross the aisle and confabulate with Arun Jaitley. I had, on at least four different occasions, run across to him and Venkaiah Naidu to clarify the provisions of the Bill. All this was in the full glare of the entire House and led Sitaram Yechury to remark that there had been a case of 'match fixing' between the Congress and the BJP. Venkaiah Naidu took us to the brink but after I had spoken to him, he was gracious enough to withdraw his amendments. And, unlike in the Lok Sabha two days earlier, the TV cameras recorded the entire proceedings.

The next day, Gargi Parsai of *The Hindu* captured that action-packed evening which had left me completely exhausted and drained:

'Match-Fixing by Congress, BJP' in RS Gives Birth to Telangana

Dramatic scenes marked the passage of the Telangana Bill in the Rajya Sabha when all the amendments moved by the Opposition members were either defeated by voice-vote or not to put to vote by the Chair on the grounds that there was disorder in the House.

Every time an Opposition party member, particularly from the BJP, pressed for [a] division of votes, Rural Development Minister Jairam Ramesh—who was a member of the GoM on Telangana and a key architect of the Bill—would rush to the Leader of the Opposition Arun Jaitley who would gently gesticulate to him to 'relax'. More than twice BJP leader M. Venkaiah Naidu sought 'division' but was quick to catch on to the situation as Mr. Ramesh would rush back to the Treasury Benches and from there give an 'explanation' or 'an assurance' which would 'satisfy' Mr. Naidu.

A repeat of the scene at least five times prompted CPI(M) leader Sitaram Yechury to charge that there was 'match fixing' between the ruling party and the main Opposition party. [...]

There were some anxious moments for the ruling party

as much of the points the Opposition members were raising had been answered in the Prime Minister's statement on special package and other incentives. When Mr. Naidu insisted on seeking replies about finances, Mr. Ramesh realised that the member had not been given the Prime Minister's statement. He rushed to Mr. Shinde and took his copy of the statement to Mr. Naidu. When Mr. Jaitley also asked for a copy, Mr. Ramesh came to the Prime Minister and took his copy to hand over to the Leader of the Opposition.[73]

As I came out of the Rajya Sabha at 9 p.m. or so, Telangana MPs of the Congress party, both from the Lok Sabha and the Rajya Sabha, lifted me onto their shoulders and filled my mouth with sweets. But sadly, my colleagues from Seemandhra were sullen and came up to me to say that I had written their political obituaries, as indeed that of the Congress, in the new state of Andhra Pradesh.

---

[73] Parsai, 2014.

19

The Final Touches

With Parliament having given its approval to bifurcation, I turned my attention to matters requiring urgent follow-up. I felt this was a moral obligation on my part.[74] The first task was to identify, in the minutest detail, what actions would have to be taken and by whom once the Act received the President's approval. My intention was that our government should do the maximum as long as it was in power and not assume that its responsibility had ended once Parliament had passed the Bill. Suresh Kumar, Vineel Krishna and I prepared this document and handed it over to the Home Minister. But there were some actions I took myself, even though technically the GoM had ceased to exist, and everyone was in election-mode. I first wrote to the Deputy Chairman of the Planning Commission, Montek Singh Ahluwalia:

---

[74]It was a similar sentiment that prompted me to accompany the newly-elected Chief Minister of the successor state of Andhra Pradesh, N. Chandrababu Naidu, when he met ministers of the central government and Y.V. Reddy, Chairman of the Fourteenth Finance Commission on 30 and 31 May 2014 to follow up on the implementation of the Andhra Pradesh Reorganisation Act, 2014. Based on a draw of lots, I had been 'allotted' to the successor state of Andhra Pradesh by the Rajya Sabha Secretariat following the bifurcation.

25th February, 2014

While intervening in the debate on the Andhra Pradesh Reorganisation Bill, 2014 in the Rajya Sabha on February 20th, 2014, PM made the following commitments which have relevance for the Planning Commission:

First, for purposes of Central assistance, Special Category Status will be extended to the successor state of Andhra Pradesh comprising 13 districts, including the four districts of Rayalaseema and the three districts of north coastal Andhra for a period of five years. This will put the state's finances on a firmer footing. [...]

Third, the Bill already provides for a special development package for the backward regions of the successor state of Andhra Pradesh, in particular for the districts of Rayalaseema and North Coastal Andhra Pradesh. This development package will be on the lines of the K-B-K Special Plan (Koraput-Bolangir-Kalahandi) in Odisha and the Bundelkhand special package in Madhya Pradesh and Uttar Pradesh.

I am writing to request you to kindly initiate follow-up action on the PM's assurances as we discussed this morning.

On 1 March, the Planning Commission requested the Cabinet to approve the proposal to extend special category status to the successor state of Andhra Pradesh. The Cabinet duly did so and directed the Planning Commission to 'implement the decision to grant special category status for a period of five years to the successor state of Andhra Pradesh comprising 13 districts'. To a query regarding whether any other formality needed to be completed to execute the Cabinet's orders, the Deputy Chairman replied, 'No. It only requires the *endorsement* of the National Development Council (NDC).' He drew our attention to the fact that when Uttarakhand formally came into being in November 2000, a similar special category status was extended to it through a Cabinet decision two years later. He was clear that the *approval* of the NDC was not required. In any case, I discovered that the Uttar Pradesh Reorganisation Act, 2000 that created Uttarakhand had no provision for a 'special category status' for the new hilly state.

The allocation of state government employees had to begin right away and therefore I wrote to my colleague V. Narayanasamy thus:

25th February 2014

> You may recall that I have mentioned to you that the Department of Personnel and Training has to set up two advisory committees for the allocation of personnel to the two successor states of Telangana and Andhra Pradesh. One committee will deal with the allocation of officers belonging to the all-India Services and the other will deal with the allotment of state-level service officials.
>
> I would request you to kindly have these two committees constituted immediately.

The committee for state-level service personnel would have to deal with complex issues arising from the fact that there were local, district, zonal and multi-zonal cadres. It had to develop objective and transparent criteria for the allocation of personnel, determine cadre strength, make individual allocations and deal with representations from aggrieved employees. The allocation of officers belonging to the all-India services like the IAS and the Indian Forest Service would be, by contrast, relatively straightforward. Rajiv Sharma and I discussed the names of those who could chair these crucial committees. At his suggestion, an advisory committee for the all-India services was announced under the chairmanship of Pratyush Sinha, formerly the central vigilance commissioner; C.R. Kamalanathan, a retired IAS officer of the Andhra Pradesh cadre was to chair the all-important committee for state government employees. The Kamalanathan Committee had to decide on the allocation of some 71,000 posts between the two states (the number of employees involved was less than that figure because of vacancies) in a fair manner that would not lead to yet more discord.

I was also keen that we move quickly on the provisions regarding the sharing of water resources. Accordingly, I wrote to Ghulam Nabi Azad who held additional charge of water resources.

25th February 2014

With the passage of the Andhra Pradesh Reorganisation Bill, 2014 by both the Lok Sabha and the Rajya Sabha, the Ministry of Water Resources has to take Cabinet approval for the following:

1. Constitution of a special purpose vehicle for executing the Polavaram project.
2. Extension of the tenure of Krishna Water Disputes Tribunal-II.
3. Creation of Krishna River Management Board and Godavari River Management Board.
4. Creation of an Apex Council for Godavari and Krishna river water resources.
5. Reconstitution of the Tungabhadra Board to replace the undivided state of Andhra Pradesh by the successor states of Telangana and Andhra Pradesh.

I am sure you will follow-up on these expeditiously.

Between 28 March and 29 April, the Cabinet gave its approval to these five proposals that emanated from the Reorganisation Act. I wish this could have been done faster but such are the procedures of the Government of India. To make matters worse, the bureaucracy already sensed that we were on our way out and therefore was not moving files quickly.

◆

After the Act had been passed, we discovered an error in the following formulation in Para 6 of its Twelfth Schedule:

> 6. The power of Central Generating Stations will be allotted in such ratio to the State of Telangana and the State of Andhra Pradesh based on the actual energy consumption of the last 5 years of the relevant DISCOMS in the respective successor State.

This formulation had come from the Ministry of Power and the GoM had accepted it in toto. I kicked myself for not having foreseen the confusion it could create. It was certainly an oversight on my part. There was no use blaming the Ministry of Power. A central generating station has an 85 per cent firm allocation based on a pre-determined and objective formula and a 15 per cent allocation called 'unallocated power' that is determined by the central government based on the exigencies of the situation. What the GoM had in mind in regard to paragraph 6 was *unallocated* power and not the entire power of central power generating stations. The word 'unallocated' had got left out in the legislation although it was there in the GoM's final report. This created considerable heartburn on both sides. The Cabinet cleared the change on 1 March and subsequently an ordinance was issued.

The 1 March Cabinet meeting also considered a proposal from the Ministry of Commerce and Industry to establish a National Institute of Design in Hyderabad. This reflected the traditional mindset in the Government of India which led to Hyderabad being the location of all its investments. When the proposal came up, I immediately requested the Prime Minister to change the location from Hyderabad to either Visakhapatnam or Vijayawada. My Seemandhra colleagues, Pallam Raju and K.S. Rao, supported me and argued for Vijayawada—which is what the Cabinet decided.

I should also mention that on 27 February, I went to Hyderabad to meet my party compatriots and apprise them of the details of the Andhra Pradesh Reorganisation Act, 2014 and the special provisions it had for Seemandhra. I used this opportunity to meet, for the very first time, M. Kodandaram and his colleagues from the Telangana Joint Action Committee (TJAC) that had been spearheading the Telangana agitation for the past few years. My plea to Kodandaram was this: now that their long-standing demand had been met, it was now incumbent upon the TJAC to ensure that the bifurcation proceeded smoothly. I requested him to build an alliance with his counterpart organization in Seemandhra so that the bitterness of the past could be overcome and reconciliation could take place quickly. He responded positively to this suggestion.

◆

The schedule for the 2014 Lok Sabha and assembly polls was announced on 5 March 2014. This immediately made us a lame duck administration. But still, I felt we had an obligation to keep the bifurcation process going. Accordingly, the GoM met informally for a last time on 21 March, although not all members could attend and only the Home Minister and I could be present throughout. We had invited the Chief Secretary of Andhra Pradesh, P.K. Mohanty, to give us a detailed presentation on the actions taken vis-à-vis the Andhra Pradesh Reorganisation Act, 2014. He apprised us of the steps the state government was taking.

To follow up on this presentation, I again went to Hyderabad on 10 April 2014 and further reviewed with the Governor the implementation of the Andhra Pradesh Reorganisation Act, 2014. President's Rule had been imposed in the state on 1 March after the Chief Minister's resignation on 19 February. There were many things that had to get done before two new states could come into being and the more we accomplished prior to that date, the better it would be for all concerned. Therefore, I spent roughly three hours with the Governor and senior officers of the state administration going over the nuts and bolts of the bifurcation. In the Governor's review, we discovered that some 2.54 million files and 1.65 lakh movable assets had to be allocated. There were a total of 5.79 lakh pensioners; the February 2014 pension bill alone was a little over ₹1,200 crore, of which a little over ₹500 crore was Telangana's share. There were 1.38 lakh agreements entered into by the undivided state. All these numbers revealed the magnitude of the challenge we faced in the implementation.

The issue of high courts was sensitive and politically very volatile. The Andhra Pradesh Reorganisation Act, 2014 certainly had provisions for two separate courts but there were murmurs that the GoM had not done adequate 'justice' to the issue. I certainly did not want to leave anything to chance but at the same time knew that there was a process to be followed. Accordingly, I persuaded Anil Goswami, the Union Home Secretary, to push the matter officially with his counterpart in the Department of Justice, which he did on 24 April 2014.

Dear Ms. Anita Kaul:

You must be aware that the bifurcation of the existing State of Andhra Pradesh and the creation of a new State of Telangana would happen shortly. Article 214 of the Constitution mandates that there would be a separate High Court for every State. Part IV of the Andhra Pradesh Reorganisation Act, 2014 deals with the issue of [a] High Court. Section 30 read with Section 31 of the Act makes it clear that a separate High Court for the successor state of Andhra Pradesh would need to be set up and the existing High Court of Judicature at Hyderabad would become the High Court of Telangana. The Act also provides for a common High Court during the interregnum period until a separate High Court is set up. We have also notified the appointed day as 2nd June 2014 for the formation of the two new States.

The Act states that both the States would have a common capital for a period of ten years or until a new capital for the State of Andhra Pradesh is setup [sic], whichever is earlier. A separate High Court for the State of Andhra Pradesh in the common capital of Hyderabad would thus entail some reorganisation of the space of the High Court, [the] assignment of High Court judges and also the bifurcation of the Subordinate Judiciary.

It is hence requested that the matter be taken up with the Ld. Chief Justice of the Supreme Court drawing his attention to the provisions of the Act relating to the setting up of a separate High Court for Andhra Pradesh in the common capital of Hyderabad as well as other attendant issues to enable the expeditious formation of the new High Court for Andhra Pradesh. The issues relating to the creation of posts and underwriting of the costs can be taken up with the present State Government or the Government of the successor States subsequently.

The GoM had toiled hard and produced legislation to give effect to the bifurcation. But we knew that disputes would be inevitable especially in the transition period. And we also knew that not every operational detail could be taken care of by the law. I spoke to the

Home Minister and suggested that we create some forum for resolving disputes as and when they arose. Accordingly, on 12 May, the Ministry of Home Affairs issued an office memorandum that ran thus:

Sub: Resolution of Disputes between the two successor states of Telangana and Andhra Pradesh–Regarding

I am directed to inform that a Committee has been constituted to resolve any differences and disputes arising out of the implementation of the Andhra Pradesh Reorganisation Act, 2014 on and from the appointed day as notified as 2nd June, 2014 between the successor states of Telangana and Andhra Pradesh. The composition of the Committee shall be as follows:

1. Union Home Secretary—Chairman
2. Chief Secretary of Telangana—Member
3. Chief Secretary of A.P.—Member
4. Additional Secretary (CS)—Member Convenor

The Committee shall invite the concerned Secretary in Govt. of India as a Member-invitee, based on the subject under consideration. The Committee can also co-opt any other person as directed by the Home Secretary. The Committee shall be serviced by the Centre-State Division and will also be assisted by a technical support group to be set up by the State Govt. of Andhra Pradesh.

S. Suresh Kumar
Joint Secretary (CS)

Four days later, the Lok Sabha election results came in and the government in which I was a minister went out.

IV
RECOLLECTIONS

20

Amusing GoM Musings

While the GoM was having its meetings, I was inundated with emails from all sorts of people on matters relating to the colourful political history of the Telangana region, now about to be made a separate state.

Rajaji was mentioned in some of the emails as having ensured that the Telugus did not have control over Madras in the early 1950s.[75] In fact, a couple of messages from some amateur historians also pointed to the obstructionist role played by the 'conscience of the Mahatma' in delaying the creation of the Andhra state.

As I have documented at some length in the first chapter, Rajaji was certainly quite cussed when it came to the Andhra issue. However, what his critics overlook is the single-handed role he played in opposing Tamil demands for Tirupati and ensuring that Tirupati stayed in Andhra. In this context, Rajmohan Gandhi writes: '…that his remote ancestor Nallan Chakravarti had lived in the temple city was immaterial, as was an old Tamil text referring to Tirupati as the northern boundary of the Tamil country'.[76]

What is also forgotten is how, in December 1925, Rajaji took a 'temporary leave of absence' from Gandhiji's call for the boycott of courts and secured the acquittal of a 'panchama' (in today's language,

---

[75]Srinivasan, 2009, writes that Rajaji's reputation for shrewd manipulation and opportunism stems mainly from his handling of the Andhra issue.
[76]Gandhi, 1997.

a dalit) who had entered the temple of Tiruchannur near the famed Tirupati shrine and had been prosecuted and convicted for 'insulting religion'. And Rajmohan Gandhi writes movingly about the frequently acrimonious Rajaji–Prakasam relationship which was also marked by respect and regard. When the two had their last bitter quarrel leading up to the formation of Andhra state in 1953, Rajaji was seventy-five and Prakasam was eighty-one and their parting was very sentimental.

But the most wonderful story relating to Rajaji was narrated to me by my father-in-law who had started his IAS career in Machilipatnam and Ongole. In 1953, Devdas Gandhi, Rajaji's son-in-law (and Gandhiji's son), as the *Hindustan Times* editor, wrote to the then Chief Minister of Madras asking for an article on Tyagaraja, the greatest composer of Carnatic music who lived in the nineteenth century. Rajaji's reply to his son-in-law, made available to me by his grandson Gopal Gandhi, was characteristic and reads thus:

P. Sabanayagam, IAS
Private Secretary to the
Chief Minister of Madras

Fort St. George, Madras
September 24, 1953

Sir:

C.H.V. Pathy, your correspondent has written to Rajaji requesting him to contribute an article on poet Tyagaraja for the Andhra Supplement of your paper. Rajaji desires me to say that Sri Tyagaraja was a good Tamilian of Tanjore district and that only Tamilians know how to sing his compositions properly and that Rajaji is unable to contribute any article that will hand over Tyagaraja to the Andhras.

Yours faithfully,
P. Sabanayagam

Sri Devadas Gandhi
Editor, *Hindustan Times*, New Delhi

I had received some email messages on Jawaharlal Nehru's role in Telangana affairs. Apparently, in his speech of 1 November 1956, in Hyderabad, he had said something to the effect that Hyderabad/

Telangana's merger with Andhra Pradesh was like a matrimonial alliance with provisions for divorce if the partners in the alliance did not get along well in the future. I was intrigued. I went back to the *Selected Works of Jawaharlal Nehru* and re-read the speech delivered that day. Nowhere in the transcript does Nehru draw the marriage–divorce analogy. I then listened carefully to the audio recording of the speech available with the All India Radio and here, too, I drew a blank.

A second mystery relates to something Nehru is reported to have said in Nizamabad on 5 March 1956. One book that was released in Hyderabad when the GoM meetings were taking place[77] quoted Nehru as having said, '*Ek masoom bachchi ka ek natkhat ke saath shaadi ho raha hai. Kai din ke baad mein ittefaq nahin hone ke vaje se talaq de sakti hai.*' ('An innocent girl is getting married to a clever boy. After many days she can get a divorce if there is no compatibility.') Presumably Hyderabad/Telangana was the '*masoom bachchi*' and Andhra was the '*natkhat*'. Nehru's colourful formulation and a variation of it has become part of Telangana folklore and was even quoted by Sushma Swaraj in her speech in the Lok Sabha on 18 February 2014. The book attributes Nehru's analogy to another well-known work called *The Last Nizam* by V.K. Bawa.[78] I looked up Bawa's book and just did not find it there. I then contacted Mr Bawa and he confirmed what I had to say. Thereafter, I once more returned to the *Selected Works of Jawaharlal Nehru* and the All India Radio archives and, again, drew a blank. I was then reminded of what Gopal Gandhi had once told me about his grandfather: 'Jairam, MKG [Mohandas Karamchand Gandhi] did not say many things attributed to him but we accept them because we wish he had said them'.[79] Maybe, then, this is equally true of Nehru.

But I did not let it go at that. I got in touch with Suresh Reddy, the former Speaker of the Andhra Pradesh assembly, who is from

---

[77]Ranga Reddy, 2013. The book was released on 25 November 2013.
[78]Bawa, 1992.
[79]Examples of such immortal 'quotes' of Gandhiji include (i) there is enough in this world for everyone's need but not enough for everyone's greed; (ii) western civilisation would be a good idea; (iii) post-dated cheque on a crashing bank (a reference to the Cripps Mission offer of 1942).

Nizamabad, to find out whether he could help trace the source of Nehru's much-quoted statement. This is what he replied by email on 21 December 2015.

> Dear Jairam Ramesh Garu:
>
> Namaskaram. Your determined effort to get the documented proof of Panditji's statement is inspiring. I spoke to ex-MP Mr. Narayan Reddy who as a young volunteer put up by my grand-father for the All-India Bharat Sewak Samaj Conference remembers the incident which I believe was said at a public meeting. When Panditji announced the merger there were protests from the crowd. Sensing the mood, Panditji gave that assurance. This has been reiterated by an IFS officer who attended that meet and is alive. I am trying to access him. Newspaper archives unfortunately do not have this, as the merger then was big news.

On Indira Gandhi, the same book that mentioned Nehru's purported '*masoom bachchi-natkhat*' formulation at Nizamabad, claimed that she had been in favour of creating a separate Telangana state after the 1971 Lok Sabha election results were out and the TPS had put up a stunning performance. The book holds that she had instructed her then closest aide, P.N. Haksar, to set the ball rolling but that T.N. Kaul, her Foreign Secretary, had dissuaded her from doing so. This was apparently because of the pending case of the erstwhile Hyderabad state in the United Nations. The book asserts that Kaul recorded all this in his memoirs. This is certainly a startling statement since there is incontrovertible evidence in Parliament speeches, for instance, that Indira Gandhi was vehemently in favour of a united and integrated Andhra Pradesh.

It is certainly true that the Nizam of Hyderabad had approached the UN Security Council on 21 August 1948 on the grounds that a 'grave dispute' had arisen between Hyderabad and India regarding the former's status—whether it was to accede to India or be independent. The Security Council had considered the Nizam's cablegram on eight occasions between September 1948 and May 1949. But thereafter, with Hyderabad's accession to India, following Sardar Patel's decisive action, the dispute ceased to exist. It is also true that Hyderabad has remained on the 'list of matters of which the Security Council is seized' although no formal discussion has taken place since 24 May 1949.[80] But the claim in the book regarding Indira Gandhi wanting to concede Telangana is unverifiable. Neither the Haksar papers in the Nehru Memorial Museum & Library nor the Kaul memoirs, which I made a point of going through carefully, corroborate it.

I have drawn attention to Indira Gandhi's role in handling the Jai Telangana and Jai Andhra agitations. In the former, she had been assisted by the then Home Minister, Y.B. Chavan, and in the latter by her Minister of State for Home Affairs, K.C. Pant. I had worked closely with Pant between 1983 and 1985 and had, in fact, accompanied him on a visit to the state. He had got a 5 a.m. appointment with its colourful Chief Minister, NTR, which he found extremely inconvenient since he did not begin his day before 10 a.m. Nonetheless, he went to meet NTR. During the visit, Pant talked to me about the key role he had played in resolving the Andhra Pradesh crisis in the first six months of 1973. Little did I realize that three decades later I would end up playing a wholly different role in reconfiguring Andhra Pradesh. Life does indeed move in strange ways.

I have mentioned earlier that on 18 April 1956, the States Reorganisation Bill, 1956 had been introduced in the Lok Sabha. proposing that the new unified Telugu-speaking state be called Andhra-Telangana. There was a hilarious exchange between the Home Minister and an MP representing Visakhapatnam in Andhra state on this subject as I discovered in the Parliamentary archives, which I would occasionally dip into during the GoM assignment. The date was 26 April 1956 and the occasion was a debate in the Lok Sabha on a motion to send the Bill to a joint committee of both Houses of Parliament.

> Pandit G.B. Pant: A number of new States are being set up. The State of Madhya Pradesh which will perhaps be the biggest in area hereafter is to be formed according to the provisions of

---

[80] V.K. Bawa writes in his book that on the evening of 17 September 1948, the Nizam announced the withdrawal of his appeal before the UN Security Council in a broadcast on Hyderabad Radio.

this Bill. Telangana and Andhra will form another big State. The Legislatures of both Telangana and Andhra have suggested that the name of the new State might be Andhra Desa, instead of Andhra-Telangana.

Dr. Lanka Sundaram: Is it Andhra Desa or Andhra Pradesh?

Pandit G.B. Pant: Perhaps the Hon Member is right.

Dr. Lanka Sundaram: I would like to know from the Home Minister.

Pandit G.B. Pant: When he reminds me I should accept the correction.

Dr. Lanka Sundaram: I just wanted to know what exactly is the opinion given to the Home Minister and what he proposes to do.

Pandit G.B. Pant: It is either Desh or Pradesh; but it is not Pardesh!

In one of the meetings with Telangana MPs in the GoM, the name of Konda Lakshman Bapuji came up in some context. He was a respected leader from Telangana who, as I have pointed out earlier, had resigned from Brahmananda Reddy's Cabinet in March 1969 to spearhead the Telangana agitation. I then recalled that, in September 1975, when I first went to Carnegie Mellon University in the USA for graduate study, I met a young doctoral student called Suresh Konda who took our computer science class. I got to know him well and one day he told me about his father who was a politician in Andhra Pradesh. I had forgotten all about this and lost touch with him after I came back to India in 1980. But when the MPs mentioned Konda Lakshman Bapuji, I recalled Suresh Konda and tried to get in touch with him—only to find that he had passed away quite suddenly in May 2003 at a young age but after attaining some eminence in the field of computer security. Konda Lakshman Bapuji was his father.

On another day, I had met the Home Minister to discuss the Rayala-Telangana proposal. As I came out of North Block, a large Telugu media contingent surrounded me to ask what had transpired at the meeting and whether Rayala-Telangana was to be proposed. 'Will Telangana have ten or twelve districts?' I was asked. I did not want to reveal what had happened and so kept smiling. I thought of diverting one persistent questioner's attention by asking him what the time was. It was 11.50. I had no idea that a whole new twist would be given to an innocuous question and answer. Ten to twelve districts was the immediate story that was flashed!

On another occasion, as I was about to enter North Block, I was surrounded by about twenty TDP legislators. One of them, Chintamaneni Prabhakar, an MLA, held on to my feet and would not allow me to move. He kept saying that we should not go ahead with the bifurcation. Ultimately, I had to be rescued by the security personnel. The usual media contingent captured my embarrassment but the legislators had registered their political points and presence as well. I did not mind the protest and was quite willing to engage with the MLAs, but I was whisked off by the police and so were they.

When faced with the TDP's protests, I could not help but recall with a smile that, in April 2000, the then Chief Minister of Andhra Pradesh and the TDP supremo, N. Chandrababu Naidu had invited me to serve as a member of the state's economic advisory council—an offer which flattered me, but that I had to refuse as I was an office-bearer of the Congress party. In fact, his offer had led to my denunciation by none other than YSR himself. But YSR's attitude towards me had changed dramatically when in the period between the first and second phase of polling in the 2004 assembly elections I had, on 25 April 2004, in an interview to a leading Telugu TV channel, said, 'YSR, who led the campaign for our party is our chief ministerial candidate'. This angered all other claimants and aspirants who protested to my bosses but from that day YSR's attitude towards me changed completely. He went to the extent of ascribing a 2 to 3 per cent swing in favour of the Congress in the second phase to that statement of mine!

All of 2011 and 2012, not a day passed without Congress MPs from Telangana raising the demand for bifurcation. Very often, the Lok Sabha would get adjourned because of their protests. It was quite embarrassing to have MPs belonging to the treasury benches interrupt the work of the government. The opposition was, however, delighted that the government was being heckled by its own MPs day in and day out. On one such occasion, I told the group of MPs—Ponnam Prabhakar, G. Vivekanand, Suresh Shetkar, Sukhender Reddy, Siricilla Rajaiah and Madhu Yaskhi Goud in Hindi—'*Roz ka gana, ek hi gana*, Telangana, Telangana.' ('The song of everyday, only one song, Telangana, Telangana.') They used this slogan subsequently whenever they agitated. Likewise, I used to banter with the Seemandhra MPs and would often pull their leg by reeling off their surnames, or *'inti perus'* as they are called in Telugu, which is indeed the most poetic of languages: Daggubati, Lagadapati, Rayapati, Mekapati, apart from Tikkavarapu and Muppavarapu.[81] Many of the Seemandhra MPs and ministers were well-known industrialists who were running successful businesses and I would refer to them as 'Andhrapreneurs', although there were a couple of Telangana MPs like Nama Nageshwara Rao of the TDP and G. Vivek who occupied this category.

One day, after a particularly taxing GoM meeting, I was accosted by journalists and asked what had happened. Not wanting to say anything substantive, I looked upwards and cheerily said, 'Govinda Govinda', hinting that we were waiting for divine guidance, but inexcusably forgetting that for the Andhras such a chant had very grim overtones—overtones of 'everything is lost'. The Telugu media went to town with this faux pas.

After the Bill had been referred to the state assembly there was criticism in Andhra Pradesh that it contained references to Tamil Nadu. Some of my own colleagues protested that perhaps we had forgotten our mandate was Telangana. A few told me that perhaps the Finance Minister, who hails from Tamil Nadu, had lost track of what he had actually been asked to do. The Home Minister was curious how a reference to Tamil Nadu had crept into the Bill. I had to explain that the appearance of the word 'Tamil Nadu' in the Andhra Pradesh Reorganisation Bill, 2013 was because we were seeking to insert the word 'Telangana' serially after the words 'Tamil Nadu' in Article 168 of the Constitution and in the Representation of People Act, 1950 and 1951. It was a straightforward, mundane explanation but for two days the media had a field day having fun at our expense.

Obviously, much of the vitriol against me came from those who

---

[81] A reference to Daggubati Purandeswari, Lagadapati Rajagopal, Rayapati Sambasiva Rao, Mekapati Rajamohan Reddy, Tikkavarapu Subbirami Reddy and Muppavarapu Venkaiah Naidu.

opposed bifurcation. But I could not but help be struck by the irony here. Through the 1960s there had been a movement spearheaded in Telangana for separation from Seemandhra. And soon thereafter, in the early 1970s, there had been a Jai Andhra movement launched by leaders from the coastal districts to separate from Telangana. Prominent among these leaders was Tenneti Vishwanatham, a close associate of Tanguturi Prakasam and a champion of Vishalandhra in the 1950s.[82] The shoe was suddenly on the other foot now and it claimed the scalp of the then Chief Minister P.V. Narasimha Rao who, as we know, happened to be from Telangana.

I have mentioned the pepper spray incident in the Lok Sabha on 13 February 2014. That same evening, as we were coming out of the Rajya Sabha at around 5 p.m., two Congress MPs and close friends of mine—Hanumantha Rao from Telangana and J.D. Seelam from Seemandhra—were engaged in an animated conversation. I joined them. Both have very loud voices which they don't hesitate to use to press their viewpoints. I held Hanumantha Rao's cheek fondly and told him to relax as he was getting very agitated. I could take such liberties with him. But I did not realize that we were being photographed. This picture went viral in the media with headlines blaring, 'Jairam manhandles Hanumantha Rao'. I was accused of hooliganism and of using strong-arm tactics to muzzle the voice of Telangana. Of course, exactly a week later, Hanumantha Rao was photographed lifting me exuberantly after the Rajya Sabha had approved the creation of Telangana.

During this time, there were some emails extolling the glorious cosmopolitan history of Hyderabad. This brought back memories of growing up torn between the Karnataka and Hyderabad teams in the Ranji Trophy cricket matches. Having been born in Chikmagalur (Karnataka), it was but natural for me to support a team which boasted of greats like G.R. Vishwanath, E.A.S. Prasanna, B.S. Chandrasekhar, Brijesh Patel and V. Subramanyam. But who could not be mesmerized by a team which had M.L. Jaisimha, M.A.K. Pataudi, Abid Ali and Abbas Ali Baig? When either of the teams played, there was no doubt

---

[82]Another prominent activist of the Jai Andhra movement was Venkaiah Naidu, now a senior minister in the Narendra Modi government.

where my sympathies lay. But when they played each other, as they did in the 1975-76 Ranji Trophy final, I was on the proverbial horns of a dilemma.[83] Recently, I located a priceless photograph of these two teams thanks to V. Ramnarayan who played for Hyderabad then and could not resist including it in the book.

Speaking of Hyderabad, there were some suggestions that Telangana should be called Hyderabad[84] as that was what had been suggested in the report the SRC had submitted in March 1955. The SRC had said, 'After taking all these factors into consideration, we have come to the conclusion that it will be in the interests of Andhra Pradesh and Telangana if, for the present, the Telangana area is constituted as a separate State, which may be known as Hyderabad State, with provision of its unification with Andhra after the general elections, likely to be held in or about 1961, if by a two-thirds majority the legislature of the residuary Hyderabad State expresses itself in favour of such unification.' As it turned out, the unification took place very soon thereafter and Andhra Pradesh came into being on 1 November 1956 itself. On the other hand while some Telangana activists wanted the new state to be called Hyderabad, Seemandhra representatives invoked no less a person than Dr B.R. Ambedkar to insist on Hyderabad being a union territory. In his thought-provoking book *Thoughts on Linguistic States*, Dr Ambedkar had advocated that Hyderabad (along with Secunderabad and Bolarum) should be declared the second capital of India after being constituted as a chief commissioner's province. He wrote that 'Hyderabad is a far better city than Delhi' and that Delhi should be the capital during the winter months. It was a most interesting suggestion but perhaps too radical to be taken seriously. But I half-jokingly told my Seemandhra colleagues that on grounds of equidistance perhaps, Nagpur is better situated than Hyderabad to be the second capital!

[83]Even today, Hyderabad and Andhra are two separate teams in the Ranji Trophy matches as are Mumbai, Maharashtra and Vidharbha as well as Gujarat, Baroda and Saurashtra.
[84]As pointed out earlier, a Hyderabad state comprising of the Telugu-speaking districts of the Telangana region, the Kannada-speaking districts of the Gulbarga division and the Marathi-speaking districts of the Aurangabad division had existed between 26 January 1950 and 31 October 1956.

The GoM meeting on 12 November 2013 was very interesting. We met the political parties of the state. Indisputably, the best presentation was by Asaduddin Owaisi. I am not always a supporter of his politics, but that day he was superb. The memorandum that he handed over was the best-written, best-researched and best-referenced of all memoranda submitted by political parties. It was also quite amusing to see the CPI(M) and CPI take diametrically opposite views when in the 1940s and 1950s, the communists were united and a formidable force to reckon with both in Telangana and Andhra. It was doubly amusing because Sitaram Yechury was from Kakinada in Seemandhra while Suravaram Sudhakar Reddy, the CPI leader, was from Mahabubnagar in Telangana. But it was the presentation by the Congress party that was the most interesting, to say the least. The Deputy Chief Minister of Andhra Pradesh, Damodar Raja Narasimha, came and made a case for a separate Telangana. Thirty minutes later, his colleague seated next to him, Tourism Minister Vatti Vasanth Kumar, made an eloquent plea against bifurcation. This, of course, reflected the deep divide within the Congress party which the Antony Committee had been unable to bridge.

I had to face an hour of public embarrassment on 20 December 2013 at a function organized by *India Today* to honour the best performing states in different areas. I was the chief guest and had to give the award for the best performing state in the area of governance to none other than my friend, Kiran Kumar Reddy, Chief Minister of Andhra Pradesh. Fortunately, he was very restrained in his speech, not mentioning the impending bifurcation of the state even once and the different roles we were playing in the process. He extolled the state's achievements and I did likewise. But I could see people in the audience smiling at our discomfiture since our problems with each other were well known. On 13 February 2014, in my final official communication with him, I conveyed the centre's approval for the upgradation of about 2,285 kilometres of rural roads under the Pradhan Mantri Gram Sadak Yojana-II and I must admit that the letter was more formal than would have been under normal circumstances.

I have mentioned earlier about meeting Dr Y.V. Reddy, the Chairman of the Fourteenth Finance Commission, during the course of the GoM's deliberations. I called on him on 7 February 2014. We had known each other for almost three decades and had been colleagues in the Finance Ministry during the mid-1990s. During the course of our conversation I bemoaned my thankless position—I was being attacked by all sides. He smiled and said, 'Well, it is your fault'. I asked why. He replied, 'You should have refused to be a member of the GoM'. I told him ministers can't and don't refuse to be a member of the GoM set up by the Prime Minister and the Cabinet. He had a response to that as well: 'You should have said that as an MP from Andhra Pradesh you have a conflict of interest!' I laughed and told him that this was not something I could or indeed should have done. We let it go at that.

In an email, one person accused me of being the new Cyril Radcliffe—the man who divided the subcontinent—immortalized in W.H. Auden's poem, 'Partition'. Radcliffe stayed in Delhi for less than five weeks and never returned. My reply was that unlike the British lawyer, I knew the region that was being reconfigured very well; that I had close ties with it, with my son having studied in Hyderabad between 2002 and 2007 and with my being an MP from the region since 2004; and that I had every intention of returning to both states regularly. But the mail did get me to re-read Auden's haunting 'Partition'.

Speaking of Partition, at a public function in Hyderabad on 24 December 2015, I was introduced by the organizer as the 'father of partition' of Andhra Pradesh. I immediately protested saying 'bifurcation', not 'partition', please. Partition has immensely negative connotations in our country and bifurcation does not conjure up the images that partition does. But obviously, a reputation once established, howsoever unjustified, is very difficult to obliterate! Strictly speaking, the 2014 reorganization of Andhra Pradesh is neither 'partition' nor 'bifurcation' but a 'demerger' because the two parts were separate prior to 1 November 1956.

Finally, how the wheel of history turns. On 21 September 1973, at the insistence of Indira Gandhi, leaders of Andhra Pradesh had issued the six-point formula to bring back peace and normalcy. As I have explained in chapter 1, this formula followed the agitation launched by coastal Andhra leaders to break away from Telangana—an agitation that had followed a movement started by Telangana leaders to break away from Seemandhra. Forty years later, on 20 February 2014, another Prime Minister who had been Indira Gandhi's close economic aide for over a decade announced a six-point package, in addition to the various provisions already contained in the Reorganisation Law, to address the concerns of Seemandhra.

Postscript

As this book was being sent to press, an issue relating to the reorganization suddenly erupted. Section 26 of the Andhra Pradesh Reorganisation Act, 2014 provided for an increase in the strength of the Telangana assembly from 119 to 153 and that of Andhra Pradesh from 175 to 225. The GoM had done this after hearing a thoughtful presentation by Marri Shashidar Reddy (son of Dr M. Chenna Reddy and a leading Congress politician) on 26 November 2013. He later submitted a detailed note to the GoM on 3 January 2014. His contention, supported by many Congress leaders, was that small assemblies were a recipe for political instability, especially when a number of political parties were locked in intense competition. Shashidar Reddy even dug out a statement I had made on the less-than-desirable size of the Jharkhand assembly and submitted this to the GoM to buttress his arguments. The GoM discussed this at some length and was finally persuaded, in mid-January 2014, to make the provision for the expansion. But while going along with what he suggested, the GoM added a condition that it would be subject to Article 170 of the Constitution which froze the size of the assemblies till at least 2031-32. However, what I could not understand was the sudden scramble to push for increasing the size of the assemblies that was initiated by Chandrababu Naidu and supported by KCR. This appeared to me to be political opportunism at its cynical worst and being resorted to only to encourage defections. The spirit of what the GoM had intended was clearly being subverted. The TDP and TRS already enjoyed huge majorities in their respective states.

21

A Last Word

The initial two chapters of this book are based on archival research, some conversations with knowledgeable people and my own understanding of political history. The subsequent chapters are based on my personal involvement and participation.

The first wave of the reorganization of states—in the 1950s and 1960s—that created Andhra Pradesh, Kerala, Karnataka, Maharashtra, Gujarat, Punjab and Haryana was predominantly based on language considerations, although the rising aspirations of castes like the Reddys and Kammas in Andhra Pradesh, the Lingayats and Vokkaligas in Karnataka and the Marathas in Maharashtra also played a role.

The second wave—in the 1970s and 1980s—focussed on the northeastern region where new states came into being on either an ethnic basis to fulfil the aspirations of hill tribes in some places like Meghalaya; or to deal with secessionist movements like in Mizoram; or on strategic considerations as in Arunachal Pradesh.

The third wave, in 2000, was driven by the larger social agenda of the RSS and the political strategy of the BJP, anchored in expanding their support base among tribal and other backward caste (OBC) communities. To be sure, there were long-standing movements, especially in Jharkhand, but the dominant stimulus for reorganizing Bihar, Madhya Pradesh and Uttar Pradesh—with the BJP in power in New Delhi—came from the

Hindutva ideology.[85]

However, while the push for reorganisation may well have come from the BJP, there was support from other quarters as well. Digvijaya Singh of the Congress was Chief Minister of Madhya Pradesh in 2000 when that state was bifurcated by the Atal Bihari Vajpayee government. However, earlier, in 1994, he himself had got a resolution passed by the state assembly in favour of a separate Chhattisgarh state. Other senior Congress leaders of the state like Arjun Singh, Shyama Charan Shukla and Motilal Vora were also supporters of a separate Chhattisgarh.

In Uttar Pradesh, the BJP was in power when it was bifurcated in 2000 and that made the process relatively easy. In any case, by the mid-1990s, Mulayam Singh Yadav, the UP strongman, had softened his opposition to the creation of a hill state and went to the extent of 'provoking regional mobilisation in Uttarakhand as part of an attempt to hold together a political coalition in the plains of his state'.[86] While there was opposition to the inclusion of Udham Singh Nagar and Haridwar districts in Uttarakhand during the actual bifurcation process, this opposition was soon overcome.

The case of Bihar is more complex. Lalu Prasad was Chief Minister when it was bifurcated to create Jharkhand. Why did he agree to it especially since Jharkhand contributed something like 70 per cent of undivided Bihar's revenues? To be sure, he did declare that Jharkhand would be formed over his dead body but that proved to be an empty threat. It is possible that, embroiled in the fodder scam and at the mercy of the CBI (Central Bureau of Investigation), Lalu Prasad wanted to keep on the right side of the Vajpayee government. It is also possible that Lalu was influenced by his mentor Jayaprakash Narayan who had advocated the formation of Jharkhand way back in the mid-1970s to fulfil the aspirations of tribal communities. Lalu Prasad may also have realized that the populous north Bihar region would have little scope for industrialization if Jharkhand remained part of Bihar. The Bihar assembly finally agreed to the bifurcation of the state, subject to a ₹1,79,900 crore financial package by the central government. That this

---

[85]This has been well analyzed in Louise Tillin's *Remapping India*, 2014.
[86]Tillin, 2014, p. 157.

package subsequently did not materialize is a separate point.

What is beyond doubt is that the disputes in Uttar Pradesh and Bihar over bifurcation were nothing like what was to be experienced in Andhra Pradesh. Perhaps the stakes in Andhra Pradesh were much higher. While the reasons for this certainly need to be analyzed and understood, it is not for me to do so since I was, at once, too far from the scene when the decision was taken and too near the scene after the decision was taken. However, I am firmly convinced about one thing: the presence of Hyderabad and its indubitable attractions just did not allow other places in the undivided state to develop and flourish. Whatever the larger merits and demerits of the bifurcation may be, I strongly believe that other cities in the new state of Andhra Pradesh—like Visakhapatnam, Vijayawada, Guntur and Tirupati—now have a bright chance for a take-off.

All political parties concerned, barring the CPI(M), supported the creation of Telangana. In the face of such overwhelming backing, the question was not 'whether Telangana' but 'when Telangana'. The long history of the demand for Telangana discussed in the very first chapter should also not be forgotten. However, the creation of Telangana was certainly not based on language. It also had little to do with administrative efficiency. There was definitely a Telangana movement launched by influential political leaders to give themselves relevance—like Chenna Reddy in the late 1960s and KCR in the first decade of this century. But a movement has to have some foundation. And that foundation in the case of Telangana, according to its protagonists, was its continued backwardness and neglect. Rayalaseema, of course, is more backward than Telangana but there has been no strong separatist movement in that region like in Telangana. Ironically, Rayalaseema produced powerful Chief Ministers like N. Sanjiva Reddy, D. Sanjeevaiah, Kotla Vijayabhaskar Reddy, Chandrababu Naidu and YSR himself. Kiran Kumar Reddy, too, hails from Rayalaseema.

Economic neglect, political marginalization and domination by powerful and resourceful castes from the coastal areas were routinely given as reasons by Telangana leaders to justify their agitation for a separate state. However, there was something deeper at work as I discovered when I spent time with the charismatic balladeer, Gummadi

Vittal Rao, popularly known as Gaddar. Some scholars have pointed out that 'cultural production in the form of song-performance and fiction' gave strength to historical memory and provided an impetus to the Telangana movement.[87] It is indeed ironical that the Telangana movement of the late 1990s and the first decade of this century followed NTR's regime, which was based on the assertion of Telugu pride and self-respect. Clearly that assertion came to be seen as 'hegemonic' by large sections of Telugus living in Telangana who saw their distinctive identity as a being under assault.

The bifurcation of Andhra Pradesh proved hugely contentious and controversial. The dominant political party at that time in the state—the Congress—was itself deeply divided, with the Chief Minister aggressively opposing what his own national leadership had decided after a long period of consultations.[88] The issue of Hyderabad dominated the discourse with both sides laying claim to it. Once it became abundantly clear that it was not being shared but was being 'given' to one of the two claimants, all hell broke loose. In this acrimonious atmosphere, political communication, outreach and trouble-shooting by Congress leaders from Delhi entrusted with that job did not seem to have had much impact. With the benefit of hindsight, it could be argued that the stridently obstructionist Chief Minister should have been sacked but, truth be told, at that time there appeared no other option but to persist with him.

I started this narrative by underscoring what this book is *not* about. It is really not about *why* Telangana came into being. Nor is it about the history of the Telangana movement, and there certainly has been

---

[87]The best example of such an analysis is Srinivasulu, 2011.

[88]However, factionalism was rampant even in Nehru's time, as the correspondence in *Selected Works of Jawaharlal Nehru,* Second Series, Volume 63, edited by Madhavan K. Palat, 2015, reveals. In the late 1960s, Brahmananda Reddy, as Chief Minister of Andhra Pradesh, blessed an agitation for locating a steel plant in the state which he knew would embarrass the Union Minister of Steel and Mines who happened to be N. Sanjiva Reddy, his predecessor. The fact that Sanjiva Reddy lost his chief ministership first in 1960 to D. Sanjeevaiah to become Congress president and then the two swapped jobs in 1962 reflects the intensity of factional fights within the Congress even in the Nehruvian era.

one going back to the late 1940s and early 1950s. Rather, it is about *how* Telangana came into being once a decision had been taken to create it and *what* decisions got taken in that process. It does not deal with the merits of the bifurcation of Andhra Pradesh, only with its mechanics. The reason for this is simple: I have no inside knowledge of the 'why' nor can I shed any new light on it over and above all the speculation that already exists in the public domain.

Instead, this book is a first-person, insider narrative of the process of bifurcation, as observed and recorded by someone who participated in it closely. Further, the perspective is Delhi-centric. It does not get into the debates that took place in the Andhra Pradesh assembly or in other fora in the state. It tells the story of how Telangana was created as I saw it and that too during a limited period between 8 October 2013 and 14 May 2014 when, by forces that I can only ascribe to that mysterious force called 'destiny', I came to occupy a pivotal role in the *process* of bifurcation.

What went into the decision to bifurcate Andhra Pradesh and also what determined its timing was, honestly, unknown to me. But one thing did become clear when the election results were announced in May 2014. The results proved catastrophic for the Congress in the new state of Telangana and cataclysmic in the new state of Andhra Pradesh, something that the champions of bifurcation in the party had not expected. The results certainly traumatized me. It was especially painful as I had myself campaigned extensively across both Telangana and Seemandhra, touching each of the twenty-three districts and forty-two Lok Sabha seats in both regions. For a while, I began to wonder whether I had erred grievously in taking the GoM assignment as seriously as I did and whether I should not have just allowed matters to be dragged along. But such angst was momentary since I knew very well that the merits and demerits of bifurcation could not be judged by the Congress' electoral fortunes but had to be measured by more fundamental socio-economic concerns and political factors.

The manner in which the bifurcation legislation was passed in Parliament in February 2014 did not portray our democracy in good light. Sure, Parliament has supreme powers under Articles 3 and 4 of the Constitution to reorganize states but the Constitution makers envisaged full-fledged debate and discussion on the floor of both Houses in the exercise of such powers. It would be unfortunate, however, if Parliament loses its appetite for further reorganization of states as a result of the Andhra Pradesh experience—as Arun Jaitley observed might happen when we spoke after the 20 February 2014 vote. The fact is that the reorganization of India's most populous state is long overdue. Uttar Pradesh, with a current population of around 200 million, that is expected to more than double in the next three decades, is simply ungovernable in its present form.[89] Personally, I think a strong case can also be made for Vidarbha, too.

There is, I realize, too much 'I' in this narrative. I have tried to avoid that dreaded pronoun in whatever I have written so far—articles, papers and books. But in this story, it was simply unavoidable. For that, I plead guilty. The 'I' figures prominently only to be true to events as they unfolded. And wherever the 'I' figures, I have done my best to provide written evidence, as far too many books, such as this, are based on oral recollection and tend to glorify the author. There is no self-aggrandizement in these pages—only hard, verifiable facts. And, for the most part, I have tried to avoid any value judgement.

'Fools rush in where angels fear to tread', wrote the poet Alexander Pope over three centuries ago. So, have I taken a huge risk in putting together this account when memories are still fresh, when wounds are still raw, when tempers are still frayed and when passions are still running high in both the new states? Perhaps. In the successor state of Andhra Pradesh I am still considered a villain and in the state of Telangana I am believed to have bent over backwards to appease Seemandhra sentiments. In Telangana, the comment I get to hear is that the Andhra Pradesh Reorganisation Act, 2014 has nothing but shackles for Telangana and sops for Seemandhra. And in Seemandhra, all I hear is that the Act is badly drafted and betrays the people of Seemandhra hugely. So this book cannot be an exercise in self-glorification as both sides are unhappy.

I have sometimes asked myself then why write this account? In part, this is to bring clarity in the public discourse about the nuts and

---

[89]Ramesh, 2014.

bolts of the bifurcation process, regarding which there are many myths and misconceptions. In part, it is to underline that having been part of the GoM, I tried to do as fair a job as possible in the time given to me. Additionally, the book has an academic purpose in the best sense of that term—to be an enduring contribution to the scholarship on contemporary politics and political history that will also provide useful primary source material.

I am not surprised that the Andhra Pradesh Reorganisation Act, 2014 has been bitterly criticized in both Telangana and Seemandhra. In fact, I would have been more than surprised if it hadn't been. But it seems to me that very often criticism is an alibi for the failure of the political process. In fact, in the GoM report—perhaps anticipating the attacks on the legislation that were to come later—I had written: 'The GoM would like to stress that, while the terms of reference are wide-ranging, there may well be issues arising out of the bifurcation that have not been dealt with as part of the recommendations. Such issues must necessarily be dealt with as part of the political dialogue process between the two successor states for which it is absolutely essential to maintain a climate of amity and mutual understanding.'

Chroniclers of contemporary events, especially if they are participants themselves, are not in the best position to foretell or judge the consequences of their actions. Maybe after five or ten years, a more objective and dispassionate assessment will be made of the bifurcation of Andhra Pradesh and what was accomplished by it. When such a balance sheet does get drawn up, I may or may not be around but I will have had the psychological satisfaction of having left behind my side of the story. It is a story of trying to be fair to both sides under the most trying of circumstances, and with the knowledge that if both sides ended up being unhappy the objective of being fair had indeed been fulfilled.

Annexures

Annexure 1: Gentlemen's Agreement, 20 February 1956
Annexure 2: All-Party Agreement, 19 January 1969
Annexure 3: Statement of Prime Minister Indira Gandhi on Telangana in the Lok Sabha, 11 April 1969
Annexure 4: Statement of Prime Minister Indira Gandhi on 'Mulki Rules' in the Lok Sabha, 27 November 1972
Annexure 5: Six-point Formula, 21 September 1973
Annexure 6: L.K. Advani's Letter to A. Narendra, 1 April 2002
Annexure 7: N. Chandrababu Naidu's Letter to Pranab Mukherjee, 18 October 2008
Annexure 8: N. Chandrababu Naidu's Letter to Sushilkumar Shinde, 27 December 2012
Annexure 9: YSR Congress Party Leaders' Letter to Sushilkumar Shinde, 28 December 2012
Annexure 10: Minutes of the Congress Working Committee Meeting, 30 July 2013
Annexure 11: Note Handed over by the Author to Chief Minister, Andhra Pradesh, 12 October 2013
Annexure 12: Office Memorandum, 4 June 2014: Special Responsibility of the Governor of Telengana
Annexure 13: Author's Letter to Sushilkumar Shinde Regarding Management of Water Resources, 4 November 2013
Annexure 14: Extracts from the Rajya Sabha Debate on the Polavaram Ordinance, 14 July 2014

Annexure 1

Gentlemen's Agreement, 20 February 1956

1. The expenditure/of the central and general administration of the State should be borne proportionately by the two regions and the balance of income from Telangana should be reserved for expenditure on the development of Telangana area. This arrangement will be reviewed after five years and can be continued for another five years if the Telangana members of the Assembly so desire.
2. Prohibition in Telangana should be implemented in the manner decided upon by the Assembly members of Telangana.
3. The existing educational facilities in Telangana should be secured to the students of Telangana and further improved. Admission to the colleges including technical institutions in the Telangana area should be restricted to the students of Telangana, or the latter should have admission to the extent of one-third of the total admissions in the entire State, whichever course is advantageous to Telangana students.
4. Retrenchment of services-should be proportionate, from both regions if it becomes inevitable due to integration.
5. Future recruitment to services will be on the basis of population from both regions.
6. The position of Urdu in the administrative and judicial, structure existing at present in the Telangana area may continue for five years, when the position may be reviewed by the Regional Council. So far (as) recruitment to services is concerned, knowledge of Telugu should not be insisted upon at the time of recruitment but they should be required to pass a prescribed Telugu test in two years after appointment.
7. Some kind of domicile rules, e.g., residence for 12 years should be provided in order to assure the prescribed proportion to recruitment of services for Telangana area.
8. Sales of agricultural lands in Telangana area (is) to be controlled by the Regional Council.
9. A Regional Council will be established for the Telangana area with a view to secure its all round development in accordance with its

needs and requirements.

10. The Regional Council will consist of 20 members as follows: 9 members of the Assembly representing each district of Telangana to be elected by the Assembly members of the Telangana districts separately, 6 members of the Assembly or the Parliament elected by the Telangana representatives of the Assembly, 5 members from outside the Assembly to be elected by the Telangana members of the Assembly. All ministers from Telangana area will be (its) members.

11. (a) The Regional Council will be a statutory body empowered to deal with and decide about matters mentioned above and those relating to planning and development, irrigation and other projects, industrial development within the general plan and recruitment to services insofar as they relate to Telangana area. If there is difference of opinion between the views of the Regional Council and the Government of the State, a reference may be made to the Government of India for final decision.

    (b) Unless revised earlier by agreement, this arrangement will be reviewed at the end of ten years.

12. The Cabinet will consist of members in proportion of 60 to 40 per cent for Andhra and Telangana respectively. Out of the 40 per cent Telangana Ministers one will be a Muslim from Telangana.

13. If the Chief Minister is from Andhra, the Deputy Chief Minister will be from Telangana and vice-versa. Two out of the following portfolios will be assigned to Ministers from Telangana: (a) Home; (b) Finance; (c) Revenue; (d) Planning & Development; and (e) Commerce & Industry.

14. The Hyderabad Pradesh Congress Committee President desired that the Pradesh Congress Committee Should be separated from Telangana up to the end of 1962. Andhra Provincial Congress Committee President has no objection.

The above agreement was arrived at on February 20, 1956. It was signed by (1) B. Gopala Reddi, Chief Minister of Andhra; (2) N. Sanjiva Reddi, Deputy Chief Minister of Andhra; (3) G. Latchanna, Minister in the Andhra Cabinet and Leader of the Krishikar Lok Party, a constituent of the United Congress Front, which contested the Andhra elections

(1955) and formed the Ministry; (4) A. Satyanarayana Raju, President, Andhra Provincial Congress Committee; (5) B. Rama Krishna. Rao; Chief Minister, Hyderabad; (6) K.N. Ranga Reddy, Minister, Hyderabad; (7) Dr. M. Chenna Reddy, Minister, Hyderabad; and (8) J.V. Narasinga Rao, President, Hyderabad. Provincial Congress Committee.

Annexure 2

All-Party Agreement, 19 January 1969

The following is the full text of the agreement reached between leaders of all political parties convened by the Chief Minister of Andhra Pradesh on 19 January 1969 to take steps for the implementation of Telangana safeguards

With the formation of Andhra Pradesh State on November 1, 1956 the long cherished aspiration of the Telugu-speaking people for having a state of their own was achieved, thanks to the combined efforts of leaders of the Andhra and Telangana regions. Both were concerned primarily with securing the fuller cultural and economic development of the Telugu people. The leaders of both the regions found it necessary to provide safeguards for ensuring due protection of the interests of Telangana and its development. Provisions in this regard were accordingly made in what has come to be known as the gentleman's agreement.

Though it has been the settled policy of the Andhra Pradesh Government to implement faithfully the terms of the gentleman's agreement, lapses have arisen in the implementation of the policy. In order to ensure the proper implementation of the safeguards the following decisions have been taken at a meeting of the leaders of all the political parties of the Legislature convened for the purpose by the Chief Minister.

Employment

All non-domicile persons who have been appointed either directly or by promotion or by transfer to posts reserved under the Andhra Pradesh Public Employment (Requirement as to Residence) Rules 1959 for domiciles of the Telangana region will be immediately relieved from service. The posts so rendered vacant will be filled by qualified candidates possessing domicile qualifications and in cases where such candidates are, not available the posts shall be left unfilled till qualified domicile candidates become available. Action on the above lines will be taken immediately.

All non-domicile employees, so relieved shall be provided employment in the Andhra region without break in Service and by creating supernumerary posts, if necessary.

Two senior officers will be appointed charged with the responsibility for implementing these decisions immediately and effectively.

There have been some complaints that employment has been obtained on the basis of false domicile certificates. The Government will arrange to inquire into any such complaints.

Statutory Bodies

The Andhra Pradesh Public Employment (Requirement as to Residence) Act and Rules applied to posts under the Government and local bodies only. The High Court has recently held that this Act does not apply to the Andhra Pradesh State Electricity Board. The Government, however, felt that as these bodies are state-wide organisations, reservation of posts for Telangana candidates should also be made in them as in the case of posts under the Government. The State Government will immediately file an appeal against the judgement of the High Court regarding the applicability of the APPE (RR) Rules to the Andhra Pradesh State Electricity Board.

Simultaneously the State Government will move the Government of India to make provision in the Bill extending the Andhra, Pradesh Public Employment (Requirement as to Residence) Act, for a further period of five years so as to include within its purview statutory or other corporations financed by the Government.

Integrated Lists

In all cases where the Government of, India has approved common gradation lists of Andhra and Telangana officers, or issued any directive for preparation or revision of such lists, the lists so approved, or prepared shall alone be followed for regulation of conditions of their service. In cases, however, where no such lists have been approved by the Government of India or no directive has been issued by it regarding their preparation or revision, the provisional lists being followed by the State Government shall continue to be followed, pending approval of the Government of India has given any directive regarding the equation of posts or preparation of common gradation lists, such directive shall be followed by the State Government without any further correspondence.

Surplus Funds

The Telangana surpluses will be determined on the following basis:
(a) The existing method of allocation of expenditure and receipts to either region will continue.
(b) The Telangana surpluses for each year will be computed by adding to the net revenue surplus of the Telangana region of that year the difference between one-third of the total capital expenditure of the State in that year and the actual capital expenditure in the Telangana region in that year.
(c) So far as statutory or other boards and corporations, functioning on a State-wide basis financed by the State Government are concerned, they will, for the purpose of computing Telangana surpluses, be treated as if they were State-wide Government departments, and as if their receipts and expenditure were booked in Government accounts. In the case of Andhra Pradesh State Electricity Board, however, the expenditure on power generation and high tension transmission lines only will be apportioned between the two regions in the manner indicated above. Expenditure on distribution lines and rural electrification will be booked to each region as per actuals.
(d) The Industrial Trust Fund which is being operated exclusively for the Telangana region, will continue to be so utilized. To work out on the basis of the above principle the exact Telangana surpluses which have accrued since the formation of the Andhra Pradesh State and to avoid any controversy in this regard the Comptroller and Auditor-General of India will be requested to depute, a senior officer of the rank of an Accountant-General. He will be requested to give his finding before February 28, 1969.

Development

The Telangana surpluses so determined will be fully utilized for development of Telangana region during the next five years. Any Telangana surpluses accruing in future will be worked out at the end of each financial year and due provision will be made for its utilization in the Telangana region in succeeding year. Half-yearly review of expenditure in the Telangana region will be undertaken by the Government and a copy of the review will be furnished to the Regional Committee and Members of the Legislature.

We also take note that there are backward areas in the Andhra region and they also deserve immediate attention. For the removal of imbalance it shall be the endeavor of the Government to give top priority to the rapid economic development of those areas also so that employment opportunities could improve to mitigate the hardship faced by the unemployed.

Education

Steps will be taken to afford better educational opportunities to students, irrespective of region, in the capital city of Hyderabad with effect from the ensuing academic year.

We trust that by taking energetic action on the above lines the grievances voiced in the Telangana region will be fully redressed, The cultural enrichment and economic development of the Telugu people should continue to be our primary concern. It must be borne in mind that maintenance of unity and tranquility in the State is essential to create a proper climate for attracting larger investment in the State leading to economic progress and creation of more employment opportunities for the younger generation.

Nothing should, therefore, be done which would in any way lead to fissiparous tendencies in our society. We of different political persuasions firmly resolve to bend our energies towards achieving quicker development and fuller integration of our State. Andhra Pradesh holds a prominent position on the map of India, and in order to be able to contribute our own share to the national integration of the country, it is of paramount importance that within our own State we achieve full unity.

Therefore, we vehemently and unequivocally condemn the slogan raised in some quarters for the creation of separate Telangana State.

The signatories to the statement are:

1. Mr. J. Chokka Rao
2. Mr. K. Achuta Reddi
3. Mr. V.B. Raju
4. Mr. P. Narasingha Rao
5. Mr. Ch. Rajeswara Rao
6. Mr. Badrivishal
7. Mr. Y.V. Krishna Rao
8. Mr. P.V. Narasimha Rao
9. Mr. Jupudi Yagnarayana
10. Mr. Kulupu Prabhakara Rao
11. Mr. V. Rama Rao
12. Mrs. Roda Mistry
13. Mr. C. Janga Reddi
14. Mr. A. Vasudeva Rao
15. Mr. Sultan Salahuddin Ovasi
16. Mr. P. Narasa Reddi
17. Mr. J. Ranga Reddi
18. Mr. J. Vengal Rao
19. Mr. P. Goverdhan Raddi
20. Mr. T. Purushothama Rao
21. Mr. K. Ramachandra Reddi
22. Mr. M. Kamaluddin
23. Mr. Erram Satyanarayana
24. Mr. Ch. Murthi Raju
25. Mr. K. Raimallu
26. Mr. K. Sudharsana Reddi
27. Mr. Kakani Venkatarathnam
28. Mr. M.N. Lakshminarasaiah
29. Mr. Kaja Ramanatham
30. Mr. T. Ramaswami
31. Mr. Siddha Reddi
32. Mr. N. Ramachandra Reddi
33. Mr. Arige Ramaswamy
34. Mr. N. Prasada Rao
35. Mr. Peddireddi Thimmareddi
36. Mr. J.V. Narasinga Roa
37. Mr. K.V. Narayana Reddi
38. Mr. B.V. Gurumurthy
39. Mr. Md. Ibrahim Ali
40. Mr. G. Latchanna
41. Mr. Vavilala Gopalakriniah
42. Mr. Narasimha Reddi
43. Mr. Chenchurama Naidu
44. Mr. Konda Lakshman

Annexure 3

Statement of Prime Minister Indira Gandhi on Telangana in the Lok Sabha, 11 April 1969

Mr. Speaker: Sir, during the last few weeks, I have conferred with my colleagues in Government and Party the Leaders of the Opposition in Parliament, the Chief Minister of Andhra Pradesh, political leaders of some parties from Telangana and other parts of Andhra Pradesh as well as others, on the prevailing situation in Andhra Pradesh.

2. These talks have been held in a spirit of free and frank exchange of views and with the object of evolving constructive steps to meet the genuine problems of the people inhabiting Telangana. We had to keep in mind the importance of finding urgent and positive solutions which would further the objective of providing immediate as well as long-term answers to the needs of the people in the Telangana region and, at the same time, of maintaining and strengthening the unity and integrity of Andhra Pradesh. The overall aim is to ensure that the pace of development and the expansion of employment opportunities in Telangana is accelerated, and conditions are created for the balanced development of all parts of Andhra Pradesh through cooperative and shared efforts on the people living there.

3. With this objective a number of specific measures have been decided upon as follows:—

    (i) A high-powered Committee will be appointed by the Central Government with a retired or serving Supreme Court Judge as Chairman and an eminent Economist with knowledge of State finances together with a senior representative of the Comptroller and Auditor General as Members.

    The committee will go into the varying estimates and representations and determining the surplus relatable to Telangana which was expected to have been spent on the development of the Telangana region. The Committee shall report to the Union Government by the end of the next month.

    (ii) Discussions will take place immediately between representatives of the Union Finance and Home Ministries, the Planning Commission and the State Government regarding the manner in which the requisite financial resources could be found to take good the surpluses relatable to Telangana.

(iii) At the suggestion of the Chief Minister, it has been agreed that a high-powered Telangana Development Committee shall be constituted immediately, composed of the Chief Minister, Andhra, as its Chairman, and a Member of the Planning Commission, the Ministers of the Andhra Cabinet belonging to the Telangana region and the Chairman of the Regional Committee for Telangana as its Members.

The main functions of the Committee will be to identify within the overall framework of the Five Year Plans, the programmes and schemes relatable to the Telangana region with reference to the physical as well as financial targets to be achieved: to review from time to time the actual implementation and working of these progammes and schemes; and to advise the State Government on appropriate decisions that may be considered necessary.

(iv) There will also be a Plan Implementation Committee at official level, presided over by an Adviser of the Planning Commission, and composed of representatives of the Union Finance and Home Ministries and the State Government, with the object of detailed periodic review of the actual implementation of Plan programmes and schemes relating to the accelerated development of the Telangana region.

This Committee will meet every quarter and make its report to the Chief Minister and to the Prime Minister.

(v) In order to ensure adequate coordination as well as effective and the Chief Minister will consider what further delegation of powers, if any, need be made in favour of the authorities specially entrusted with the task of the dealing with the problems of the Telangana region.

(vi) The possibility of providing for appropriate constitutional safeguards in the matter of public employment in favour of people belonging to the Telangana region will be examined by the Government of India in consultation with a Committee of Jurists.

(vii) At the suggestion of the Chief Minister, it has also been agreed that the high powered Central Advisory Committee which was set up under the State Reorganisation Act of 1936 (which is headed by the Chairman of the U.P.S.C. and composed of a retired High Court Judge and a retired Law Secretary of the Union Govt.) will undertake a very early visit to Hyderabad, in order to examine expeditiously the grievances of the public servants of various categories and make appropriate recommendations to the Union Home Ministry.

The Union Home Ministry will also devise an urgent programme within a definite time schedule, with the object of deciding any outstanding cases relating to the integration of the Services.

The Chief Minister has assured that the State Government shall implement promptly any decisions that the Government of India may give in the light of the advice tendered by the Central Advisory Committee or the State Advisory Committee.

(viii) In order to ensure the continuous attention of the Central Government towards the problems of the Telangana region, at the suggestion of the Chief Minister it has been agreed that the Prime Minister will hold review meetings, every six months, with the Chief Minister and his other colleagues in the high-powered Telangana Development Committee referred to earlier. The Deputy Prime Minister, the Union Home Minister, such other Union Ministers whose presence may be found necessary, and the Deputy Chairman of the Planning Commission will also be associated with these meetings.

4. The accelerated development of the Telangana region, and the balanced economic development of the State as a whole, and objectives which can be secured in an atmosphere not only of peace and tranquillity but also of amity, understanding and cooperation between people inhabiting different parts of the State. In the course of his talks with me, the Chief Minister indicated his desire to make, in consultation with me, appropriate political arrangements which would promote these objectives.

5. There was recognition in the course of various discussions, of the importance of restoring an atmosphere of complete peace and

harmony in Andhra Pradesh. May I take this opportunity of appealing the people of Telangana to end the present agitation, and of inviting them to extend their wholehearted cooperation in the fulfilment of various positive measures evolved as a result of these discussions, and any other measures that may be devised hereafter. Towards this end, I propose to continue further, the process of discussions with the widest possible section of public opinion in Andhra Pradesh.

6. I should like to assure the people of Telangana as well as those of other parts of Andhra Pradesh, that their genuine problems will receive the continuous and sympathetic attention of the Central Government.

Annexure 4

Statement of Prime Minister Indira Gandhi on 'Mulki Rules' in the Lok Sabha, 27 November 1972

Last week this house had occasion to discuss the situation in Andhra Pradesh arising out of the Supreme Court judgment regarding the Mulki Rules. In certain parts of that state there have been violent incidents resulting in loss of life and damage to public property. This has caused deep distress to us in the house and to people all over the country. I had appealed to all sections in the state and all political parties to help in the effort to restore public tranquillity and to bring about a climate of confidence and trust.

We had hoped that it would be possible for the leaders of the State to come to an agreement through discussions between themselves. however, this did not happen, and the Chief Minister of Andhra Pradesh and his colleagues wanted the Central Government to take decisions on all matters relating to the Mulki Rules.

During the last few weeks, my colleagues and I have held discussions with the Andhra Pradesh leaders and representatives of different sections of the people. These discussions revealed an overwhelming desire of the people of Andhra Pradesh for a solution within the framework of the existing integrated State. After the most earnest consideration of the issues involved, we have taken certain decisions which I should like to place before the House in the course of this Statement.

At the time of the formation of the State of Andhra Pradesh in 1956, it was realized that the people of Telangana would need some safeguards in the matter of public employment, and an agreed formula was evolved by the representatives of the Andhra and Telangana regions. As a matter of national policy, residential qualification for public employment was removed in other areas, yet Parliament, enacted the Public Employment (Requirement as to Residence) Act, 1957, in order to provide for posts in the subordinate services in the Telangana area being filled subject to the requirement of residence in that area. This law was envisaged as a temporary measure and was to expire to March, 1974; however, it was struck down by the Supreme Court early in 1969. Since then the question of devising suitable measures to secure representation of the people of Telangana region in the public services of the State has been engaging the attention of the Central and State Governments. The recent judgment of the Supreme Court has brought about a new situation requiring the adoption of further measures to give effect to the objectives envisaged earlier.

It is common knowledge that the Mulki Rules are applicable only to certain posts under the State Government and are not applicable to recruitment to the All India Services, to posts in the Central Government offices and the public sector undertakings of the Central Government.

The measures decided upon are as follows:—

(i) The residential qualification prescribed in the Mulki rules will apply only for the purpose of recruitment to non-gazetted posts and posts of Tehsildar, Civil Assistant Surgeon and Junior Engineer in the Telangana region. However, in the case of composite offices, such as the Secretariat, the offices of the Heads of Departments and common institutions of the State Government, these Rules will apply for the purpose of filling the second vacancy in every unit of three direct recruitment vacancies in non-gazetted posts.

(ii) These safeguards will remain operative in the Telangana region up to the end of the December, 1930. However, in the cities of Hyderabad and Secunderabad, the safeguards will continue only up to the end of the December, 1977. This distinction has been made because the State Capital is located to these cities.

(iii) In order to provide adequate avenues of promotion to the Government servants working in each of the two regions, the various service cadres will be regionalized up to the first or second gazetted level. This will not, however, apply to the services which act as direct feeders to the All India Services.

(iv) Educational facilities, including those in the technical and professional fields, which are available at present to Telangana students in the cities of Hyderabad and Secunderabad will not be adversely affected. In these cities the facilities will be suitably expanded and these additional facilities will not be subject to any restrictions on the basis of residence.

(v) For the cities of Hyderabad and Secunderabad, there will be a composite police force, the details of which will be worked out in consultation with the State Government.

Necessary legislation to give effect to the decisions, mentioned above, will be brought before the House shortly. The Central Government will devise suitable machinery to ensure the proper functioning of these arrangements.

The above mentioned decisions have been taken, keeping in view the requirement's of the integrated State, the legitimate interests of the people of both the regions in the matter of public employment and education, and the assurances given in this House. Government hopes that these decisions will receive general acceptance in the State and will be implemented in a spirit of understanding co-operation and accommodation.

I appeal in particular to all Members of Parliament to help in maintaining peace in all parts of Andhra Pradesh.

Annexure 5

Six-point Formula, 21 September 1973
Statement issued by the leaders of Andhra Pradesh

1. We have had several discussions with Central leaders as well as amongst ourselves on the problems facing the people of Andhra Pradesh. We are satisfied that the present misgivings about the future of the State can be completely removed on action being taken in accordance with the following principles:—

    (1) Accelerated development of the backward areas of the State and planned development of the State capital with specific resources earmarked for these purposes and appropriate association of representations of such backward areas in the State legislature along with other experts in the formulation and monitoring of development schemes for such areas should form the essential part of the developmental strategy of the State. Constitution at the State level of a Planning Board as well-as Sub-Committees for different backward areas should be the appropriate instrument for achieving this objective.

    (2) Institution of uniform, arrangements throughout the State enabling adequate preference being given to local candidates in the matter of admission to educational institutions and establishment of a new Central University at Hyderabad to argument the exiting educational facilities should be the basis of the educational policy of the State.

    (3) Subject to the requirements of the State as a whole, local candidates should be given preference to specified extent in the matter of direct recruitment to (i) non-gazetted posts (other than in the Secretariat. Offices of Heads of Department, other State level offices and institutions and the Hyderabad City Police) (ii) corresponding posts under the local bodies and (iii) the posts of Tahsildars, Junior Engineers and Civil Assistant Surgeons. In order to improve their promotion prospects, service cadres should be organised to the extent possible on appropriate local

basis up to specified gazetted level, first or second, as may be administratively convenient.

(4) A high power administrative tribunal should be constituted to deal with the grievances of services regarding appointments, seniority, promotion and other allied matters. The decisions of the Tribunal should ordinarily be binding on the State Government. The constitution of such a tribunal would justify limits on recourse to judiciary in such matters.

(5) In order that implementation of measures based on the above principles does not give rise to litigation and consequent uncertainty, the Constitution should be suitably amended to the extent necessary conferring on the President enabling powers in this behalf.

(6) The above approach would render the continuance of Mulki Rules and Regional Committee unnecessary.

2. We are convinced that the accelerated development of the backward areas and planned development of the State capital are the major factors which will help in successfully implementing the above principles, We would, therefore, urge upon the Central Government to take a generous view in the matter of financial assistance to the State for the development of these areas.

Clarifications on Six-Point Formula
Statement issued by Andhra Pradesh Leaders on 22nd October 1973

1. We discussed amongst ourselves and the Central leaders the various aspects and implications of the six-point formula which has received overwhelming support from all shades of public opinion in Andhra Pradesh and else where in the country. The formula was intended to indicate the basic approach to promote the accelerated development of backward areas, a balanced development of the State as a whole and to provide equitable opportunities to different areas of State in the matter of education, employment and career prospects in public services, with a view to achieve of fuller emotional integration of the people of Andhra Pradesh. It will be for the Government of Andhra Pradesh and the Government of India to formulate specific,

comprehensive and practicable schemes in the light of the approach set out in the six-point forumla. We, however, appreciate that it would be advantageous to elaborate the more basic aspects of the formula to promote a better understanding of its approach.

2. The formula lays stress on accelerated development of backward areas. We discussed the question whether it would be possible to specify straightway what the backward areas in the State are Backward areas will require to be identified in the light of objective factors and in consultation with Planning Commission. This task will have to be left to the popular Government to be completed with atmost expedition.

3. Schemes for development of all such areas, will have to be drawn up and resources required for implementing such schemes should be earmarked, not only out of the general resources of the State Plan but also out of the special assistance from the Centre. In the process of preparing suitable schemes as well as earmarking resources, the State Planning Board should necessarily have an important role. The role of the State Board in overall co-ordination between the general Plan Scheme and special programmes for accelerated development of backward areas will also have to be emphasised. It will, therefore, have to be an effective organisation consisting of the Chief Minister, some of the colleagues, expert people's representatives and others.

4. The Committees for the different backward areas should be agencies to assist the Planning Board in the formulation of development schemes for such areas, particularly in regard to matters where knowledge of local conditions is of importance and subsequent monitoring of the implementation of such schemes. These Committees should hence have a substantial number of the representatives of the people familiar with local conditions and problems. The composition of these Committees should, however, be such as to make them business like, compact and knowledgeable. In order that these Committees enjoy the full support and backing of Government it may be considered if the Chief Minister himself could be their Chairman.

5. Programme in the State Plan to develop the infrastructure of the State will benefit the capital city. Other schemes intended specifically for urban development, housing, water supply, expansion of educational and medical facilities etc., also from part of the State Plan. The formula

contemplates that special assistance from the Centre to supplement these programmes would also be available. As the formula emphasised the importance of the planned development of the capital city, Government may also consider the constitution of a suitable Capital Development Authority.

6. Taking into account the broad scope and functions of the Planning Board and its role in co-ordination, it may be advantageous to designate it as Andhra Pradesh Planning and Development Board and its Sub-Committees as Planning and Development Committees for the respective areas. Other details regarding composition for functions, procedures and role of the Committee will have to be left to the Government.

7. In regard to the services the basic approach of the formula is that the people of different areas should have equitable employment and career prospects. The concepts of local candidates and local areas are interrelated because local candidates will be identified with reference to a local area. In specifying any local areas it should not be necessary to go below the level of a district. For recruitment to Class IV posts and posts of L.D.C. and equivalent in district officer, the district will then be the local area. For other categories of posts it would be desirable to group contiguous districts into divisions. We, however, visualise that the State as a whole may consist of five or six divisions, the twin cities including the cantonment being constituted into a separate division.

8. A local candidate can be a person residing in the concerned local area or who has studied in an institution situated in that area leading to the educational qualifications prescribed for the post or a pass in the Matriculation/equivalent examination whichever is lower. In cases where no educational qualifications are at all required, residence can be the only test. In other cases, it may be advantageous to adopt the criterion of study in a local institution. Where necessary either of the criteria could also be adopted ensuring however that a candidate is not regarded as belonging to more than one local area. To obviate hardship, suitable exemptions will require to be formulated. The minimum period of residence of study in a local institution should be reasonable, neither being illusory nor excessive. In the course or

our deliberations we found that it should not be difficult to specify such a reasonable, minimum after explaining to the people of the State the different aspects of the problem.

9. The extent of preference for local candidates should in no case be 100%. In case of Class I V posts it can be 80%. For all other non-gazetted posts the extent of preference should be 70% and for gazetted posts it should be 60%. It will, however, have to be borne in mind that substantial employment potential may develop in different local areas on account of major development projects. These will have to be equitably shared between different areas in the State and special arrangements for this purpose may be necessary. Suitable remedial measures will have to be devised in cases where the institution of revised administrative arrangements affect the employment of the candidates from the twin cities.

10. In regard to the agency for recruitment, posts entrusted to the State Public Service Commission may continue with the Commission. It will no doubt require separate consideration whether any special measures are called for in regard to the scope, strength, status and efficient functioning of the Commission to enable the Commission to discharge its responsibilities. Where any category of posts is excluded from the purview of the Commission it may be advantageous initially to constitute district / divisional committees to make recruitment for such posts.

11. We are satisfied that the six-point formula provide all the necessary policy directives for comprehensive detailed schemes to be drawn up and implemented in due course. The association of the Central Government in the implementation of the six-point formula will make available to the State Government the necessary expertise and national guidance. As soon as a popular Government is restored in Andhra Pradesh the stage would be set for the State and the Centre to take upon themselves without any delay the implementation of the formula.

Annexure 6

L.K. Advani's Letter to A. Narendra, 1 April 2002

D.O. No. 16014/1/2002-SR

L. K. ADVANI
HOME MINISTER

Dear Shri Narendra Ji, — 1 APR 2002

   Please refer to the matter raised in the Lok Sabha on 26.2.2002 under Rule 377 regarding need for creation of a separate State of Telangana.

   I have had the matter examined. The Government of India is of the view that regional disparities in economic development can be tackled through planning and efficient use of available resources. The Government, therefore, do not propose creation of a separate State of Telangana.

   With regards,

Yours sincerely,

(L.K.ADVANI)

Shri A.Narendra, M.P.,
16, Windsor Palace,
New Delhi-110001.

Ministry of Home Affairs, North Block, New Delhi - 110001 INDIA
"Please visit our website at http://mha.nic.in"

Annexure 7

N. Chandrababu Naidu's Letter to Pranab Mukherjee, 18 October 2008

NARA CHANDRABABU NAIDU
PRESIDENT
Telugudesam Party &
Leader of Opposition, A.P. Legislative Assembly
Government of Andhra Pradesh

Tele : 91(40)-30699999
Fax: (O) 91(40)-23542108
(R) 91(40)-23547845
Mobile: 9948710904
http://www.chandrababunaidu.com
e-mail: ncbn@chandrababunaidu.com
ncbn@telugudesam.com

Hyderabad,
18th October, 2008.

Respected Shri Pranab Mukherjee ji,

In continuation of our earlier letter wherein we had conveyed our views on Telangana Issue, we wish to inform you that after taking into active consideration the sentimental and emotional intensity of the people in Telangana region and the subsequent developments, the Telugu Desam party has formed a Core Committee consisting of its senior leaders in order to ascertain the views of the people on this issue. This Committee had submitted its report to the Party. The Politburo of Telugu Desam Party has discussed thoroughly on the conclusions arrived at by the Core Committee and agreed with its recommendations in favour of formation of a separate Telangana State A copy of the resolution passed by the Politburo of Telugu Desam Party is enclosed.

With kind regards,

Yours sincerely

(NARA CHANDRABABU NAIDU)

Shri Pranab Mukherjee
Minister for External Affairs
Government of India
New Delhi.

Annexure 8

N. Chandrababu Naidu's Letter to Sushilkumar Shinde, 27 December 2012

NARA CHANDRA BABU NAIDU
President
TELUGU DESAM PARTY

NTR Bhavan,
Road No.2, Banjara Hills
Hyderabad-500 033 (A.P.)
Phone : 040-30699999
Fax : 040-23542108
e-mail :ncbn@telugudesam

Dt 27.12.2012
Camp at Potkapalli Village
Karimnagar District, A.P.

Dear Shri Sushil Kumar Shinde ji,

In response to the D.O. letter No AS (CS)/PPSMisc/2012 dated 11 December 2012 of the Additional Secretary, Home Ministry, I am nominating Sri Yanamala Ramakrishnudu and Sri Kadiyam Srihari to attend the All Party Meeting on behalf of Telugu Desam Party. I would like to place the following for necessary action at your end.

Due to the political uncertainty, massive corruption, inefficient and ineffective governance by the successive Congress Chief Ministers over the past eight years, our state has suffered enormous damage in different spheres. The growth and development has taken a back seat and some of the prospective investors have backed out of the state. Agriculture and power sectors are in the worst crisis. A prosperous and booming economy of the state has been in doldrums for the last few years. As a result, the youth have suffered the worst due to the decline in the employment and the poor are losing livelihood opportunities. Therefore, as all of you are well aware, a letter was sent by me on behalf of our party on 26.09.2012 to the Hon'ble Prime Minister of India Dr.Manmohan Singh urging him to convene the All Party Meeting to settle the Telangana issue.

In this context, I would like to bring to your notice that our party has stated its opinion through its letter dated 18-10-2008 to the then Minister for External Affairs Sri Pranab Muhkejee and our letter is still with your government. We have not withdrawn our letter.

On the other hand, Sri.P. Chidambaram, the then Union Home Minister had stated in the Lok Sabha on 03.05.2012 that the Congress Party did not give its opinion. Even till date the Congress Party has not spelt out its opinion.

Therefore, our party once again requests the Government of India to take a decision on this issue to put an end to this uncertainty.

With kind regards,

Yours Sincerely,

Nara Chandrababu Naidu

To
Shri Sushil Kumar Shinde,
Minister for Home Affairs,
New Delhi

Annexure 9

YSR Congress Party Leaders' Letter to Sushilkumar Shinde, 28 December 2012

YSR CONGRESS PARTY
Plot No: 883-884, Road No 45,
Jubilee Hills, Hyderabad-500033
Fax 91 40 23382448

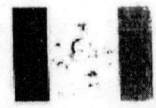

Dt: 28-12-2012

Shri **Sushil Kumar Shinde**,
Hon'ble Minister for Home Affairs
Government of India
NEW DELHI

Sir,

All Party Meeting on Telangana

We thank you sir, for your invitation to our party to participate in this meeting

The founding fathers of the Indian Constitution, under the Chairmanship of Dr B R Ambedkar gave us a comprehensive Constitution ensuring peaceful co-existence of all people belonging to different regions, religions and castes, and handed over the power of implementing the Articles to the Government of India. As part of this, the Article 3 was incorporated in the Constitution of India which gave full powers to the Central Government alone to make law whether to keep the states intact or to reconstitute them, without giving scope to involvement of the political parties and state Governments.

Therefore, unless the Central Government makes its stand clear about this issue, there is no way this can be resolved even if all the political parties in the state come up with their stand. Already the state has turned into a battle ground while development has taken a back seat because of the Central Government's imprudent actions. Despite the Government not making its stand clear as a responsible political party, we convey our stand as follows

Our party addressed this issue at the first Plenary of our party held on 8-9th July 2011. As per the decision taken in that meeting, we reiterate that our party respects the sentiments of the people of Telangana. Despite the fact that Art 3 of the Constitution authorizes the Central Government alone with the power to take decision to keep the state intact or reconstitute it, you have been playing havoc with our lives. All what we request from you is a solution acceptable to all without injustice to any one taking into consideration all aspects and problems, at the earliest, in a fair, just and equitable manner as a father would do

For YSR Congress Party

M.V.Mysura Reddy
Former MP Member Political Affairs Committee YSRCP

K.K.Mahender Reddy,
Member Central Governing Council YSRCP

Annexure 10

Minutes of the Congress Working Committee Meeting, 30 July 2013

A meeting of the Congress Working Committee was held at 5.30 pm. on 30th July, 2013 at 10, Janpath, New Delhi to discuss issues relating to the demand for separate State of Telangana. The meeting was presided over by the Congress President, Smt. Sonia Gandhi. The following Members and Invitees were present:

Members
1. Dr. Manmohan Singh
2. Shri Rahul Gandhi
3. Shri Ahmed Patel
4. Shri Ajay Maken
5. Smt. Ambika Soni
6. Shri B.K. Hari Prasad
7. Ch. Birender Singh
8. Dr. C.P. Joshi
9. Shri Digvijaya Singh
10. Shri Ghulam Nabi Azad
11. Shri Gurudas Kamath
12. Smt. Hemo Prova Saikia
13. Shri Janardan Dwivedi
14. Shri Luizinho Faleiro
15. Shri Madhusudan Mistry
16. Shri Mohan Parkash
17. Shri Motilal Vora
18. Shri Mukul Wasnik
19. Smt. Sushila Tiriya

Invitees (for this meeting)
1. Shri P. Chidambaram
2. Shri Sushilkumar Shinde

Confirmation of Minutes

The minutes of the extended CWC meeting held on 19th January, 2013 was duly confirmed.

Telangana Issue

The Congress Working Committee discussed in depth. Various aspects of the demand, for the formation of the separate state of Telangana. The Committee acknowledges that the decision to create a separate state of Telangana has not been an easy decision. It has been taken after the widest possible consultations and taking into account the chequered history of the demand for a separate State of Telangana since 1956. The Congress Working Committee appeals to all Congressmen and women as well as to all the residents of the State of Andhra Pradesh to extend their fullest cooperation so that this resolution can be implemented in letter and spirit and in a manner that ensures peace and goodwill and progress and prosperity among all the sections of the people of both states.

The CWC resolved to request the Central Government:

1. To take steps in accordance with the Constitution of India to form a separate State of Telangana;
2. To establish, simultaneously and within a definite time frame, an institutional mechanism to address the concerns of the people of the regions of Andhra and Rayalaseema on matters relating to (but not limited to) the sharing of river waters, generation and distribution of electricity, safety and security of all residents in all the three regions, and the guarantee of the fundamental rights of all residents;
3. To declare that Hyderabad Will be the common capital of both States for a period often years after the formation of the State of Telangana and to put in place legal and administrative measures to ensure that both State Governments can function efficiently from the common capital during the said period of ten years;
4. To assist in the building of a new capital for the residuary State of Andhra Pradesh within a period of ten years;
5. To declare the Polavaram irrigation project as a National project and

to provide adequate funds to complete the same;
6. To identify the special needs of the backward regions/districts of Andhra Pradesh and to provide adequate funds for the development of those areas; and
7. To assist the Government of Andhra Pradesh and, after the formation of the State of Telangana, assist both State Governments to maintain law and order and ensure peace and harmony in all the regions/districts.

The meeting ended at 6.30 pm. with vote of thanks to the Chair.

Annexure 11

Note Handed over by the Author to Chief Minister, Andhra Pradesh, 12 October 2013

LEGAL POSITION REGARDING THE CREATION OF A NEW STATE UNDER THE INDIAN CONSTITUTION

The issues which impinge on the creation of new state(s) are dealt with under Article 2, 3 and 4 of the Constitution.

Article 2: Admission or establishment of new States.—*Parliament may by law admit into the Union, or establish, new States on such terms and conditions as it thinks fit.*

Article 3: Formation of new States and alteration of areas, boundaries or names of existing States-- *Parliament may by law---*

(a) form a new State by separation of territory from any State or by uniting two or more States or parts of States or by uniting any territory to a part of any State;
(b) increase the area of any State;
(c) diminish the area of any State;
(d) alter the boundaries of any State;
(e) alter the name of any State; Provided that no Bill for the purpose shall be introduced in either House of Parliament except on the recommendation of the President and unless, where the proposal contained in the Bill affects the area, boundaries or name of any of the States, the Bill has been referred by the President to the Legislature of that State for expressing its views thereon within such period as may be specified in the reference or within such further period as the President may allow and the period so specified or allowed has expired Explanation I In this article, in clauses (a) to (e), State includes a Union territory, but in the proviso, State does not include a Union territory Explanation II The power conferred on Parliament by clause (a) includes the power to form a new State or Union territory by uniting a part of any State or Union territory to any other State or Union territory

Article 4: Laws made under Article 2 and 3 to provide for the amendment of the First and the Fourth Schedules and supplemental, incidental and consequential matters---*(1) Any law referred to in Article 2 or Article 3 shall contain such provisions in the amendment of the First Schedule and the fourth Schedule as may be necessary to give effect to the provisions of the law and may also contain such supplemental, incidental and consequential provisions (including provisions as* to representation in Parliament and in the Legislature or Legislatures of the State or States affected by such law) as Parliament may deem necessary.

(2) No such law as aforesaid shall be deemed to be an amendment of the constitution for the purposes of Article 368.

SCOPE OF ARTICLE 2

This Article provides that foreign territories which, on acquisition, become part of the territory of India under Article 1(3)(c) can by law be admitted into the Union under Article 2. Such territories have to be admitted into the Union or may be constituted into the States on such terms and conditions as Parliament may think fit; and such territories can also be dealt with by law under Article 3 (a) or (b)

SCOPE OF ARTICLE 3

When the writers of Constitution were drafting Article 3, our nation was not fully integrated or well organized as some Princely States were not included and States Reorganization Commission was working on forming linguistic states. Keeping in view the need for formation of new states, an enabling provision giving power to the Parliament was incorporated in Article 3. For this purpose the Constitution provided a simple and easy process for 'reorganizing' a new state. Article 3 says that Parliament can enact a law to reorganize the existing states by separating new state out of territories of the existing states, or by uniting two or more states or parts of states, or by uniting any territory to a part of any state, or by altering their boundaries, or by separating territory from, or increasing or diminishing the area of, or by changing the name of, a state. If the Parliament acts as per these provisions of the Constitution, it will automatically effect a change in the Schedules, without necessitating a separate Constitutional Amendment. The Bill approved by the Parliament would change those schedules to suit the new state. Hence Constitutional Amendment is also not required.

2. The steps for creating a new state are as follows: A bill on a new state has to be recommended by the President. In India it is the Executive i.e the Union Cabinet based on a proposal of the Department of States, Ministry of Home Affairs, GoI which requests the President to do that. **Article 3 makes it clear that the Parliament is the sole authority on making a decision on a new state.** President

then refers the bill to the State Assembly for **its views** giving it a certain period of time. Parliament is not obligated to follow the views of State Assembly. If the State Assembly does not express its opinion within the specified period of time, the bill could be introduced in the Parliament after the expiry of the specified period.

3. The convention started within the Home Ministry in the re-organisation process started in 2000 has been that the process of creation of a new state starts with a Resolution passed by the State Legislature that a separate State be formed from its existing territory. However, this is not mandatory and raises the following questions. Why did the authors of the constitution put complete responsibility of creating new states ONLY with the Parliament? Why did they not provide a bigger role for a State Assembly other than expressing 'its views' on the topic?

4. To understand the intentions behind a certain clause in our Constitution the Constituent Assembly Debates (CAD) can be referred to. When the Constituent Assembly was deliberating in November 1948 on the scope and content of Article 3, there was a proposal by Prof. KT Shah that the **legislation constituting a new State from any region of a State should originate from the legislature of the State concerned.** Had this procedure been approved, the power to decide the statehood of a region seeking separation would have been vested with the State legislature dominated by the elite of developed regions. Opposing the same and using the then demand for an Andhra Province as an example, Shri K Santhanam stated as under: "I wonder whether Professor Shah fully realises the implications of his amendment. If his amendment is adopted, **it would mean that no minority in any State can ask for separation of territory… unless it can get a majority in that State legislature.** Take the case of Madras Province for instance. The Andhras want separation. They bring up a resolution in the Madras Legislature. It is defeated by a majority. There ends the matter. The way of the Andhras is blocked altogether. They cannot take any further step to constitute an Andhra province." Thus Article 3 emerged in its current form.

5. It is thus the Constitutional intent that **the will of the people of a region to form a separate State be the sole criterion for the Centre to initiate the process of State formation.** This is the Constitutional benchmark for creating a new State for a

region, as amply demonstrated in the deliberations of the Constituent Assembly and as reflected in the current phraseology of Article 3 of the Constitution of India. This interpretation of Article 3 prevailed over creation of many new states in modern India thereby nearly doubling the number of states in the last fifty years.

The sole exception to the plenary power of the Parliament under article 3 is that of the State of Jammu and Kashmir which has its own Constitution and it would not be possible for the Parliament of India to increase or diminish the area of J&K, to alter its name or boundaries in the manner provided under articles 3 and 4, unless the Legislature of J&K consents.

The plenary powers of the Parliament were confirmed again by the Supreme Court in the case Mullaperiyar Environmental Protection Forum vs U.o I on 27/2/2006 when it observed that: The creation of new States by altering territories and boundaries of existing States is within the exclusive domain of Parliament. The law making power under Articles 3 and 4 is paramount and is not subjected to nor fette3red by Article 246 and Lists II and III of the Seventh Schedule. The Constitution confers supreme and exclusive power on Parliament under Articles 3 and 4 so that while creating new States by reorganisation, the Parliament may enact provisions for dividing land, water and other resources; distribute the assets and liabilities of predecessor States amongst the new States; make provisions for contracts and other legal rights and obligations. The constitutional validity of law made under Articles 3 and 4 cannot be questioned on ground of lack of legislative competence with reference to the lists of Seventh Schedule. The new State owes its very existence to the law made by the Parliament. It would be incongruous to say that the provision in an Act which gives birth to a State is ultra vires a legislative entry which the State may operate after it has come into existence........The power of Parliament to make law under Article 3 and 4 is plenary and traverse over all legislative subjects as are necessary for effectuating a proper reorganisation of the State.

6. **Supreme Court Verdict**

A constitutional democracy also refers to legal verdicts as well as Presidential References under Article 143(1) to the Supreme Court which decide on the interpretation and set a precedent on applicability of a certain clause from Indian constitution.

Back in 1960 a Bill was introduced in the Indian Parliament proposing the formation of Maharashtra and Gujarat. This Bill was referred by the President to the State Assembly to obtain their views. Upon receiving the views, the Bill was passed in the Parliament. A petition was filed against this by **Shri. Babulal Parate** in High Court of Bombay:

His contention was that the said Act was passed in contravention of the provisions of Art. 3 of the Constitution, since the Legislature of Bombay had not been given an opportunity of expressing its views on the formation of the composite State. **The High Court dismissed the petition.**

In this case, *Babulal Parante v. State of Bombay,* 1960 AIR SC 51, 1960 SCR (1) 605, the Supreme Court explained the provisions of Article 3 as follows:

The period within which the State Legislature must express its views has to be specified by the President; but the President may extend the period so specified. If, however, the period specified or extended expires and no views of the State Legislature are received, the second condition laid down in the proviso is fulfilled in spite of the fact that the views of the State Legislature have not been expressed.

The intention seems to be to give an opportunity to the State Legislature to express its views within the time allowed; **if the State Legislature fails to avail itself of that opportunity, such failure does not invalidate the introduction of the Bill.**

Prior to the amendment of provision in 1955 (5th Constitutional Amendment) the view so the State Legislature were to be ascertained not only with respect to the proposals to introduce the bill but also with respect to the 'provisions' of the Bill. The amended proviso has omitted these words and it now requires only a reference of the Bill which comes within the purview of article 3. Now an opportunity is given to the concerned State Legislature and the Government to express their views without giving them a veto. If they fail to avail the opportunity, the Bill can take its due course, and they are then bound to accept the award of the Union Parliament.

Thus is there nothing in the proviso to indicate that Parliament must accept or act upon the views of the State Legislature.

7. Clearly, Indian Constitution envisioned a situation where a state may refuse to provide its view or provide negative views about a formation of a new state, and therefore gave full powers to Indian Parliament to go ahead with its decisions irrespective of opposition from the State Assembly.

8. It is also not necessary to make a fresh reference to the State Legislature nor is any fresh reference recommendation of the President required every time an amendment of the proposal contained in the Bill is moved and accepted in accordance with the rules of procedure of Parliament. The States Reorganisation Bill, 1956 when referred to the Bombay Legislature, proposed for the reorganisation of the State of Bombay into three separate units, namely, (i) U T of Bombay, (ii) State of Maharashtra and (iii) State of Gujarat. But the Bombay State Re-organisation Act provided for a composite state of Bombay. In the same Babulal Parate vs State of Bombay, the Supreme Court held that even though it was a substantial modification that does not mean that it was not a proper amendment of the original proposal or that the State Legislature had no opportunity of expressing its views on all aspect os the subject matter of the proposal. Mention may be made that the views of the State Legislature are not binding on the Parliament. This view has also been reiterated in the Supreme Court judgment where a challenge was made to the previous State Reorganisation Acts enacted in the year 2000 in the case Pradeep Choudhury and others vs. U.o.I in Transfer Case (Civil) No. 62 of 2002[1]. The Supreme Court in its judgment delivered on 5th May, 2008 had held that consultation with the State Legislature although is mandatory but its recommendations were not binding on the Parliament. 'Consultation' in a case of this nature would not mean concurrence. It also inter-alia held that even in a case where substantive amendment is carried out,

---

1 http:\\judis.nic.in/supremecourt/imgs1.aspx?filename=34543

the amended Parliamentary Bill need not be referred to the State Legislature again for obtaining its fresh views.

9. Effect of Re-organisation of territories on existing laws.

In the case of State of Maharashtra vs. Narayan Shamrao Puranik reported in (1982) 3 SCC 519, the Court held that such powers vested by virtue of an Act under Article 3 would continue to exist unless specifically repealed by an act of Parliament. It observed that, *'The Act is a law under Article 3 for reorganisation of States. Article 4 of the Constitution provides that the law referred to in Article 3 may containe "such supplementary, incidental and consequential provisions, as Parlaiemnt may deem necessary'.... These powers continue to exist by reason of Part V of the Act, unless Parliament by law otherwise directs. The Act is a permanent piece of legislation on the statute book. Section 14 of the General Clauses Act, 1897 provides that, where, by any Central Act or Regulation, any power is conferred, then unless a different intention appears, that power may be exercised from time to time as occasion arises.'* The Supreme Court in Ram Kishore vs. UoI (AIR 1966 SC 644) made it clear that when an adjustment or reorganisation of territories takes place, the existing laws as well as administrative orders in a particular territory continue to be in force and continue to be binding upon the successor state, so long as they are not modified, changed or repudiated by the successor state. This position was further amplified by the Supreme Court in State of Punjab vs Balbir Singh (AIR 1977 SC 629) in which it held that, *"When there is no change of sovereignty and it is merely an adjustment of territories by the reorganisation of a particular State, the administrative orders made by the Government of the erstwhile State continue to be in force and effective and binding on the successor States until and unless they are modified changed or repudiated by the Governments of the successor States. No other view is possible to be taken. The other view will merely bring about chaos in the administration of the new States.'*

10. Article 3 and the State Legislature under Article 356.

On July 5th, 1966, the President made his proclamation under Article 356 regarding the State of Punjab and declared that the powers of the Legislature of the said State shall be exercisable by or under the authority of Parliament. He suspended certain provisions of the Constitution in relation to Punjab which were the proviso to Article 3 and clause 1 and sub-clause (a) of clause (2) of Article 174. The validity of the relevant sections of the Punjab Re-organisation Act 1966 was challenged on the ground that the views of the Punjab legislature were not ascertained while making changes in the boundaries of the State in Manohar Lal vs UoI (AIR 1970 Delhi 178(180)). However it was held that in view of the clear power conferred by Article 356(1)(a)(b) to declare that 'the power of the Legislature of the State shall be exercisable by or under the authority of the Parliament', it enacted the Punjab Re-organisation Act by which all the powers of the Legislature of the concerned State to make laws were conferred on the President. This situation arose only as a direct consequence of the legislature being unable to meet for any purpose whatever during the period when the Governor's power to summon the legislature was itself suspended. Thus, article 3 remains validly in use, without referring the bill to the State Legislature to express its view where the State is under the President's rule.

11. **Effect of article 255**.

Under article 3, a bill can be introduced on fulfilling two conditions: (i) recommendation of the President, and (ii) reference of the Bill to the Legislature of the affected State. But article 255 debars the courts from enquiring into the validity of a law on the ground that the Bill was introduced without such recommendation, but article 255 shall not apply to the State of J&K.

SCOPE OF ARTICLE 4

The effect of Article 4 is that the laws relatable to Article 2 or 3 are not to be treated as constitutional amendments for the purpose of Article 368, which means that if legislation is competent under Article 3, it would be unnecessary to invoke Article 368. In fact using this provision, Article 371 was amended when new States were created - Bombay Reorganisation Act of 1960 when Maharashtra and Gujarat were formed and in 1971 when Article 371 (B) was amended by the North Eastern Areas (Reorganisation) Act.

The Supreme Court in Mangal Singh vs UoI in (1967) 2 SCR 109 had rejected the argument for a constricted reading of Article 4 by specifically observing as follows:

'On the plain reading of Article 4, there is no warrant for the contention advanced by counsel for the appellants that the supplemental, incidental and consequential provisions, which by virtue of Article 4 Parliament is competent to make, must be supplemental, incidental or consequential to the amendment of the First or the fourth Schedule. The argument that if it be assumed that Parliament is invested with this wide power it may conceivable exercise power to abolish the legislative and judicial organs of the State altogether is also without substance. We do not think that such power is contemplated by Article 4. Power withy which Parliament is invested by Articles 2 and 3 is power to admit, establish, or form new States which conform to the democratic pattern envisaged by the Consitt8ition; and the power which parliament may exercise by law is supplemental, incidental or consequential to the admission, establishment or formation of a State as contemplated by the Constitution, and is not power to override the constitutional scheme. No state can therefore be formed, admitted or set up by law under Article 4 by Parliament which has not effective legislature, executive and judicial organs.'

Annexure 12

Office Memorandum, 4 June 2014: Special Responsibility of the Governor of Telangana

No. 12012/05/2014-SR
Government of India
Ministry of Home Affairs
(Centre-State Division)
******

NDCC-II, New Delhi
Dated the 4th June, 2014

OFFICE MEMORANDUM

Subject: **SPECIAL RESPONSIBILITY OF THE GOVERNOR OF TELANGANA**

The undersigned is directed to say that Section 5 of the A.P. Reorganization Act (the Act) envisages a common capital of Hyderabad (GHMC area) for the two States of Telangana and Andhra Pradesh for a period not exceeding ten years. Section 7 has provided for a common Governor for the two States of Telangana and A.P. for a period that the President determines. Section 8 casts a special responsibility on the Governor with respect to the issues of law and order, safety and security of citizenry and vital installations as well as the management and allocation of government buildings in the common capital as given below:

Section 8 Responsibility of Governor to protect residents of common capital of Hyderabad

8. (1) On and from the appointed day, for the purposes of administration of the common capital area, the Governor shall have special responsibility for the Security of life, liberty and property of all those who reside in such area.
(2) In particular, the responsibility of the Governor shall extend to matters such as law and order, internal security and security of vital installations, and management and allocation of Government buildings in the common capital area.
(3) In discharge of the functions, the Governor shall, after consulting the Council of Ministers of the State of Telangana, exercise his individual judgment as to the action to be taken.
Provided that if any question arises whether any matter is or is not a matter as respects which the Governor is under this sub-section required to act in the exercised of his individual judgment, the decision of the Governor in his discretion shall be final, and the validity of anything done by the Governor shall not be called in question on the ground that he ought or ought not to have acted in the exercise of his individual judgment.
(4) The Governor shall be assisted by two advisors to be appointed by the Central Government.

2. In order to ensure that the provisions regarding the special responsibility of the Governor is implemented smoothly vis-à-vis the Government of Telangana, the following amendments to the State Business Transaction Rules are proposed:

   a) The Governor shall have power to call for any record or information or decision of the Council of Ministers or any authority relating to the responsibilities

envisaged under Section 8 of the A.P. Reorganization Act, 2014. The Commissioners of Police and the S.P. of Ranga Reddy District shall furnish periodical reports of law and order to the Governor in addition to special reports on all grave and specially grave crimes in the common capital area.
b) The Governor shall have the power to issue a direction in accordance with the provisions of law or regulation.
c) The Governor will be assisted by Advisor/s appointed by Government of India. The Governor shall allot the responsibilities between the Advisors as deemed fit from time to time.
d) For the purposes of matters falling under law and order, internal security and security of vital installations, as well as the two Police Commissionerates currently operating in the common capital area i.e. the Hyderabad and the Cyberabad and Commissionerates, and for the district of Ranga Reddy, the Home Secretary of the State of Telangana shall brief the Governor on all matters mentioned above as well as those that have special significance and Governor may convey his views which shall be placed before the appropriate authority. Governor's advice shall prevail.
e) A Special Cell headed by an officer of rank not below the rank of Inspector General in both the Commissionerates and with a senior officer in the office of S.P. Ranga Reddy to deal with hate crimes and crimes related to extortion or any other specified crime and ensure speedy trial, shall be set up. Wide publicity would be given to the contact numbers of the officers of this cell so as to enable citizens to contact them directly.
f) A Special Cell to deal with issues concerning internal security and security of vital installations with a senior officer in-charge shall be set up in both the Commissionerates and in the office of S.P. Ranga Reddy. The Special Cell shall also identify sensitive establishments/institutions and report to the Governor through the Government of Telangana on the adequacy or otherwise of the security arrangements of the said establishment/installation. The Cell shall undertake a review of the existing security provided by the Special Protection Force (SPF), Central Industrial Security Force (CISF) etc., and suggest additional measures, if considered necessary, to ensure fool proof security of the notified installations. The Governor may suggest measures to strengthen the security arrangement based upon the information made available and the threat perceptions, which shall be binding. A Nodal Officer from the senior management cadre shall be appointed in all the notified vital installations, who shall be responsible for furnishing periodical review reports on the security status of the installation and for implementation of the recommendations of the Special Cell.
g) A Police Service Board comprising DGP Telangana and the Commissioner of Police, Hyderabad and Cyberabad should be set up exclusively for the State of Telangana in the context of law and order administration of the common capital area of Hyderabad to handle the transfer and postings of all officers including DCPs, ACPs and SHOs. The police force of Hyderabad and Cyberabad Commissionarates shall be a joint force comprising of elements from Andhra & Telangana, on fair share basis in higher supervisory posts i.e., Deputy

Commissioners of Police, Addl.Commissioners of Police & Commissioners of Police. In case of officers drawn from residual State of Andhra Pradesh, a Police Service Board on the lines of Telangana, will propose a panel of names. The Governor shall have the power to approve and suggest such changes as he deems fit, as per his best judgment.

h) In case the Governor considers it necessary in view of the situation, as per his best judgment, to requisition additional forces for deployment, he would ask the State Government to examine this issue and communicate the decision to the Governor. This decision will be subject to review u/s 8 of the Act and the Governor's decision shall be final after such review.

i) The Governor can call for a report or assessment from the State Government of Telangana on any acts of omission and commission by any official and direct the Government to conduct an enquiry and take appropriate action as per law.

j) In case of exigencies, the Governor can call for a report or assessment from the State Government or Telangana upon which he can ask the State Government specifically for reallocation of the staff on a temporary basis in case of any contingency.

k) The management and allocation of buildings to all the Departments of both the successor States shall be decided by the Governor on the recommendations of the Committee of Senior Officers constituted for the purpose keeping in view the requirement and availability of accommodation. The decision of the Governor shall be final

l) To ensure the safety of property of the common capital of Hyderabad, the Collectors of Hyderabad and Rangareddy Districts as well as the Commissioner of GHMC shall set up Grievance Cells for the redressal of grievances and affected parties shall have the right to represent themselves. The Governor can issue necessary directions to the officials of the State Government of Telangana for the protection of the property rights of the aggrieved..

3. You are requested to send your comments on the above mentioned principles or take necessary action for amending the Business Transaction Rules of the Govt. of Telangana immediately on the lines suggested above.

(S. Suresh Kumar)
Joint Secretary to the Govt. of India
Ph. 23438100
jscs@nic.in

To
Dr. Rajeev Sharma,
Chief Secretary,
Govt. of Andhra Pradesh
Hyderabad

Annexure 13

Author's Letter to Sushilkumar Shinde Regarding Management of Water Resources, 4 November 2013

जयराम रमेश FTS No. 70058/M (RE)
JAIRAM RAMESH   4/11/2013

ग्रामीण विकास मंत्री
भारत सरकार
कृषि भवन, नई दिल्ली-110114
MINISTER OF RURAL DEVELOPMENT
GOVERNMENT OF INDIA
KRISHI BHAVAN, NEW DELHI-110 114

November 4, 2013

My dear Sushil Kumarji,

I am sending you a note that I have just prepared for consideration of the GOM to look into the bifurcation of the State of Andhra Pradesh and the formation of a new State of Telangana.

This note deals with a part of item (vi) of the GoM's Terms of Reference and focuses on the sharing of river water and irrigation resources. It has been prepared after wide consultations with officials and experts from all over the State of Andhra Pradesh. I have also gone by provisions relating to water resources in earlier legislations on reorganisation of UP, Punjab, Bihar and Madhya Pradesh. I have also had the benefit of going through a number of representations and notes submitted to the GOM on this subject.

I hope this note will be useful for the deliberations of the GoM.

With warm regards, personal

Yours sincerely,

(Jairam Ramesh)

Shri Sushil Kumar Shinde,
Home Minister.
North Block
New Delhi

Encl: as above

Enclosure: River Water Sharing Issues

I

The Three Challenges:

There are three challenges that need to be addressed with regard to sharing of Krishna and Godavari rivers between Telangana State and residuary state of Andhra Pradesh.

- ➤ Allocation and protocol for sharing surplus water of Krishna River for projects, completed or in-progress, based on surplus water in Krishna River.The surplus water includes surplus flows in Krishna River and the inter-basin transfer to Krishna River through Polavaram and Dummugudem –Nagarjunasagar Tailpond projects.

- ➤ An institutional mechanism to ensure availability of water in both States as per the award given by Tribunals.

- ➤ Completion of incomplete projects - where land acquisition, rehabilitation & resettlement and execution of works may fall in both the States like Polavaram and Dummugudem – Nagarjunasagar Tailpond projects.

II

Allocation and protocol for sharing surplus water of Krishna River:

A number of projects based on surplus water have come up on Krishna River. Some of the projects are completed and while some projects are under construction. These projects benefit both Telengana and Seemandhra regions. Some of the projects are taken up in anticipation of the inter-river basin transfers to Krishna with the completion of Polavaram project and Dummagudem-Nagarjunasagar Tail pond project. When the river receives abundant surplus water as estimated then water is available for any of the projects based on assured or surplus waters. However, such abundant flows in the Krishna River is often an exception.

After bifurcation of State, there will be serious problem for release of water for various projects in the event of deficit flows in Krishna River. Presently, there are no protocols or principles regarding the release of water to projects as all projects are within a one state and the decisions are taken by the CM. It is also not possible for the newly formed State of Telengana and the residuary state of AP to meaningfully adjudicate these issues on a season to season basis considering the competing demands of both the regions.

Therefore, the Union Ministry of Water Resources should commission a technical study in consultation with the State of AP and freeze allocations to each project based on surplus water and evolve an operational schedule/protocol for release of water to each project, in the event of deficit flows. This exercise should be completed and notified before reorganization of the State of AP, and same should be binding on the newly formed State of Telengana and residuary State of AP.

III

Institutional mechanism and principles governing the sharing of Krishna and Godavari River waters between the State of Telangana and residuary State of Andhra Pradesh:

There shall be a 2-tier institutional mechanism to manage sharing of Krishna and Godavari River water and irrigation sources, between the State of Telangana and residuary State of Andhra Pradesh, optimally and strictly in accordance with the awards made, by the Tribunals under Inter-State River Disputes Act, 1956, duly following the principles laid down below; after reorganization of the State of Andhra Pradesh.

This 2-tier mechanism shall consist of:

A. **Apex Council on Krishna and Godavari River water (ACKG)**

- Consisting of Minister of Water Resources, GoI, as Chairman, Chief Ministers of both the States; Ministers of the Water resources from both States; Chief Secretaries and Secretary of Water Resources of both States;

- The Council is empowered to oversee the management of the Reservoirs by it's technical body i.e. Krishna and Godavari River Board (KGRB);

- The Council is empowered to sanction proposals for construction of new projects if any based on Krishna or Godavari River water, after getting the proposals appraised and technically cleared by the Krishna and Godavari River Board (KGRB).

B. **Krishna and Godavari River Board (KGRB)**

- Consisting of a Chairman to be appointed by GoI and comprising of Chief Engineers and other officials, taken on deputation basis from both the States, as well as appropriate representation from the GOI and independent experts as members.

- The Board is primarily responsible to manage and maintain the reservoirs of the irrigation projects including the hydel power projects on Krishna and Godavari Rivers strictly in accordance with the awards made by the Tribunal to each project in the State of Telangana and residuary State of AP.

- The Governments of the successor States shall at all times provide the necessary funds to the Board to meet all expenses (including the salaries and allowances of the staff) required for the discharge of its functions and such amounts shall be apportioned among the successor States, in such proportion as the Central Government may, having regard to the benefits to each of the said States, specify.

- The Board shall be under the control of the Central Government and shall comply with such directions, as may from time to time, be given to it by that Government.

- The Board may with the approval of the Central Government delegate such of its powers, functions and duties as it may deem fit to the Chairman of the said Board or to any officer subordinate to the Board.

- The Central Government may, for the purpose of enabling the Board to function effectively, issue such directions to the State Governments of Telengana and the residuary State of AP and the State Governments shall comply with such directions.

- The Board may, with the previous approval of the Central Government and by notification in the Official Gazette, make regulations consistent with this Act and the rules made there under, to provide for:

    - regulating the time and place of meetings of the Board and the procedure to be followed for the transaction of business at such meetings;

    - delegation of powers and duties to the Chairman or any officer of the Board;

    - the appointment, and the regulation of the conditions of service, of the officers and other staff of the Board;

    - any other matter for which regulations are considered necessary by the Board.

- Administration maintenance and operation of the head works of the following Dams, Reservoirs or head works of Canals and works appurtenant there to:

    1. Jurala
    2. Bhima Lift Irrigation
    3. Nettempadu
    4. Koil Sagar Lift Irrigation
    5. Kalwakurthy Lift Irrigation
    6. Srisailam Reservoir and the head works of Srisailam Right bank canal and Srisailam left Bank Canal
    7. Nagarjunasagar Dam and the head works of the left canal and right canal
    8. Telugu Ganga
    9. Handri-Neeva
    10. GaleruNagari
    11. Velugonda

> The Board will be assisted by Central Industrial Security Force (CISF) in the day to day management of reservoirs.

> The Board is also responsible for taking up appraisal of any proposal for construction of new projects on Krishna or Godavari Rivers and give technical clearance, after satisfying that such projects do not negatively impact the availability of water as per the Tribunal awards for the projects already completed or taken up, before reorganization of the State.

C. **Principles governing the functioning of the 2-tier mechanism:**

(i) The operation protocol notified by the Ministry of Water resources with respect to surplus waters shall be binding on both the State.

(ii) In the event of conflicting demand of water for irrigation and power, the requirement of water for irrigation will take precedence.

(iii) In the event of conflicting demand of water for irrigation and drinking water, the requirement of water for drinking water purpose will take precedence.

(iv) The allocations made by the Tribunals with regard to various projects on Krishna and Godavari Rivers or for the regions of erstwhile State of Andhra Pradesh, in respect of assured water or surplus flows would remain same.

(v) Future allocations, if any, to be made on excess flows by any Tribunal in future will be binding on both State of Telangana and residual State of Andhra Pradesh.

(vi) All completed projects on the Godavari and Krishna rivers will operate based on assured or surplus waters allocated by the Tribunals or specific allocations made by union Government for projects based on surplus water.

(vii) All on-going projects on the Godavari and Krishna rivers will operate based on assured or surplus waters allocated by the Tribunals or specific allocations made by union Government for projects based on surplus water.

(viii) The Board will also manage the disaster/drought/flood in the two rivers of Krishna and Godavari and will have adequate authority to get its order implemented on a real-time basis.

(ix) No new projects based on surplus water on Krishna or Godavari rivers can be taken up by the State of Telangana or residual State of Andhra Pradesh without obtaining sanction from the Apex Council on Krishna and Godavari River water (ACKG). All such proposals need to be first appraised and technically cleared by KGRB, before sanction by the Apex Council on Krishna and Godavari River Water.

(x) Execution of ongoing projects and future new projects on Krishna and Godavari rivers will be the responsibility of the State government concerned where the project is located. After the completion of the project, the Krishna and Godavari River Board (KGRB) will take over the management and maintenance of the reservoirs.

(xi) In case of non-implementation of the decision by either of the state, the defaulting state will bear the responsibility and will face financial and other penalties imposed by Government of India.

D. Reconstitution of the Tungabhadra Board

Tungabhadra Board will be reconstituted with representation from both new State of Telengana and the residuary State of AP. It will continue over see release of water to High level Canal, Low level canal and Rajolibanda diversion scheme.

IV

Completion of projects that will become Inter-State after bifurcation:

1. **Polavaram Project**:
   Polavaram will be declared as a National Project and it will be completed with due regard to all environmental and Rehabilitation & Resettlement (R&R) considerations. The revenue division of Bhadrachalam will be part of the residuary State of the AP as major submergence will be in this division.

2. **Dummugudem – Nagarjunasagar Tailpond Project**:
   The construction (including the completion of any work already commenced) of the Dummugudem–Nagarjunasagar Tailpond Project shall be undertaken by the Central Government on behalf of the successor States.

***

Annexure 14

Extracts from the Rajya Sabha Debate on the Polavaram Ordinance, 14 July 2014

SHRI JAIRAM RAMESH (ANDHRA PRADESH): Mr. Deputy Chairman, Sir, I rise to speak in support of the Andhra Pradesh Reorganisation (Amendment) Bill, 2014.

Sir, on the 20th of February, 2014, I was sitting where Mr. Venkaiah Naidu is sitting today, and had occasion to speak on this very issue. Today from this side I have to repeat much of what I had presented to the House on the 20th of February when the Rajya Sabha had passed the Andhra Pradesh Reorganisation Bill.

Sir, the President gave his assent to the Andhra Pradesh Reorganisation Bill; and the Andhra Pradesh Reorganisation Act, 2014 was gazetted on the 1st March. Section 91 of the Andhra Pradesh Reorganisation Act reads as follows:

'(1) The Polavaram Irrigation Project is hereby declared to be a national project.

(2) It is hereby declared that, it is expedient in the public interest that the Union should take under its control the regulation and development of the Polavaram Irrigation Project for the purposes of irrigation.

(3) The consent for the Polavaram irrigation project shall be deemed to have been given by the successor State of Telangana; and

(4) The Central Government shalt execute the project and obtain all requisite clearances including environmental, forests, and rehabilitation and resettlement issues.'

Sir, the Polavaram project has the same emotive and iconic appeal to the people of Andhra Pradesh as the issue of Hyderabad was to the people of Telangana. The Polavaram project has been under discussion for many years. The momentum gathered alter the award of the Godavari Waters Dispute Tribunal in 1080 and in the last decade or so, the final technical designs of the Polavaram project had been finalised.

Sir, briefly what is the Polavaram project? It is a multipurpose project. The Polavaram project will irrigate about 7,00,000 acres in the

Godavari Basin of Andhra Pradesh. It will generate about 960 MW of power. It will transfer about 80 tmc of water from the Godavari Basin to the Krishna Basin which will benefit Telangana, Karnataka and Maharashtra.... (Interruptions). It will also supply 23 tmc of drinking water to Visakhapatnam. Broadly this is the configuration of the Polavaram multipurpose project. It was conceived of as a multipurpose project. It was under discussion for a long time. The technical design was frozen by the Central Water Commission. Thereafter the cost estimates were firmed up. In 2010 and 2012 prices, the Polavaram multipurpose project was estimated to cost Rs. 16,000 crores. Out of Rs. 16,000 crores, roughly 32 per cent of the expenditure has already been incurred.

Sir, I have been to Polavaram on three occasions in three different capacities. I have been to Polavaram as Member of Parliament, I have been to Polavaram as Minister for Environment and Forests and I went to Polavaram as Minister of Rural Development and Member of the GoM on Telangana. There is no doubt in my mind, and I want to say this with all the force at my command, that while the Polavaram project has many benefits, it is also a project that will involve substantial rehabilitation and resettlement of families. It is estimated that roughly 45,000 families will have to be relocated. Hundreds of villages presently—I will come to that number 35,000 families in Khammam district, nearly 7,000 families in West Godavari district and nearly 3,000 families in East Godavari district, making a total of 45,000 families in the undivided State of Andhra Pradesh, in the districts of Khammam, East Godavari and West Godavari, will have to be relocated. ...(Interruptions)...

SHRI V. HANUMANTHA RAO: Sir, what he is saying...(Interruptions)...

SHRI JAIRAM RAMESH: Mr. Rao, will you please give me a chance to speak?... (interruptions).

MR. DEPUTY CHAIRMAN: Mr. Hanumantha Rao, what are you doing? Your own Member is speaking. ... (Interruptions)... Nothing will go on record. Only what Shri Jairam Ramesh is saying will go on record. Nothing else will go on record. ...(Interruptions)... Please sit down. Why are you worried? Please sit down.

SHRI JAIRAM RAMESH: I am requesting my friends to have patience.

I have explained this. ...(Interruptions)...I will explain it once again.

MR DEPUTY CHAIRMAN: Your own Member is speaking. Show some respect.

SHRI JAIRAM RAMESH: There are nearly 2,000 families in Malkangiri district of Odisha and nearly 1,000 families in Dantewada district of Chhattisgarh who are also going to be resettled and relocated on account of the Polavaram project. Sir, when I was Minister for Environment and Forests, I issued a Show Cause Notice for stopping work on the Polavaram project till such a time the concerns of Odisha and Chhattisgarh had not been met. The then Government of Andhra Pradesh went to the Supreme Court, filed an affidavit and made a commitment that they would build protective embankments at an expenditure of Rs. 600 crores to minimize submergence in Odisha and Chhattisgarh. ...(Interruptions)... This matter was taken up by...

SHRI BAISHNAB PARIDA: Sir,[1]

MR. DEPUTY CHAIRMAN: That is not going on record.

SHRI JAIRAM RAMESH: I myself had written to the Chief Ministers or Odisha and Chhattisgarh asking them for public hearings...(interruptions)...

MR. DEPUTY CHAIRMAN: Please sit down. ...(Interruptions)...

SHRI JAIRAM RAMESH: ...to be completed in Malkangiri and Dantewada, but neither the Odisha Government, nor the Chhattisgarh Government has yet given permission for these public a hearings. But I want to place on record here that the erstwhile Government of undivided Andhra Pradesh had filed an affidavit in the Supreme Court committing to an expenditure of Rs. 600 crores to build protective embankments to avoid submergence in the States of Odisha and Chhattisgarh. The bulk of the resettlement has to be done in Khammam district, West Godavari district and East Godavari district. Sir, it is a fundamental rule of administration that by and large resettlement takes place in contiguous areas; it takes place broadly in the areas where people are living. Sir, Section 3 of the

---

[1]Not recorded.

Andhra Pradesh Reorganisation Act draws the boundaries of the State of Telangana and makes an exception in the case of Khammam where certain villages were to be transferred from Khammam district to East Godavari district to reinstate the position, as the Home Minister mentioned, which prevailed before 1959. Now this Section was put in order to ensure that the submergence takes place in one State and resettlement also takes place in one State. It cannot be that the people who are going to be relocated are living in one State and the people who are going to be benefited are in another State. Therefore, in order to assuage the concerns of the people of Andhra Pradesh that resettlement will be done. These villages in these seven Mandals of Khammam District, that is, 134 villages, to be precise, based on a G.O. issued in 2005, were to be transferred to the successor State of Andhra Pradesh,. ... (Interruptions)...

MR. DEPUTY CHAIRMAN: Mr. Reddy, please sit down.

SHRI JAIRAM RAMESH: Sir, it the hon. Members have a little patience, I will take them through the chronology of events, and I will be totally frank and transparent in the chronology of all the events that have taken place so far.

Sir, in the original Bill that was sent by the UPA-II Government to the Andhra Pradesh Legislative Assembly, there was no provision for the transfer of area from the Khammam District to the East Godavari District. The original Bill had the provision for only the implementation of the Polavaram Project. On the 7th of February, 2014, the Union Cabinet met, based on all the representations that the GoM, that was headed by the former Home Minister, Shri Sushilkumar Shinde, had received, and after discussing this matter with the cross-sections of people from Telangana and Andhra Pradesh, the Union Cabinet, in its meeting on 7th February decided that seven Mandals would be transferred from the Khammam District to the East Godavari District, except the Bhadrachalam town and the holy Ram temple in the Bhadrachalam town. This was objected to by Telangana on the grounds that connectivity would be impaired and that the access to Bhadrachalam would not be through Telangana but would be through the successor State of Andhra Pradesh. The Union Cabinet then met again on the 12th of February to take note of these concerns, and on the 12th of February, the Union Cabinet overruled its decision of the

7th of February and, instead of transferring the seven Mandals, decided to transfer the submerged villages alone. This was the Cabinet decision of 12th February that only submerged villages, partially submerged and fully submerged, would be transferred from the Khammam District to the East Godavari District. Sir, then, after 12th February, the Bill came to the Lok Sabha on the 18th of February and it came to the Rajya Sabha on the 20th of February. When it came to the Rajya Sabha, the Prime Minister made a detailed statement. There were six points in that statement. And point No. 4 of the statement of the former Prime Minister, Dr. Manmohan Singh, read as follows: 'I would like to reassure hon. Members that if any further Amendments are needed to facilitate smooth and full rehabilitation and—resettlement for the Polavaram Project, they will be given effect to at the earliest. Our Government will execute the Polavaram Project. Let there be no doubt about it.' This was a statement which was welcomed on the 20th of February, and this was a solemn commitment made by the Prime Minister after he had discussions with various political leaders in the run-up to the consideration of the Bill in the Rajya Sabha. Sir, I have already mentioned to you that the first time the Union Cabinet met on the 7th of February, it transferred the Mandals. This was objected to by Telangana. On the 12th of February, the Union Cabinet I said, 'No Mandals, but transfer submerged villages.' This was objected to by the Seemandhra or the successor State of Andhra Pradesh. So, keeping in mind what the then Prime Minister said on the 20th of February, the COM went back to the Drawing Board and tried to find a solution that would satisfy both Telangana and Andhra Pradesh. The first solution, full mandal, was not acceptable to Telangana and the second solution, submerged villages, was not acceptable to Andhra Pradesh. So, we had to come up with a third alternative, and, Sir, on the 1st of March, the Union Cabinet met and considered the third alternative, which the hon. Home Minister just now mentioned, that some Mandate would be transferred in full, and in one Mandal, only submerged villages would be transferred and the Bhadrachalam Town and the Bhadrachalam Temple would remain under the control of the new State of Telangana.

This was the third time the Union Cabinet met on the first of March and we were ready with an ordinance then, but, the election code was in operation. We could not issue the Ordinance and rightly so, and we left it to the successor Government. We hoped it was UPA-III but it became NDA-II. But we accepted the fact that there would be continuity and whichever Government will be there, whoever be the Prime Minister, he or she Would respond and uphold the solemn commitment made by Dr. Manmohan Singh. So, Sir on the first of March the contours of the ordinance had been drawn up, the mandate that were to be transferred had been drawn up, the villages that were to be transferred had been drawn up and Sir, I have no hesitation in saying that the Andhra Pradesh (Amendment) Bill 2014, brought forward by the Union Home Minister, is word for word a repetition of the Cabinet decision taken on the first of March 2014. I do not want hon. Members to be under any doubt or suspicion; Comma, full stop, Word, spellings are identical. Whatever the Cabinet had decided on the first of March, Whatever was contained in the draft Ordinance drawn up by the UPA-II Government has been new incorporated as the Andhra Pradesh Reorganisation (Amendment) Bill, 2014. Sir,..

DR. K. KESHAVA RAO: Sir,...

SHRI JAIRAM RAMESH: When you have your chance you contradict me. But let me put forward my point of View.

MR. DEPUTY CHAIRMAN: Dr. Keshava Rao, I am not allowing you. ...(Interruptions)...

SHRI JAIRAM RAMESH: Sir, I am not yielding.

MR DEPUTY CHAIRMAN: He is not yielding

SHRI JAIRAM RAMESH: I am not yielding. I have listened to them patiently. I expect them to listen to me patiently. Sir, the Polavaram project will involve massive resettlement. Let us be under no illusions. It is not an easy project to implement. Almost 45,000 to 50,000 families have to be relocated. This is on par with the relocation that has taken place on *Sardar Sarovar* and we are still seeing the controversy on *Sardar Sarovar*. This is on par with the resettlement that has taken place in Indira Sagar in Madhya. So, this is a gigantic project. It will bring major benefits to the States of Andhra Pradesh and other States but it will also involve very substantial submergence, it will also involve substantial resettlement and rehabilitation. Sir, this Parliament in September 2013 has passed a new Land Acquisition Law. Mr Rajnath Singh, when he was in the Lok Sabha, was the lead speaker in supporting that new law and the main difference between the 2013 Land Acquisition Law and the 1894 Land Acquisition Act is that the 2013 law passed by Parliament unanimously has provisions for R&R. It is actually Land Acquisition, Resettlement and Rehabilitation Act, 2013. So whatever resettlement and rehabilitation has to be done by the State of Andhra Pradesh will have to be done in consonance with the new law that Parliament has passed in 2013 which makes it incumbent. What I am saying, Sir, is very, very important and I would wish my colleagues from Telangana to hear me carefully. The new law makes it incumbent upon the R&R to be completed before the submergence actually happens. We have had a very poor track record of resettlement and rehabilitation in our country and that has created all sorts of social problems. It is because of this that the 2013 Land Acquisition Act marks a departure from the past and said unless you are able to convince the people who are going to be displaced and almost 45-50 per cent of the families to be displaced are going to be tribal families. We are not going to be able to get the full benefits of the project. Sir, while supporting the Andhra Pradesh Reorganisation (Amendment) Bill, 2014, my earnest appeal to the successor State of Andhra Pradesh, is that by all means implement the Polavaram project but implement it in a manner that R&,R is done democratically. It is done sensitively.

It is done humanely and it is done as per the provisions of law that Parliament has passed. It should not be the case that Polavaram project comes up and people are still waiting for resettlement and rehabilitation. It should not be the case that Polavaram Project is constructed and contractors have made maximum benefit from the project, but families are still waiting for their houses, families are still waiting for their land, families are still waiting for electricity. Sir, I am fully conscious, I do not need any sermons from my friends in Telangana. Having been Minister of Environment and Forest, I am fully conscious of the environmental impact and the R&R impact of projects like Polavaram. These are project which are difficult to implement. These are the decisions that are taken under the most difficult circumstances. It is not a black and white case. It is not an open and shut case. It has huge benefits. But, it also presents

OLD HISTORY, NEW GEOGRAPHY ■ 229

huge challenges. I think, given the background of the Andhra Pradesh Reorganisagtion Act, as I mentioned right in the beginning, I would like my Telangana friends to please remember this. For Telangana, Hyderabad became an emotive litmus test issue. For Andhra Pradesh...

श्री वी. हनुमंत रावः आप हैदराबाद की बात कैसे कह सकते हैं? (व्यवधान)

MR. DEPUTY CHAIRMAN: Please, sit down...(Interruptions)... आप लोग बैठिए...(व्यवधान) हनुमंत जी, बैठिए ...(व्यवधान)....What is this?...(Interruptions)... Congressmen troubling Congressmen!...(Interruptions)...Why are you disrupting? Your own Member is speaking...(Interruptions)...

SHRI JAIRAM RAMESH: Sir, I cannot out shout my colleague, Mr. Hanumantha Rao...(Interruptions).

MR. DEPUTY CHAIRMAN: If you interrupt like this, I will not allow you to speak...(Interruptions)...I will not call your name. I am telling you...(Interruptions)...Interrupters will not be given time to speak in the House...(Interruptions)...I am telling you...(Interruptions)...

SHRI V. HANUMANTHA RAO: What is he speaking about Hyderabad?... (Interruptions)...

SHRI JAIRAM RAMESH: I can understand his anguish.... (Interruptions)...But, I do want to mention that Polavaram is an emotive issue for the successor State of Andhra Pradesh.

MR. DEPUTY CHAIRMAN: I told you to conclude. Please conclude.

SHRI JAIRAM RAMESH: Polavaram is not just an emotive issue; it is also vital, bread and butter, water resources issue for the successor State of Andhra Pradesh. I believe, in the fitness of things, in the grand architecture of Andhra Pradesh reorganisation, a conscious decision was taken by the UPA Government with the support of all political parties that Polavaram will be implemented as a National Project by following all environmental and R&R norms.

MR. DEPUTY CHAIRMAN: Okay. Now, please, conclude.

SHRI JAIRAM RAMESH: So, Sir, I would like to end by saying that this is an important commitment made by the erstwhile Government being taken forward by the present Government. It demonstrates continuity in our democratic system of governance. I support the Andhra Pradesh Reorganisation (Amendment) Bill and I would like to make once again an appeal to the Government of Andhra Pradesh of which the BJP is an ally and partner in the Government that the Polavaram Project be implemented in a manner that gives confidence to the people, but R&R will be done democratically, humanely, sensibly and in consonance with the 2013 Act.

With these words, I thank you for giving me this opportunity...

गृह मंत्री (श्री राजनाथ सिंह): आप हैदराबाद डिप्टी चेयरमैन सर, मैं तो आपको ही धन्यवाद देना चाहता हूँ कि आपने इस विधेयक पर चर्चा करने के लिए बहुत सारे सम्मानित सदस्यों को अवसर प्रदान किया है। (व्यवधान) मेरी यह इच्छा भी थी कि इस सदन के अधिक से अधिक सम्मानित सदस्य इस संवेदनशील मुद्दे पर जो चर्चा हो रही है, उसमें भाग लें और उन्होंने भाग लिया। चर्चा की शुरूआत श्री जयराम रमेश जी ने की और वहाँ से लेकर आगे कई सम्मानित सदस्यों ने इस पर अपने विचार रखेए जिनके नाम की चर्चा मैं आगे करूँगा।

डिप्टी चेयरमैन सर, मैं आपके माध्यम से यह कहना चाहूँगा कि जयराम रमेश जी ने जो चर्चा प्रारंभ की है, वह बहुत ही हेल्दी है और हर व्यक्ति द्वारा हेल्दी डेमोक्रेसी में उसकी सराहना की जानी चाहिए।

References

Austin, Granville. 1966. *The Indian Constitution: Cornerstone of a Nation*. Oxford University Press.

Basu, Durga Das, 2015. *Shorter Constitution of India*. Lexis News, reprint edition.

Bawa, V.K. 1992. *The Last Nizam*. Penguin.

Choudhary, Valmiki, ed. 1991. *Dr Rajendra Prasad: Correspondence and Select Documents*. Volume 15. Allied Publishers.

Das, Durga, ed. 1974. *Sardar Patel's Correspondence, 1945-50*. Volume IX. Navajivan Publishing House.

The Collected Works of Mahatma Gandhi. 1977. Volume 69. Publications Division, Ministry of Information and Broadcasting, Government of India.

———. 1979. Volume 75. Publications Division, Ministry of Information and Broadcasting, Government of India.

Fotedar, M.L. 2015. *The Chinar Leaves*. HarperCollins.

Gandhi, M.K. 1942. 'The Andhras', *Harijan*, 29 March.

Gandhi, Rajmohan. 1997. *Rajaji: A Life*. Penguin.

Gopal, S. 1979. *Jawaharlal Nehru: A Biography*. Volume 2. Oxford University Press.

———. 1986. *Selected Works of Jawaharlal Nehru*. Second Series. Volume 4. Oxford University Press.

———. 1990. *Selected Works of Jawaharlal Nehru*. Second Series. Volume 10. Oxford University Press.

———. 1992. *Selected Works of Jawaharlal Nehru*. Second Series. Volume 14, Part I. Oxford University Press.

———. 1994. *Selected Works of Jawaharlal Nehru*. Second Series. Volume 16, Part II. Oxford University Press.

———. 1995. *Selected Works of Jawaharlal Nehru*. Second Series. Volume 17. Oxford University Press.

———. 1996. *Selected Works of Jawaharlal Nehru*. Second Series. Volume 18. Oxford University Press.

———. 1996. *Selected Works of Jawaharlal Nehru*. Second Series. Volume 19. Oxford University Press.

———. 1997. *Selected Works of Jawaharlal Nehru*. Second Series. Volume 20. Oxford University Press.

———. 1999. *Selected Works of Jawaharlal Nehru*. Second Series. Volume 24. Oxford University Press.

———. 2002. *Selected Works of Jawaharlal Nehru*. Second Series. Volume 31. Oxford University Press.

———. 2003. *Selected Works of Jawaharlal Nehru*. Second Series. Volume 32, p. 5. Oxford University Press.

Harrison, Selig. 1960. *India: The Most Dangerous Decades*. Princeton University Press.

King, Robert. 1998. *Nehru and the Language Politics of India*. Oxford University Press.

Kunhi Krishnan, T.V. 1971. *Chavan and the Troubled Decade*. Somaiya Publications.

Moon, Vasant, ed. 1989. *Dr. Babasaheb Ambedkar Writings and Speeches*. Volume 1. Publication Department, Government of Maharashtra.

Munshi, K.M. 1967. *Pilgrimage to Freedom*. Bharatiya Vidya Bhavan.

Nag, Kingshuk. 2011. *Battleground Telangana: Chronicle of an Agitation*. HarperCollins.

Nanda, B.R. 2002. *Selected Works of Govind Ballabh Pant*. Volume 16. Oxford University Press.

Nehru, B.K. 1997. *Nice Guys Finish Second*. Viking.

Palat, Madhavan K., ed. 2015.*Selected Works of Jawaharlal Nehru*, Second Series, Volume 63, Oxford University Press.

Parsai, Gargi. 2014. 'Match-Fixing by Congress, BJP' in Rajya Sabha Gives Birth to Telangana, *The Hindu,* 21 February.

Pawar, Sharad. 2015. *On My Terms: From the Grassroots to Corridors of Power*. Speaking Tiger.

Rajeswar, T.V. 2015. *India: The Crucial Years.* HarperCollins.

Ramesh, Jairam. 2014. 'Uttar Pradesh is Ungovernable', *Mint*, 3 August.

Ram Reddy, G. and Sarma, B.A.V. 1979. *Regionalism in India: A Study of Telangana*. Concept Publishing Company.

Ram Reddy, G. 1989. 'The Politics of Accommodation: Caste, Class and Dominance in Andhra Pradesh'. In *Dominance and State Power in India,* Volume I edited by Francine Frankel and M.S.A. Rao. Oxford University Press.

Ranga Reddy, Captain Lingala Pandu. 2013. 'States Reorganization: A Case Study of Andhra Pradesh.' Voice of Telangana.

Rao, C.H. Hanumantha. 2010. *Regional Disparities, Smaller States and Statehood for Telangana*. Academic Foundation.

———. 2011. 'Srikrishna Committee Report on Telangana: Recommendations at Variance with Analysis', *Economic & Political Weekly*, 46(5), pp. 33–36.

Rao, K.V. Narayana. 1973. *The Emergence of Andhra Pradesh*. Popular Prakashan.

Reddy, B. Muralidhar. 2014. 'We Cannot Rush T-Bill, Says Jairam Ramesh', *The Hindu*, 17 February.

Reddy, K.V. Ranga. 2009. *The Struggle and the Betrayal: The Telangana Story*. Vignyana Sarvovara Prachuranulu.

Schwartzberg, Joseph E. 2009. 'Factors in the Linguistic Reorganisation of Indian States'. In *Language and Politics in India*, edited by Asha Sarangi. Oxford University Press.

Sen, Mohit. 2003. *A Traveller and the Road: Journey of an Indian Communist*. Rupa.

Srinivasan, Vasanthi. 2009. *Gandhi's Conscience Keeper: C. Rajagopalachari and Indian Politics*. Permanent Black.

Srinivasulu, K. 2011. 'Discourses on Telangana and Critique of the Linguistic Nationality Principle'. In *Interrogating Reorganisation of States: Culture, Identity and Politics in India* edited by Asha Sarangi and Sudha Pai. Routledge.

Tillin, Louise. 2014. *Remapping India: New States and Their Political Origins*. Oxford University Press.

Viswanatham, Tenneti. 1992. *Supplement to the Journey of My Life, 1937-1957: An Autobiography of Tanguturi Prakasam*. p. 221. Translated by I.V. Chalapati Rao. Prakasam Institute of Development Studies, Booklinks Corporation.

Weiner, Myron and Katzenstein, Mary with Narayana Rao, K.V. 1981. *India's Preferential Policies*. University of Chicago Press.

Acknowledgements

Rajiv Sharma, Suresh Kumar and Vineel Krishna—the three civil servants who worked very closely with me during the GoM process—have gone through an early draft of the manuscript and made very valuable suggestions.

Saye Sekhar was always available for clarifications. Sanjaya Baru and C. Rammanohar Reddy generously shared their insights on the history of the Telangana agitation, as did Syed Jafri on the Naxalite movement in the state of Andhra Pradesh. Jafri Sahib also helped me track down the 'signatories' to the September 1973 six-point formula. I have also benefitted from a reading of the manuscript by Kalpana Kannabiran.

I thank a couple of my senior political colleagues and senior officials who do not wish to be named for sharing their recollections of the December 2009 period.

D. Ramesh of the Parliament Library helped me enormously in tracking down Parliament debates and other documents.

Deepa Bhatnagar of the Nehru Memorial Museum & Library (NMML), New Delhi, enabled access to the Rajaji and Sri Prakasa collections which contain their letters to Jawaharlal Nehru.

Ritu Vajpeyi-Mohan was insistent that there be a historical context to my original idea of writing only on the GoM process. I am glad she stood firm. The context gives this book a wider appeal.

All letters, emails, notes, memoranda and other written material used or quoted in the book have been deposited in the NMML and are available freely for review and use.

Index

Advani, L.K., 45, 128
Ahluwalia, Montek Singh, 144
Ahmad, Shakeel, 48
Ali, Abid, 163
Ali, S. Fazl, 22
All India Majlis-e-Ittehadul Muslimeen (AIMIM), 53, 76, 79
Ambedkar, B.R., 6, 164
Anantapur, 75–77
Andhra Pradesh, 23-25, 28, 48, 83–84.
   capital selection, 83–84
   distribution of assets and liabilities, 113 116, 136
   domicile rules for employment, 29, 32–33
   establishment of a central university, 34–35
   establishment of education institutions, 109–110, 114
   GoM meeting on bifurcation, 71–74
   governor, 85–89, 128–129 137
   grant of special category status, 131-132, 135
   internal security issues, 67, 90–92
   jihadi terrorism and coastal security, 91
   recognized political parties of, 49–50
   six-point formula, for peace in, 34–35, 132, 166
   Srikrishna Committee report on bifurcation of, 50–54, 56, 77, 79
   Thirteenth Schedule, 113–116
   undivided, 72, 75
   water resource management, 93–99
Andhra Pradesh Public Employment (Organisation of Local Cadres and Regulation of Direct Recruitment) Order, 1975, 35
Andhra Pradesh Reorganization Act, 2014, 116, 173
   Section 8, 86–89
   Sections 46 (2) and 46 (3), 115-116
Andhra Pradesh Reorganization Bill, 2013/2014, 118–19, 128–133
   allocation of state government employees, 146
   discussion in the Lok Sabha, 128–133
   discussion in the Rajya Sabha, 134–143
   final touches, 144–151
   pepper spray incident in the Lok Sabha, 125–127
   relevance for the Planning

Commission, 144–145
Section 95, 110–111
water resource management, 146–147
Andhra province, creation of, 5–11
    as Andhra Pradesh, 25
    Justice Wanchoo's recommendations, 17, 20
    Nehru's views, 9, 11–12, 16–18
    Sriramulu's fast and martyrdom, 13–16
Anjaiah, T., 36, 100
Antony, A.K., 55–56, 66, 68, 70, 165
Articles of the Constitution of India
    Article 3, 57, 72–73, 172
    Article 4, 73, 172
    Article 4(2), 86, 129
    Article 168, 162
    Article 315, 119
    Article 368, 112, 129
    Article 370, 34
    Article 371-D, 34–35, 67, 109–111
    Article 371-H, 86, 129
Auden, W.H., 166
Aurangabad, 9
Azad, Ghulam Nabi, 54–57, 66, 68, 70, 146
Azad, Maulana, 5, 26

Babri Masjid demolition, 50
Babulal Parate vs The State of Bombay and Another, 73
Baig, Abbas Ali, 163
Bapuji, Konda Lakshman, 31, 160
Baru, Sanjaya, 39
Basu, D.D., 73
Bhadrachalam town, 105
Bharatiya Janata Party (BJP), 38–39, 44–46, 52–53, 56, 79, 98, 125–127, 130, 135, 137, 142–143, 168
Bhave, Acharya Vinoba, 11, 28

Bhoodan movement, 28
Bihar Reorganisation Act, 2000, 39n47
Bodoland, 47
Bombay Reorganisation Act, 1960, 112
Bulganin, N.A., 28

Calling Attention Motion, 53
capital selection committee, 83–84
Chakravarti, Nallan, 155
Chandrasekhar, B.S., 163
Chavan, Y.B., 31, 159
Chhattisgarh, 39, 72, 90, 101–102, 169
Chidambaram, P., 42, 44, 47–48, 54–57, 66, 68–69, 111, 126, 128
Chiranjeevi, K., 70, 135
common governor, idea of a, 85–89
Communist Party of India (CPI), 53, 61, 165
Communist Party of India (Marxist) [CPI(M)], 43, 53, 61, 142, 165, 170
Congress party, 11, 32, 36, 41, 53–54, 57, 68, 70, 125, 134
Congress Working Committee (CWC), 7–9, 19, 23, 40, 55–56, 58, 68–70, 72
    resolution of 30 July 2013, 68, 70, 103
Constitution (Fifth Amendment) Act, 1955, 73
Constitution (32nd Amendment) Act, 1973, 34
Cyberabad, 39

Dar, S.K., 5, 6
Dar Commission, 5–6
Das, Jatin, 16
Deo, V. Kishore Chandra, 70
Desai, Morarji, 21
Deshmukh, Vilasrao, 69
Dravida Munnetra Kazhagam (DMK), 55, 61

Forest Rights Act, 2006, 103

Gandhi, Devdas, 156
Gandhi, Gopal, 156
Gandhi, Indira, 29, 30–336, 158–159 166, 169
Gandhi, Mahatma, 4, 13
Gandhi, Rajmohan, 155–156
Gandhi, Sonia, 40, 55–56, 130
Gentlemen's Agreement, 24, 29
Giri, V.V., 31
Gopal, S., 12
Gorkhaland, 47
Goswami, Anil, 81, 149
Goud, Madhu Yakshi, 131, 161
Greater Hyderabad Municipal Corporation (GHMC), 81
Greyhounds Training Centre, 92
Group of Ministers (GoM), 58, 65–70, 77–78, 82–84, 86–90, 175
  Andhra Pradesh Reorganization Bill, 2013, 118–119, 128–133, 157–169
  apportioning of assets and liabilities, 114–116
  matter of re-transferring Bhadrachalam revenue division, 104–106
  power allocation, 147–148
  on reorganisation legislation, 72, 87, 94-95, 104, 110–112, 142
Gudiwada, 37
Gulbarga, 9
Guntur, 20, 51, 83, 170

Haksar, P.N., 158–159
Hari, Sabbam, 125
Hindupur, 37
Hyderabad state, 9, 13, 23, 27, 29–30, 131–132, 163–164
  tussle for, 78–81
Hyderabad–Vijayawada corridor, 39

ITC Limited vs Agriculture Produce Market Committee and Others, 73

Jai Andhra movement in 1972-73, 33, 111, 159, 163
Jai Telangana movement, 33, 159
Jaitley, Arun, 128, 132, 134–135 142, 171
Jayashankar, K., 61
Jharkhand, 39, 72, 90-91, 120, 169
JVP Committee, 6–7, 11, 15, 16

Kalam, A.P.J., 61
Kamaraj, K., 86
Karat, Prakash, 60
Karimnagar, 32, 75, 90
Kaul, Anita, 150
Kaul, T.N., 158–159
Kavitha, 103
Khammam, 75, 90, 102-105, 108, 119
Khan, Muhammed, 73
Khrushchev, Nikita, 28
Kodandaram, M., 148
Krishna, Vineel, 91, 95, 144
Kruparani, Killi, 70
Kumar, G.V. Harsha, 125
Kumar, S. Suresh, 88, 144
Kumar, T. Vijay, 91
Kumar, Arun, 125
Kumar, Vatti Vasanth, 165
Kumar of Vizianagaram, Maharaj, 4
Kunzru, H.N., 22
Kurnool, 20-21, 26, 51, 75, 77, 82, 83

Lakshmi, Botcha Jhansi, 131
Lakshmi, Panabaka, 70, 131
Left-wing extremism, 58, 90

Madhya Pradesh Reorganisation Act, 2000, 39n47
Madras city, 8–9, 12-20
Mahapatra, Rabinarayan, 141

Maran, Dayanidhi, 61
Maru Pradesh, 47
Modi, Narendra, 88, 107
Moily, M. Veerappa, 66, 68, 70
Mukherjee, Pranab, 40, 44, 46, 48–49, 55, 62
Mulki Rules, 29, 32
Mullaperiyar Environment Protection Forum vs Union of India and Others, 74

Nagarjuna Sagar Dam, 26, 93
Naidu, N. Chandrababu, 38–39, 49, 56, 79, 161
  on Telangana's development, 38
Naidu, M. Venkaiah, 44, 46, 98, 102, 128, 132, 136–137, 138–142, 144
Nalgonda, 28, 37, 51
Narasimha, Damodar Raja, 55, 165
Narasimhan, E.S.L., 88
Narayanasamy, V., 66, 68, 70, 146
Narendra, A., 45
Nath, Kamal, 126, 130
National Common Minimum Programme (NCMP), 60–61
National Dairy Development Board (NDDB), 72
National Development Council (NDC), 145
Naxalite movement, 31, 37, 52, 90
Nehru, Jawaharlal, 5–9, 11, 23, 158, 169, 172
  Andhra province, creation of, 11–12, 16–18
  on issue of language and the linguistic reorganization of states, 21–22, 20n27
  on SRC's recommendations, 26–28
Nizam of Hyderabad, 158
North-Eastern Areas (Reorganisation) Act, 1971, 35, 112

October 1917 Revolution in Russia, 43
Organisation for Counter Terrorist Operations (OCTOPUS), 92
Osmania University, 43
Owaisi, Asaduddin, 76, 131, 165

Panikkar, K.M., 22
Pant, Govind Ballabh, 21, 23, 25, 33, 34, 159–160
Pant, K.C., 33, 159
Partition Committee, 8
Pataudi, M.A.K., 163
Patel, Ahmed, 55, 56, 70
Patil, R.K., 21
Patnaik, Naveen, 102
Peoples' War Group (PWG), 37, 91
Polavaram project, 100–108, 119, 121, 136, 141, 147
  areas under submergence, issue of, 105–108
  attractiveness of, 100
  embankments and drainage sluices, 102–105
  environmental clearance issues, 102
Prabhakar, Chintamaneni, 161
Prabhakar, Ponnam, 131, 161
Pradeep Choudhury and Others vs Union of India Transfer Case (Civil), 74
Pradhan Mantri Gram Sadak Yojana-II, 165
Praja Rajyam Party, 53
Prakasa, Sri, 11, 17
Prakasam, T., 6, 8-9, 13–17, 20–21, 156
Prasad, Rajendra, 5-6, 19, 21
Prasad, Ravi Shankar, 139
Prasanna, E.A.S., 163
Prathap, A. Sai, 125
Public Employment (Requirements as to Residence) Act, 1957, 29–30, 32
Punjab, 29, 35, 79, 80, 98, 168
Punjab Reorganisation Act, 1966, 35
Purandeswari, D., 70

Radcliffe, Cyril, 166
Radhakrishnan, S., 4, 15
Raja, D., 61
Raja, P.S. Kumaraswamy, 8–9
Rajagopal, Lagadapati, 125, 162
Rajagopalachari, C. (Rajaji), 6, 8–9, 11–20, 155–156
Rajaiah, Siricilla, 161
Rajeswar, T.V., 30
Raju, A. Satyanarayana, 25, 181
Raju, M.M. Pallam, 70, 118, 121, 148
Ramadoss, S., 47
Ram Janmabhoomi movement, 38
Ranga, N.G., 5
Rao, Hanumantha, 163
Rao, J. Vengal, 35–36
Rao, K. Chandrasekhar (KCR), 39–42, 43-44, 61, 89, 103, 131, 170
Rao, K.S., 70, 118, 121, 148
Rao, K.V.P. Ramachandra, 41
Rao, N.T. Rama (NTR), 37-38, 56, 159, 171
Rao, P.V. Narasimha, 32-33, 36, 38, 163
Rao, R. Sambasiva, 125
Rashtriya Janata Dal (RJD), 61
Rayalaseema region, 5, 75, 98, 120
Rayala-Telangana region, 51, 75–77, 160
Reddy, A. Venkatarami, 76
Reddy, Jaipal, 86, 130
Reddy, Janardhana, 38
Reddy, K. Brahmananda, 28, 30, 31, 35, 36, 160
Reddy, K. Vijaya Bhaskara, 38
Reddy, Kiran Kumar, 55, 70, 72, 133, 165, 170
Reddy, K.K. Mahender, 57
Reddy, Kotla Surya Prakash, 70, 76
Reddy, M. Chenna, 28, 30, 32, 36, 38, 170
Reddy, Modugula Venugopala, 126

Reddy, M.V. Mysura, 56
Reddy, N. Raghuveera, 76
Reddy, N. Sanjiva, 8, 16, 28, 31, 86, 170
Reddy, Sukhender, 161
Reddy, Suravaram Sudhakar, 165
Reddy, Suresh, 157
Reddy, Y.V., 116, 165
Reddy, Y.S. Rajasekhara (YSR), 40–42, 43, 79, 94, 161, 170
Rehabilitation and Resettlement (R&R) policy, 2005, 102
reorganization of states, 20–22
  in 2000, 170
  between 1956 and 1966, 168
  in the 1970s and 1980s, 168
Representation of People Act, 1950 and 1951, 162
Rosaiah, K., 41, 43–44, 47, 103
Roy, Saugata, 131

Sambamurti, Bulusu, 14
Sanjeevaiah, D., 28, 170
Sarin, H.C., 33
Satyanarayana, Botcha 55
Seelam, J.D., 70, 163
Seemandhra. *See* Andhra Pradesh
Selected Works of Jawaharlal Nehru, 157
Sharma, Rajiv, 82, 88, 95, 146
Shetkar, Suresh, 131, 161
Shinde, Sushilkumar, 54–56, 65, 68, 69, 71, 88, 109, 137, 143
Sibal, Kapil, 128, 135
Singh, Digvijaya, 55–56, 70, 169
Singh, Manmohan, 40, 55–57, 132, 133,
Singh, Master Tara, 29
Singh, Rajnath, 88, 107, 108, 230
Singh, Raman, 101
Singhvi, Abhishek, 47
Sitaram, Swami, 11, 14, 17
Sitaramayya, Pattabhi, 6, 8, 25

Sivaramakrishnan, K.C., 82, 83
special category status, 131-132
Sri Bagh Pact of 1937, 20
Srikrishna, B.N., 50, 51
Srikrishna Committee report on bifurcation of Andhra Pradesh, 52–53, 56
Srinivas, D., 40
Sriramulu, Potti, 13, 15, 44
States Reorganization Bill, 1956, 25, 159
States Reorganization Commission (SRC), 22–23, 24, 26, 48, 93, 164
Subramanya, V., 163
Subramanyam, R., 91
Sukthankar, Y.N., 19-20
Sundaram, Lanka, 25, 160
Swaraj, Sushma, 126, 128, 130, 157

Tamil, Telugu, Kannada and Kerala regions, formation of
  during British rule, 4
  Congress Working Committee (CWC) on, 7–9, 19, 23
  Dar Commission on, 5–6
  JVP Committee report on, 15, 16
  Partition Committee report, 8
Telangana Joint Action Committee (TJAC), 56, 148
Telangana Praja Samithi (TPS), 30, 31, 158
Telangana Rashtra Samithi (TRS), 39-41, 52, 57, 59, 60, 77, 79

Telugu Desam Party (TDP), 38–39, 40–41, 47, 49, 52, 56, 79, 108, 126, 134, 161–162
Thackeray, Bal, 69
Tirupati, 38, 107, 115, 155, 156, 170
Trinamool Congress (TMC), 130, 131

Union of India vs Valluri Basavaiah Chaudhary, Etc., Etc., 73
United Progressive Alliance (UPA), 40, 41, 55, 59, 60–61
Uttarakhand, 39, 72, 120, 145, 169
Uttar Pradesh Reorganisation Act, 2000, 39, 145

Vajpayee, Atal Bihari, 39, 169
Vaze, S.G., 22
Vidarbha, 40, 47, 173
Vijayawada, 11, 60, 82, 115, 125, 148, 170
Visakhapatnam, 82, 90, 100, 115, 141, 148, 159
Vishwanath, G.R., 163
Vishwanatham, Tenneti, 163
Vivekanand, G., 131, 161

Wanchoo, K.N., 17
Warangal, 31, 75, 90

Yadav, Lalu Prasad, 61, 169
Yechury, Sitaram, 61, 135, 142, 165
YSR Congress Party, 56–57, 126